JOHN DONNE

The Divine Poems

JOHN DONNE
from the effigy by Nicholas Stone in St. Paul's Cathedral

JOHN DONNE

The Divine Poems

EDITED WITH

INTRODUCTION AND COMMENTARY

BY

HELEN GARDNER

SECOND EDITION

★

OXFORD

AT THE CLARENDON PRESS

1978

Oxford University Press, Walton Street, Oxford OX2 6DP

OXFORD LONDON GLASGOW
NEW YORK TORONTO MELBOURNE WELLINGTON
KUALA LUMPUR SINGAPORE JAKARTA HONG KONG TOKYO
DELHI BOMBAY CALCUTTA MADRAS KARACHI
IBADAN NAIROBI DAR ES SALAAM CAPE TOWN

© *Oxford University Press 1978*

First published 1952
Second Edition 1978

British Library Cataloguing in Publication Data
Donne, John
    The divine poems. – 2nd ed. – (Oxford English texts).
    I. Title II. Gardner, *Dame* Helen, b. 1908
    III. Series
    821'.3   PR2246   77–30283
    ISBN 0–19–812745–6

*Printed in Great Britain
at the University Press, Oxford
by Vivian Ridler
Printer to the University*

PREFACE TO THE SECOND EDITION
(1978)

NEW material and fresh information that have come to light
in the quarter of a century since I edited Donne's *Divine
Poems* make necessary some correction and modification of
statements in the introduction and commentary and some recon-
sideration of the presentation of the text. In revising I have borne
in mind both the interests of economy and the value to scholars of
keeping page references the same in both editions. I have therefore
confined myself to such alterations as could be made without total
resetting, and provided supplementary notes at the end of the
volume. A description of the changes made in this new edition,
which would normally find a place in this preface, is given in an
introduction to the supplementary notes.

PREFACE TO THE FIRST EDITION
(1952)

IN setting out to edit the *Divine Poems* of John Donne I had two purposes. I wished to print the 'Holy Sonnets' in what I believe to be their right order, to display their dependence in subject and treatment on the tradition of formal meditation, and to argue that the majority were written well before Donne was ordained. My second purpose was to annotate the poems, particularly 'A Litany'. To do this it was necessary to re-examine the text. A third purpose thus developed: to find a solution to the problem presented by the fact that the first edition of Donne's poems is posthumous, and that, while no copies in holograph are known to have survived, the poems exist in a great many manuscript copies which antedate the first edition.

The 'Holy Sonnets' are printed here in three sets. The first set consists of the twelve sonnets which were printed in the first edition of 1633 and which appear in the same order in the two most reliable groups of manuscripts. There is high textual authority for printing these twelve together in this order. But there is good internal authority also. When these twelve sonnets are read in this order they can be seen to form a sequence. The four sonnets which were interpolated among these twelve in the second edition of 1635 are printed together, arranged in a logical order from their subject-matter. They also, in this order, form a short sequence. This leaves the three sonnets which are only extant in the Westmoreland manuscript standing by themselves. They are quite distinct in their subjects and treatment from the other sixteen, as well as from each other.

In general, discussion of the dates of poems is to be found in the Commentary; but the problem of the date of the 'Holy Sonnets' is a complicated one, and is so important for a just appreciation of Donne's religious development that I have preferred to treat the question, together with the related questions of their right order and interpretation, in the second part of the Introduction. In the same way, I have taken out of the Commentary and treated in

Appendices certain controversial matters which demand longer discussion than a Commentary can include.

No poet more needs or more repays commentary than Donne. When I was beginning my work, the late Dr. F. E. Hutchinson urged me to comment as fully as possible. Experience has shown me the wisdom of his advice. It has constantly happened, when I had thought that I had made sufficient comment on a poem, that a question from a pupil or a friend called my attention to a phrase which I had thought it unnecessary to annotate, but which on reflection proved either to be obscure, or to bear a meaning which was not the apparently obvious one. An editor who adopts the policy of full annotation runs the risk of incurring the censure which Johnson passed on a note by Warburton: 'It explains what no reader has found difficult, and, I think, explains it wrong.' But with a poet so difficult as Donne the plain meaning is sometimes overlooked, and a wrong explanation may at least provoke someone else to provide the right one. The attempt to understand the exact meaning of the words, and to recognize the sources or the field of reference of a poem brings great rewards. Indeed it places some poems in quite a fresh light.

The work on the text is embodied in the Textual Introduction and in textual notes. The textual note is always printed first, and the exegetical note follows as a separate paragraph. A reader who is not interested in textual matters can thus avoid them altogether. Since Sir Herbert Grierson's edition of 1912 two important manuscripts have come to light. Both were discovered by Mr. Geoffrey Keynes: the first he gave to the Cambridge University Library, where it is Additional MS. 5778; the other, the Luttrell manuscript, is in his own library, and he has generously allowed me to give the first description of it. With the help of the Cambridge manuscript, it has been possible to carry further Sir Herbert Grierson's analysis of the manuscripts of Group I. I argue that the collection which these manuscripts contain is a collection made by Donne himself in 1614, when he was thinking of publishing his poems. Since the largest and best portion of the edition of 1633 was taken from a very good manuscript of this group, my argument, if accepted, places the major part of Donne's poems on a secure textual foundation.

The Luttrell manuscript is also of great importance. It is the source of the O'Flaherty manuscript, which was itself the main source of the additional poems and corrections in the second edition of 1635. I have demonstrated, I hope conclusively, that this second edition is a derived and not a substantive text.

My text is a critical one, based on the first printed version of each poem, emended from the manuscripts. But emendation is in accordance with a theory of textual transmission set out at length in the Textual Introduction. The Group III manuscripts preserve in some poems a version which differs from the version in Groups I and II and appears to represent an earlier state of the text. All Group III readings which may thus be regarded as genuine earlier readings are recorded in the critical apparatus, which allows readers to see Donne at work revising his poems. The textual notes give fuller information on manuscript variants. The manuscript copies of Donne's poems are so widely scattered that consultation of more than a few is impossible for most students. An apparatus should be selective; but readings which should not appear there have a place in the notes if they throw light on the line of transmission. They may also serve to establish the relationships of any fresh manuscripts which may be discovered.

I have to thank many people for their help: Dr. Paul Maas for discussing textual problems; Dr. H. W. Garrod for help with Donne's Latin verse; Dr. R. W. Hunt for answering palaeographical questions; Dr. Percy Simpson for discussing problems of punctuation; Miss Dorothy Whitelock, Dr. C. T. Onions, and Mr. G. V. Smithers for help with difficult points of syntax; Mrs. H. R. Ing for assistance with problems of versification; and Mrs. Kenneth Leys for discussing Church History. I am particularly indebted to Professor F. P. Wilson for reading and criticizing the Textual Introduction; to Mr. Hugh Macdonald for much helpful advice; and to Miss Lucy Hutchinson for assistance in preparing my manuscript for the press and for reading the proofs. Among those particularly known for their work on Donne, I have to thank Mr. I. A. Shapiro for answering questions about Donne's letters; Mrs. Simpson for reading many sections of my work at various stages; and Mr. John Hayward for advice on problems of presentation and reading the Introductions and Appendices. By good fortune Professor W. Milgate, of Sydney University, was in Oxford working on Donne from 1948–50, and I can hardly exaggerate what I owe to the fact that we were working together on the manuscripts.

I am indebted to the trustees of the Henry W. Berg and Albert A. Berg Collection in the New York Public Library for permission to print the three sonnets and to quote variants from the Westmoreland manuscript; to the Huntington Library for permission to quote variants from the Bridgewater manuscript; and to the Houghton Library, Harvard University, for permission to quote variants from the Carnaby, Dobell, Norton, O'Flaherty, and Stephens manuscripts. I have to thank the librarians of these institutions for supplying me with photostats and information. I am similarly indebted to the Master and Fellows of Trinity College, Cambridge; the Provost and Fellows of Trinity College, Dublin; the Dean and Chapter of St. Paul's Cathedral; and to their respective librarians, Mr. H. M. Adams, Mr. Joseph Hanna, and Mr. Gerald Henderson. I should like also to express my gratitude to the officials and assistants of the Bodleian Library, and those in the Manuscript Departments of the Cambridge University Library and the British Museum.

This edition owes much to the generosity of private owners. I must thank particularly Mr. Geoffrey Keynes for allowing me to examine the Leconfield and Luttrell manuscripts; and Mr. Wilfred Merton, who most kindly deposited the Dowden manuscript of poems and two manuscripts of sermons in the British Museum for my use. I have also to thank his Grace the Duke of Portland, who through his librarian, Mr. Francis Needham, placed the Welbeck manuscript temporarily in the Bodleian Library; and Mr. Richard Jennings, who allowed me to collate the John Cave manuscript and to examine his fine copy of the edition of 1633.

I wish in conclusion to acknowledge what should be obvious without any acknowledgement from me here, the debt I owe to Sir Herbert Grierson's edition of 1912. All new work on Donne is based on his. But beside this impersonal debt which all lovers of Donne owe to him, I should like to thank him for his personal kindness and encouragement when I first told him of my wish to edit the *Divine Poems*, for the pleasure I had in discussing with him my interpretation of the 'Holy Sonnets', and for the interest he has taken in the progress of the work. I should like to join with his name that of another much beloved student of the seventeenth century, the late Dr. F. E. Hutchinson. His beautiful copy of the *LXXX* and *Fifty Sermons*, bound together, a gift to me from Mrs. Hutchinson, stands on my shelves, and has been, in the later stages of my work, a daily reminder of his warm sympathy and wise advice in its earlier stages. The last debt I have to acknowledge is a much older one. If this book bore a dedication, it would be to the memory of Florence Gibbons, sometime senior English mistress at the North London Collegiate School, with whom, twenty-six years ago, I first read the *Divine Poems* of John Donne.

H. G.

ST. HILDA'S COLLEGE
    OXFORD

CONTENTS

REFERENCES AND ABBREVIATIONS

QUOTATIONS from Donne's poems, other than the *Divine Poems*, are taken from the following editions: *The Elegies and the Songs and Sonnets*, edited by Helen Gardner (Oxford, 1965); *The Satires, Epigrams and Verse Letters*, edited by W. Milgate (Oxford, 1967); and *The Anniversaries, Epithalamions and Epicedes*, edited by W. Milgate (Oxford, 1978). These are referred to as

> Gardner, *Elegies etc.*
> Milgate, *Satires etc.*
> Milgate, *Anniversaries etc.*

The Poems of John Donne, edited by H. J. C. Grierson, 2 vols. (Oxford, 1912), is referred to as

> Grierson

Quotations from the *Sermons*, *Essays in Divinity*, *Ignatius His Conclave*, and *Devotions upon Emergent Occasions* are from the following modern editions: *The Sermons of John Donne*, edited by G. R. Potter and Evelyn M. Simpson, 10 vols. (University of California Press, Berkeley and Los Angeles, 1953–62); *Essays in Divinity*, edited by Evelyn M. Simpson (Oxford, 1952); *Ignatius His Conclave*, edited by T. S. Healy, S.J. (Oxford, 1969); *Devotions upon Emergent Occasions*, edited by John Sparrow (Cambridge, 1923). These are referred to as

> *Sermons*
> Simpson, *Essays*
> Healy, *Ignatius*
> Sparrow, *Devotions*

Quotations from other prose works are from the original editions and the following forms of reference are used:

Pseudo-Martyr	*Pseudo-martyr.* 1610
Biathanatos	*ΒΙΑΘΑΝΑΤΟΣ.* (1646)
Letters	*Letters to Severall Persons of Honour.* 1651
Tobie Mathew Collection	*A Collection of Letters, made by Sr Tobie Mathews K^t.* 1660

Other References:

Bald	*John Donne: A Life*, by R. C. Bald. Oxford, 1970
Chambers	*The Poems of John Donne*, edited by E. K. Chambers (The Muses' Library). 2 vols. 1896
Concordance	*A Concordance to the English Poems of John Donne*, by H. C. Combs and Z. R. Sullens. Chicago, 1940

E.L.H.	*A Journal of English Literary History*
Essays and Studies	*Essays and Studies by Members of the English Association*
Golden Legend	*The Golden Legend*, edited by F. S. Ellis (Temple Classics). 7 vols. 1900
Gosse	*The Life and Letters of John Donne*, by Edmund Gosse. 2 vols. 1899
Hayward	*John Donne Dean of St Paul's Complete Poetry and Selected Prose*, edited by John Hayward (Nonesuch Press). 1929
Herbert, *Works*	*The Works of George Herbert*, edited by F. E. Hutchinson. Oxford, 1941
Keynes	*A Bibliography of Dr John Donne*, by Geoffrey Keynes, fourth edition. Oxford, 1973
Migne, *P.G.*, *P.L.*	J. Migne, *Patrologia Graeca* and *Patrologia Latina* (The references given are to volume and column)
J.E.G.P.	*A Journal of English and Germanic Philology*
M.L.N.	*Modern Language Notes*
M.L.R.	*The Modern Language Review*
M.P.	*Modern Philology*
N. and Q.	*Notes and Queries*
O.E.D.	*The Oxford English Dictionary*
P.M.L.A.	*Publications of the Modern Language Association of America*
R.E.S.	*The Review of English Studies*
Simpson, *Prose Works*	*A Study of the Prose Works of John Donne*, by Evelyn Simpson, second edition. Oxford, 1948
Taylor, *Works*	*The Whole Works of Jeremy Taylor*, edited by R. Heber (15 vols. 1822), revised by C. P. Eden. 10 vols. 1847–54
T.L.S.	*The Times Literary Supplement*
Walton, *Lives*	When specific reference is not given to a particular early edition, quotations are taken from the reprint of the 1675 edition of the *Lives* in the World's Classics, and page references are to that edition

GENERAL INTRODUCTION

I. THE RELIGIOUS POETRY OF JOHN DONNE

'LET no pious ear be offended', wrote Dr. Johnson, 'if I advance, in opposition to many authorities, that poetical devotion cannot often please. . . . Contemplative piety, or the intercourse between God and the human soul, cannot be poetical. Man admitted to implore the mercy of his Creator and plead the merits of his Redeemer is already in a higher state than poetry can confer.'[1] A critic of our own century T. S. Eliot, although he did not go as far as Johnson did, suggested that religious poetry—that is, poetry whose subject is not the doctrines of religion, but man worshipping or man at prayer—gives a limited kind of pleasure. He confessed to some sympathy with those lovers of poetry who think of religious poetry as 'a variety of *minor* poetry'; who feel that

the religious poet is not a poet who is treating the whole subject matter of poetry in a religious spirit, but a poet who is dealing with a confined part of this subject matter: who is leaving out what men consider their major passions, and thereby confessing his ignorance of them;

and he went on to speak of a kind of poetry which is 'the product of a special religious awareness, which may exist without the general awareness which we expect of the major poet'.[2] Neither Johnson, in asserting that devotion is unfitted for poetic treatment, nor Eliot, suggesting that religious poetry treats a too limited range of human experience, has spoken more harshly of poetical devotion than Andrew Marvell, who, in 'The Coronet', lays bare the fundamental problem of religious poetry: the 'wreaths of Fame and Interest' with which devotion is mingled. In all poetry which attempts to represent the intercourse between an individual soul and its Maker there is a conflict between the ostensible emotion—adoring love, absorbed in the contemplation of its object, or penitence, overwhelmed by the sense of personal unworthiness—and

---

[1] 'Life of Waller', *Lives of the Poets*, ed. G. B. Hill (Oxford, 1905), i. 291.
[2] 'Religion and Literature', *Essays Ancient and Modern* (1936), p. 97.

the artist's actual absorption in the creation of his poem and his satisfaction in achieving perfect expression.

This conflict is present in much lyric poetry. It is at the root of the long debates on the sincerity of love poets. The love poet escapes Johnson's charge, for it could be claimed that the inventions of poets have bestowed upon the passion of love an ideal beauty, and that they have, in fact, conferred upon it a higher state than it has by nature. He escapes Eliot's charge also. For, although Johnson dismissed love as 'only one of many passions' and said that it 'has no great influence upon the sum of life', almost all men and women delight, in imagination if not in reality, in loving and being beloved. But the love poet, like the divine poet, may come under Marvell's condemnation, if we abandon the old doctrine of imitation and forget that both are only feigning: the love poet creating an image of himself in love, the divine poet creating an image of himself at prayer. To create his image, the divine poet must omit more of himself than the love poet. Man in love is various, and may display himself in all his moods. Man at prayer is aiming at a different kind of constancy from the lover's, for the object of his passion is not itself variable. He is at pains to banish or transform certain elements in his nature. Although in one sense it might be said to be natural for men to pray, prayer is not a natural activity. We cannot help missing the image of the natural man in the poet's image of the spiritual man. But without the poet's image of the spiritual man our poetry would be poorer, and our imagination of life would be narrowed.

Donne's religious poetry is the work of a man in whom the general awareness of which Eliot speaks was certainly present. Equally certainly that awareness is limited in his devotional poetry. He remains a wit in his divine as in his secular verse; but the 'fierce endeavour' of his wit is tamed: the outrageous element has disappeared. His Maker is more powerfully present to the imagination in his divine poems than any mistress is in his love poems. There he argues confidently, an expert in the casuistry of love. Over the argument and the wit of the divine poems hangs the knowledge of the futility of argument: 'But who am I, that dare dispute with thee?' Although the sense of strain in the divine poems is partly a product of the circumstances in which they were written—they belong in the main to Donne's melancholy middle years, and are the work of an older and sadder man than the brilliant author of the *Elegies* and the *Songs and Sonnets*—a sense of strain is possibly inherent in their nature. The divine poet is to some degree committed to showing himself as he would be rather than as he is, and is thus always in danger of overspending his spiritual capital. Yet although we may not regard the *Divine Poems* as Donne's greatest poems, they are great poems of their kind. They are deeply characteristic of their author, in spite of the limitations of the genre; and they have to many readers given one of the most powerful images in our poetry of 'man admitted to implore the mercy of his Creator and plead the merits of his Redeemer'.

One reason for their power is that Donne, though in many other ways a remarkable human being, is not remarkable for any spiritual gifts and graces which we recognize at once as extraordinary and beyond the experience of the majority of mankind. For all his genius as a poet, his intellectual vivacity and his passionate and complex temperament, his religious experience seems, as with most of those who profess and call themselves Christians, to have been largely a matter of faith and moral effort. In his early poetry there is nothing to suggest a latent spirituality. He is by nature arrogant, egotistical, and irreverent. His mind is naturally sceptical and curious, holding little sacred. In his love poetry he is only rarely tender and almost never humble: 'How blest am I in this discovering thee' is his most characteristic note. In his almost total blindness to the beauty of the natural world he reveals a lack of that receptivity, that capacity for disinterested joy which is one of the marks of the spiritual man. This differentiates him at once from a poet with whom he is often compared, Gerard Manley Hopkins. But there is one poem of his youth, the third Satire, which shows that in spite of his temperament the young Donne was genuinely religious; if by a religious person we understand a person to whom the idea of God not only is self-evident, but brings with it a sense of absolute obligation.

Donne's family tradition was one of unbroken loyalty to the Roman Church and he described in the candid and dignified preface to *Pseudo-Martyr* how strong a hold the 'Romane religion' had on him, both from natural piety and from respect for the virtue and learning of his early teachers.[1] He declared that those who knew him were well aware that he used no 'inordinate hast, nor precipitation' in binding his conscience 'to any locall Religion', even though his delay endangered his career and reputation.[2] The third Satire would seem to belong to this period, when Donne, in Walton's phrase, 'betrothed himself to no Religion that might give him any other denomination than *a Christian*'. He had plainly when he wrote it moved away from the Roman position. The only authority recognized in the poem is the authority of conscience; and the appeal made to antiquity, 'aske thy father which is shee, Let him aske his', is the Protestant appeal to primitive tradition against the Roman assertion of the authority of the continuing Church. But the poem shows that if Donne had rejected the Roman obedience, he had derived from his upbringing an unquestioning acceptance of the claim of religion. The argument rests on two assumptions: that the search for 'true Religion' is the primary duty of a moral being, and that truth exists and can be known. The satire is directed not so much against the differing Christian confessions as against the insufficient reasons for which men adhere to them—from unthinking conservatism or unthinking love of novelty, from laziness and the desire to avoid trouble, or from a shallow scepticism which thinks credal differences unimportant. There is no trace in this poem of the philosophic scepticism sometimes attributed to Donne in his

[1] 'I was first to blot out, certaine impressions of the Romane religion, and to wrastle both against the examples and against the reasons, by which some hold was taken; and some anticipations early layde upon my conscience, both by Persons who by nature had a power and superiority over my will, and others who by their learning and good life, seem'd to me justly to claime an interest for the guiding, and rectifying of mine understanding in these matters' (*Pseudo-Martyr*, sig. B2ᵛ).

[2] 'And although I apprehended well enough, that this irresolution not onely retarded my fortune, but also bred some scandall, and endangered my spirituall reputation, by laying me open to many mis-interpretations; yet all these respects did not transport me to any violent and sudden determination, till I had, to the measure of my poore wit and judgement, survayed and digested the whole body of Divinity, controverted betweene ours and the Romane Church. In which search and disquisition, that God, which awakened me then, and hath never forsaken me in that industry, as he is the Authour of that purpose, so is he a witnes of this protestation; that I behaved my selfe, and proceeded therin with humility, and diffidence in my selfe; and by that, which by his grace, I tooke to be the ordinary meanes, which is frequent praier, and equall and indifferent affections' (*Pseudo-Martyr*, sig. B3).

youth. He takes for granted that 'the intellect, which is made for truth, can attain truth, and, having attained it, can keep it, can recognize it, and preserve the recognition'.[1] In the most famous lines of the poem Truth stands on a hill. It is not a will-o'-the-wisp flickering above a swamp, or an uncertain light beckoning us into the mazes of a wood. We may be temporarily at a standstill, or forced to make our way deviously; or we may have gone wrong— but if we have, something tells us we have missed our way, for we know our general direction. The maxim 'Doubt wisely' has for its complement 'Keepe the truth which thou'hast found'; and the mysteries of religion are likened to the sun, which cannot be looked at directly, but whose existence is not in doubt: we walk, indeed, in its light.

The root of Donne's religious development can be seen in the third Satire.[2] It is significant that his first religious poem is not a divine poem, but a satire. In the proper senses of both words Donne is a moral, not a metaphysical poet. His subject is the relation of human beings to each other, or to a God who is the Hebrew God of Righteousness and Love, not the 'God of the philosophers'. What metaphysical ideas he has—and, as C. S. Lewis once observed, they are worked rather hard, like a stage army—he explores not for their own sake, but for the light they throw on his true subject, the heart of man. In his sermons he is far more remarkable as a moral than as a dogmatic theologian, and on mystical theology he has almost nothing to say. 'Morall Divinity becomes us all', he wrote, 'but Naturall Divinity, and Metaphysick Divinity, almost all may spare.'[3] When he was in Germany, as Doncaster's chaplain, in 1619, he wrote to Sir Tobie Mathew, who had changed in the opposite direction, from Canterbury to Rome:

We are fallen into so slack and negligent times, that I have been

[1] J. H. Newman, *A Grammar of Assent*, ch. vii, § 2. John Sparrow has pointed out that Donne never in later life reproached himself for having been an atheist; see 'Donne's Religious Development', *Theology* (March 1932).

[2] The essential consistency of Donne's religious position from the third Satire through the Sermons is ably argued by Dominic Baker-Smith in 'John Donne's *Critique* of True Religion', *John Donne, Essays in Celebration*, ed. A. J. Smith (1972), pp. 404–32.

[3] Simpson, *Essays*, p. 88.

sometimes glad to hear, that some of my friends have differed from me in Religion. It is some degree of an union to be united in a serious meditation of God, and to make any Religion the rule of our actions.[1]

Donne, when he reached maturity, decided that the fundamentals of the Christian Faith were preserved in the Established Church of his country, accepting its claim to be 'the Church of God in England'. The claims of the Roman See and the 'additions' of the Roman Church in the 'Trent Articles' did not commend themselves to his intellect or conscience. But he did not confuse these questions with what to him were the essentials of religion: 'a serious meditation of God' and the acceptance of the moral obligations such a meditation imposes. Like many complicated persons, Donne has his simplicities.

The transformation of the Jack Donne who wrote the *Satires* and *Elegies* into Dr. John Donne, Dean of St. Paul's, was not the result of a sudden revelation of truths unknown before, or of any sudden moral revulsion. There is no trace of any period of religious or moral crisis in Donne's works. The change was a gradual one, brought about by the circumstances of his life and the maturing of his mind and temperament. His marriage was in a worldly sense disastrous; it brought him to poverty and the distress of seeing his wife and children poor. The disappointments of his middle life broke his health and spirit. But he himself traced his desire to seek God to his love for his wife;[2] and, writing before his ordination, he thanked God for his marriage, which by 'confining his affections' had delivered him from the 'Egypt of lust', and for his poverty and loneliness which had afforded him opportunity to 'feed upon both thy Mannaes, thy self in thy Sacrament, and that other, which is true Angells food, contemplation of thee'.[3] A cynic might say that Donne began to take his religion seriously only when its rivals, the world and the flesh, withdrew their batteries. But the story of Donne's marriage silences cynicism. His acceptance of the responsibilities of a husband and a father had, as its parallel, his acceptance of the

---

[1] *Tobie Mathew Collection*, p. 337.

[2] Cf. 'Holy Sonnets' (Westmoreland), 1. 5–6:

> Here the admyring her my mind did whett
> To seeke thee God; so streames do shew the head.

[3] Simpson, *Essays*, pp. 75 and 96.

responsibilities of religious belief. The religion he had learnt as a child, whose central teaching he had not repudiated, however much he may have ignored it, reasserted its claim upon his conscience. It was strong enough to preserve him from the temptations of 'our old subtle foe' in his middle years: temptations to sins more deadly, because less generous, than those of his youth—envy, bitterness, and despair. During these years of illness, disappointment, perpetual anxiety, and humiliating financial dependence, he began to write divine poems, and they show us the continuity of his religious life. The habits of devotion they reflect are those he must have been taught as a child, which he took up again—he may never have abandoned them—with adult seriousness and adult intensity. In his devotional conservatism, his retention of traditions of Christian prayer and worship which did not seem to him incompatible with the Protestant position, he is like others of his generation, the generation in which the distinctive tradition of Anglicanism becomes clearly apparent. It is the generation which came to maturity while Hooker was writing *The Laws of Ecclesiastical Polity*.[1] But while Andrewes, Donne's elder contemporary, searched ancient office-books and liturgies to compose his eclectic *Preces Privatae*; to Donne, medieval ways of devotion were familiar and natural.

This is most obvious in '*La Corona*', the date of which is uncertain.[2] '*La Corona*' is a single poem, made up of seven linked sonnets,

---

[1] Donne's admiration for Hooker is well known from the epigram he wrote in his copy of Covell's *Defence*:

Ad Autorem
Non eget Hookerus tanto tutamine; Tanto
Tutus qui impugnat sed foret Auxilio.
(Keynes, p. 267)

Their relation has not, however, received the recognition it deserves. What is sometimes called 'orthodox Anglicanism'—although the term is hardly allowable for what is a temper of mind and not a system of doctrine—came to exist because men of Donne's calibre learned from Hooker how to see particular controversies in the light of certain philosophic principles. Hooker did not tell them what to think, but how to think. Donne's debt to Hooker is not a verbal one; but his treatment of law, for instance, in *Pseudo-Martyr* constantly recalls Hooker. To read the *Essays in Divinity* or the Sermons, after a re-reading of Hooker, is to feel at once that Donne has absorbed Hooker's conception of the *via media* so deeply that it has become the basis of his own thinking. Donne is too often spoken of as accepting something which, in fact, he helped to establish.

[2] Dated by Grierson July 1607. I originally accepted Grierson's date; but David Novarr has argued cogently against it. See below pp. 55–56 and supplementary notes, p. 151.

each of which celebrates not so much an event in the life of Christ as a mystery of faith. Those brought up in a different tradition might well wonder why Donne should devote one sonnet of his seven to the Finding in the Temple, and omit all reference to the events of the Ministry, except for a brief reference to miracles. The emphasis on the beginning and close of the life of Christ is characteristic of medieval art, whether we think of a series of windows like those at Fairford, or of the medieval dramatic cycles. It was dictated by the desire to present with simplicity the Christian scheme of man's redemption. The popular devotional equivalent of this emphasis upon the plan of salvation was the meditation on the Fifteen Mysteries of the Rosary, and reference to them explains at once why Donne would find it natural to pass directly from the Finding in the Temple to the events of Holy Week.[1] Habits of prayer, like other early habits, can survive modifications of a man's intellectual position. It is doubtful whether Donne felt there was anything particularly Catholic in concentrating on the Mysteries of the Faith, or in addressing his second and third sonnets to the Blessed Virgin, or in apostrophizing St. Joseph in his fourth; but it is also doubtful whether anyone who had been brought up as a Protestant would have done so.

'La Corona' has been undervalued as a poem by comparison with the 'Holy Sonnets', because the difference of intention behind the two sets of sonnets has not been recognized. The 'La Corona' sonnets are inspired by liturgical prayer and praise—oral prayer; not by private meditation and the tradition of mental prayer. They echo the language of collects and office hymns, which expound the doctrines of the Catholic Faith, recalling the events from which those doctrines are derived, but not attempting to picture them in detail. Instead of the scene of the maiden alone in her room at Nazareth, there is a theological paradox: 'Thy Makers maker, and thy Fathers

---

[1] The Joyful Mysteries are: the Annunciation, Visitation, Nativity, Presentation, Finding in the Temple; the Sorrowful Mysteries are: the Agony, Scourging, Crowning with Thorns, Bearing of the Cross, Crucifixion; the Glorious Mysteries are: the Resurrection, Ascension, Coming of the Holy Ghost, Assumption, Coronation. Donne's 'rectified devotion' naturally omits the last two, which have no basis in Scripture.

mother'. The scandal of the Cross is presented not by a vivid picture of its actual ignominy and agony, but by the thought that here the Lord of Fate suffered a fate at the hand of his creatures. The petitions with which the last three poems end, though couched in the singular, are petitions which any man might pray. Each is the appropriate response to the mystery propounded. It is not surprising to find that the first sonnet of the set is a weaving together of phrases from the Advent Offices in the Breviary, and that the second draws on the Hours of the Blessed Virgin. As always happens with Donne, direct dependence on sources weakens as he proceeds.[1] But the impulse with which he began 'La Corona' is clearly visible in the first two sonnets. His 'crowne of prayer and praise' was to be woven from the prayers and praises of the Church. It is possible that he chose to use the sonnet, a form he had used before this only for epistles, because he wished to write formally and impersonally: to create an offering of beauty and dignity. 'La Corona' is perhaps no more than a religious exercise, but it is an accomplished one. The sonnets are packed with meaning, with striking and memorable expressions of the commonplaces of Christian belief. The last line of each, repeated as the first line of the next, is both a fine climax and a fine opening. Unlike the majority of Elizabethan sonneteers, Donne has chosen the more difficult form of the sonnet. He follows Sidney in limiting the rhymes of the octave to two, and employs Sidney's most favoured arrangement of those rhymes in two closed quatrains. He alternates between two arrangements of the rhymes of the sestet.[2] His seventh sonnet

---

[1] This process can be seen in the 'Holy Sonnets', and, to take a very different kind, the *Elegies*. Donne appears to have begun his career as a love poet by a close imitation of the Ovidian elegy, but he transforms it by a passion outside Ovid's range, a dramatic intensity Ovid did not attempt, and a kind of wit beyond the scope of the 'sweet witty soul of Ovid', so that the finest of the Elegies do not suggest Ovid at all.

[2] The first, third, and fifth sonnets have a closed quatrain and a couplet; the second, fourth, sixth and seventh, an open quatrain and a couplet. This second arrangement is Sidney's favourite; the first is also found in *Astrophel and Stella*, but only in three sonnets. Apart from the obvious attraction of the drama and wit of *Astrophel and Stella*, a work whose relation to the *Songs and Sonnets* has not been sufficiently discussed, Donne would naturally be drawn to Sidney's, rather than to the looser 'Elizabethan' form of the sonnet. Sidney combined the final couplet, which suits his and Donne's natural rhetorical gift so well, with a stricter organization of the whole poem. Donne could find in the Sidneian form, as he did in his own complex stanzas, the artistic pleasure of overcoming 'Rimes vexation'.

presented a problem; if it contrasted with his sixth, it would be the same as his first. He chose the lesser evil, and repeated the form of the sixth sonnet in the seventh, in order to make the last lead round again to the first and form a circle.

'A Litany', which can be dated with some certainty in 1608,[1] is less successful than 'La Corona', but more interesting. Donne has cast his 'meditation in verse' into the formal mould of a litany. On the other hand, he has employed a stanza of his own invention. The contrast between the simple traditional outline of the poem and the intricacies of the separate stanzas is the formal expression of the poem's ambiguity. It appears impersonal, but is, in fact, highly personal. It tells us much, though indirectly, of its author's mind at the time when it was written, not least because it is in some ways uncharacteristic of him. It has the special interest of poems which are the product of a period of transition, when in the process of re-shaping a personality some elements are stressed to the exclusion of others. 'A Litany' is remarkable for a quality which is rare in Donne's poetry, though it is often found in his letters and sermons, sobriety. Although it is the wittiest of the *Divine Poems*, startling in paradox, precise in antithesis, and packed with allusions, its intellectual ingenuity and verbal audacity are employed to define an ideal of moderation in all things. Grierson stigmatized it as 'wire-drawn and tormented'. 'Wire-drawn' it may be called with justice; it analyses temptations with scrupulosity, and shows a wary sense of the distinctions that divide the tainted from the innocent act or motive. But 'tormented' seems less just, even if we confine the word to the style. The ideal which is aspired to is simplicity of motive, 'evennesse' of piety, and a keeping of 'meane waies'. Something of this ideal is already realized in the deliberate care with which the aspiration is expressed. At first sight the poem may appear over-ingenious. On further acquaintance it comes to seem not so much ingenious as exact; less witty, and more wise.

We know from Donne's letter to Goodyer, in which he refers to its composition,[2] that 'A Litany' was written during an illness and

---

[1] Its date depends on our dating of *Biathanatos*; see p. 81 and supplementary notes, p. 154.

[2] *Letters*, pp. 31–37; the relevant passage is quoted in full on p. 81.

in a mood of dejection. The 'low devout melancholie' of 'La Corona' is here regarded as sin from which Donne prays to be delivered in the first verse. It is very closely connected with Donne's two long exercises in casuistry: *Biathanatos*, in which he argued the most searching problem in personal ethics, whether a man may ever rightly take his own life; and *Pseudo-Martyr*, in which he debated under its pressing topical form the perennial problem of which things are Caesar's. It is a casuist's poem and shows traces both of the current debate on the Oath of Allegiance[1] and of Donne's personal searchings of conscience in his years of failure, when he was still hoping for worldly success and, if Walton is right, had already been offered and had rejected advancement in the Church. Donne, who was 'subtle to plague himself', must have been conscious of the contrast between his relatives, who for conscience' sake had chosen exile, imprisonment or death, and himself. He had conformed to the Established Church and was using his powers in its defence, and had even been offered a means of maintenance in its ministry. The rather exaggerated stress in 'A Litany' on the compatibility of the service of God with 'this worlds sweet' may reflect his need, at this time, to assure himself that the way that appears easier is not, for that reason, necessarily wrong. Intransigence may even, he hints, be a form of self-indulgence, an easy way out of the strain of conflicting duties:

> for Oh, to some
> Not to be Martyrs, is a martyrdome.[2]

But if this seems an over-subtle explanation, there is another reason why Donne should at this period pray more strongly to be delivered from contempt of the world than from over-valuing it. The temptation to despise what one has not obtained and to cry, because one has been unsuccessful, 'the world's not worth my care'

[1] See the reference to 'equivocation' in Stanza XIX.

[2] Trollope analysed this state of mind well in describing young Mr. Arabin's hesitations after Newman's secession: 'Everything was against him: all his worldly interests required him to remain a Protestant; and he looked on his worldly interests as a legion of foes, to get the better of whom was a point of extremest honour. In his then state of ecstatic agony such a conquest would have cost him little; he could easily have thrown away all his livelihood; but it cost him much to get over the idea that by choosing the Church of England he should be open in his own mind to the charge that he had been led to such a choice by unworthy motives.' (*Barchester Towers*, ch. xx.)

is strong to ambitious natures. It must have been strong to Donne
who had by nature both the melancholy and the scorn of the satirist.
If we remember the circumstances of his life at Mitcham—his
anxiety for his wife whom he had brought to poverty and for the
future of his growing family, his inability to find secure employ-
ment and his broken health—the petitions of 'A Litany' gain in
meaning. We see the passionate and hyperbolical Donne, the proud
and irritable young man of the *Satires* and *Elegies*, attempting to
school himself to patience, not rejecting with scorn a world that
has disappointed him, but praying that he may accept what life
brings in a religious spirit. His declarations that happiness may
exist in courts, and that the earth is not our prison, show an affinity
with the contemporary movement in France, which Bremond de-
scribed under the name of 'l'humanisme dévot'.[1] They also contrast
most interestingly with the pessimism of şome Jacobean writers,
particularly Webster, with whom Donne is often compared. The
dying Antonio's cry, 'And let my Sonne, flie the Courts of Princes',
and Vittoria's last words, 'O happy they that never saw the Court',
only sum up the constant Senecan despising of the world in
Webster's two greatest plays. 'A Litany' has none of this cynicism.
It is, whatever else we may say of it, a singularly unbitter poem,
although it was written at a bitter time.

   In many ways it is the most Anglican of the *Divine Poems* and
continually anticipates Donne's leading ideas as a preacher. Al-
though we may see in his restoration of the saints, whom Cranmer
had banished from the Litany, a further sign of his loyalty to 'the
ancient ways', his own praise of his poem in his letter to Goodyer
makes the typical Anglican claim of avoiding both excess and defect:

   That by which it will deserve best acceptation, is, That neither the
   Roman Church need call it defective, because it abhors not the particu-
   lar mention of the blessed Triumphers in heaven; nor the Reformed
   can discreetly accuse it, of attributing more then a rectified devotion
   ought to doe.

We may also see in the whole poem a habit of mind which has been
shaped by the practice of systematic self-examination, and thinks
more in terms of particular sins and failings than in terms of general

   [1] See the first volume of his *Histoire littéraire du sentiment religieux en France.*

and total unworthiness; but the particular sins which Donne prays to be delivered from are not the traditional sins. There is no trace of the old classifications under which the conscience can be examined: sins against God and sins against my neighbour, or the seven deadly sins and their branches. Instead the sins in 'A Litany' can all be referred back to two general philosophic conceptions: the conception of virtue as the mean between two extremes, and the related conception of virtue as the proper use of all the faculties. Donne anticipates here that ideal of 'reasonable piety' which is so familiar later in the century in the manuals of the Caroline divines. The resolute rejection of other-worldliness, the anti-ascetic and anti-mystical bias of the poem, the concentration on 'a daily beauty' and the sanctification of ordinary life, with the consequent ignoring of any conception of sanctity as something extraordinary and heroic, the exaltation of the undramatic virtues of patience, discretion, and a sober cheerfulness—all these things are characteristic of Anglican piety in the seventeenth century and after.[1] In comparison with the Roman Catholic books of devotion, which they frequently drew upon and adapted, the Anglican manuals seem to some tastes rather dry, with their stress on edification and 'practical piety' and the 'duties of daily life'. 'A Litany' has something of this dryness. It has neither the warmth of medieval religious devotion, nor the exalted note of the Counter-Reformation. It reflects the intellectuality which Anglicanism derived from its break with medieval tradition and its return to the patristic ages.

But in spite of its many felicities in thought and expression, its beauty of temper, its interest in what it tells us of Donne's mind,

[1] Cf. Taylor's *Holy Living, The Whole Duty of Man,* and Law's *A Serious Call to a Devout and Holy Life,* and such classic expressions of the Anglican spirit as Bishop Ken's Morning and Evening Hymns and Keble's Hymn 'New every morning is the love':

> We need not bid, for cloistered cell,
> Our neighbour and our work farewell,
> Nor strive to wind ourselves too high
> For sinful man beneath the sky:
>
> The trivial round, the common task,
> Would furnish all we ought to ask,—
> Room to deny ourselves, a road
> To bring us daily nearer God.

See H. R. McAdoo, *The Structure of Caroline Moral Theology* (1949), for an extended discussion of the Caroline manuals.

and its historical interest as an early expression by a writer of genius of a piety characteristic of the Church of England, 'A Litany' cannot be regarded as a wholly successful poem. It is an elaborate private prayer, rather incongruously cast into a liturgical form. Donne's letter to Goodyer shows he was aware of the discrepancy between such a 'divine and publique' name and his 'own little thoughts'. He attempted to defend himself by the examples of two Latin litanies which he had found 'amongst ancient annals'.[1] The defence is not a very cogent one. The litanies he refers to, although written by individuals, are genuine litanies, suitable for general use. Donne's poem could hardly be prayed by anyone but himself. Although he preserves the structure of a litany (Invocations, Deprecations, Obsecrations, and Intercessions), he does not preserve the most important formal element in a litany, the unvarying responses in each section. His opening invocations to the Persons of the Trinity have each a particular petition in place of the repeated 'Miserere nobis'. He is, of course, debarred by his membership of a Reformed Church from using the response 'Ora pro nobis'; instead he exercises his ingenuity in finding suitable petitions for each group of saints to make, or for us to make as we remember them. There is some awkwardness in this 'rectified devotion', which, accepting that the saints pray for men, avoids direct requests for their suffrages while suggesting fitting subjects for their intercessions; and the absence of any response makes these stanzas formally unsatisfactory. With the Deprecations, Obsecrations, and Intercessions, he makes use of the responses 'Libera nos' and 'Audi nos'; but he treats them as refrains to be modified according to each stanza, as he had loved to adapt and twist refrains in his love poetry. In one place he goes so far as to invert his response, and beg the Lord not to hear. One may sympathize with Donne's desire to find a form for his meditation; but the incompatibility between the material of the poem and the chosen form is too great. The form has had to be too much twisted to fit the material, and the material has been moulded to the form rather than expressed by it.

[1] See p. 81 where the letter is quoted. The two poems Donne refers to can be found in Migne, *P.L.* lxxxvii. 39 and 42. See supplementary notes to 'A Litany', p. 155.

Most critics have agreed in regarding 'La Corona' and 'A Litany' as inferior to the 'Holy Sonnets', which give an immediate impression of spontaneity. Their superiority has been ascribed to their having been written ten years later, and their vehemence and anguished intensity have been connected with a deepening of Donne's religious experience after the death of his wife. There can be no question of their poetic greatness, nor of their difference from 'La Corona' and 'A Litany'; but I do not believe that greatness or that difference to be due to the reasons which are usually given. The accepted date rests on an assumption which the textual history of the sonnets does not support: the assumption that the three 'Holy Sonnets' which the Westmoreland manuscript alone preserves were written at the same time as the other sixteen. These three sonnets can be called what Grierson called all the 'Holy Sonnets', 'separate ejaculations'; but the other sixteen fall into clearly recognizable sets of sonnets on familiar themes for meditation.[1] They are as traditional in their way as 'La Corona' and 'A Litany' are, and as the three Hymns are not. The Hymns are truly occasional; each arises out of a particular situation and a personal mood. But in theme and treatment the 'Holy Sonnets', if we ignore the three Westmoreland sonnets, depend on a long-established form of religious exercise: not oral prayer, but the simplest method of mental prayer, meditation. To say this is not to impugn their originality or their power. Donne has used the tradition of meditation in his own way; and it suits his genius as a poet far better than do the more formal ways of prayer he drew upon in 'La Corona' and 'A Litany'. Yet although, with the possible exception of the Hymns, the 'Holy Sonnets' are his greatest divine poems, I do not myself feel that they spring from a deeper religious experience than that which lies behind 'A Litany'. The evidence which points to a date in 1609 does not seem to me to conflict with their character as religious poems; on the contrary it accords rather better with it than does the hitherto accepted date.

Many readers have felt a discrepancy between the 'Holy Sonnets'

[1] The arguments for an earlier date for the main body of the 'Holy Sonnets', and the demonstration of their dependence on the tradition of formal meditation are set out at length in the second part of this Introduction.

and the picture which Walton gives of Donne's later years, and between the 'Holy Sonnets' and the sermons and Hymns. There is a note of exaggeration in them. This is apparent, not only in the violence of such a colloquy as 'Batter my heart', but also in the strained note of such lines as these:

> But who am I, that dare dispute with thee?
> O God, Oh! of thine onely worthy blood,
> And my teares, make a heavenly Lethean flood,
> And drowne in it my sinnes blacke memorie.
> That thou remember them, some claime as debt,
> I thinke it mercy, if thou wilt forget.

At first sight the closing couplet seems the expression of a deep humility; but it cannot be compared for depth of religious feeling with the 'Hymn to God the Father', where, however great the sin is, the mercy of God is implied to be the greater, or with such passages as the following on the phrase *virga irae*:

But truely, beloved, there is a blessed comfort ministred unto us, even in that word; for that word *Gnabar*, which we translate *Anger*, *wrath*, hath another ordinary signification in Scripture, which, though that may seem to be an easier, would prove a heavier sense for us to beare, than this of *wrath* and *anger*; this is, *preteritio, conniventia*, Gods forbearing to take knowledge of our transgressions; when God shall say of us, as he does of *Israel*, *Why should ye be smitten any more?* when God leaves us to our selves, and studies our recovery no farther, by any more corrections; for, in this case, there is the lesse comfort, because there is the lesse *anger* show'd. And therefore S. *Bernard*, who was heartily afraid of this sense of our word, heartily afraid of this preterition, that God should forget him, leave him out, affectionately, passionately embraces this sense of the word in our Text, *Anger*; and he sayes, *Irascaris mihi Domine, Domine mihi irascaris, Be angry with me O Lord, O Lord be angry with me, lest I perish!*[1]

This is the tone of the last lines of 'Good Friday':

> O thinke mee worth thine anger, punish mee,
> Burne off my rusts, and my deformity,
> Restore thine Image, so much, by thy grace,
> That thou may'st know mee, and I'll turne my face.

Both make the close of the sonnet seem facile.

[1] *Sermons*, x. 211.

The almost histrionic note of the 'Holy Sonnets' may be attributed partly to the meditation's deliberate stimulation of emotion; it is the special danger of this exercise that, in stimulating feeling, it may falsify it, and overdramatize the spiritual life. But Donne's choice of subjects and his whole-hearted use of the method are symptoms of a condition of mind very different from the mood of 'La Corona' or even from the conflicts which can be felt behind 'A Litany'. The meditation on sin and on judgement is strong medicine; the mere fact that his mind turned to it suggests some sickness in the soul. The 'low devout melancholie' of 'La Corona', the 'dejection' of 'A Litany' are replaced by something darker. In both his preparatory prayers Donne uses a more terrible word, despair. The note of anguish is unmistakable. The image of a soul in meditation which the 'Holy Sonnets' present is an image of a soul working out its salvation in fear and trembling. The two poles between which it oscillates are faith in the mercy of God in Christ, and a sense of personal unworthiness that is very near to despair. The flaws in their spiritual temper are a part of their peculiar power. No other religious poems make us feel so acutely the predicament of the natural man called to be the spiritual man. None present more vividly man's recognition of the gulf that divides him from God and the effort of faith to lay hold on the miracle by which Christianity declares that the gulf has been bridged.

Donne's art in writing them was to seem 'to use no art at all'. His language has the ring of a living voice, admonishing his own soul, expostulating with his Maker, defying Death, or pouring itself out in supplication. He creates, as much as in some of the *Songs and Sonnets*, the illusion of a present experience, throwing his stress on such words as 'now' and 'here' and 'this'. And, as often there, he gives an extreme emphasis to the personal pronouns:

> Take mee to you, imprison mee, for I
> Except you'enthrall mee, never shall be free,
> Nor ever chast, except you ravish mee.

The plain unadorned speech, with its idiomatic turns, its rapid questions, its exclamatory Oh's and Ah's, wrests the movement of

the sonnet to its own movement. The line is weighted with heavy
monosyllables, or lengthened by heavy secondary stresses, which
demand the same emphasis as the main stress takes. It may be
stretched out to

> All whom warre, dearth, age, agues, tyrannies,

after it has been contracted to

> From death, you numberlesse infinities.

Many lines can be reduced to ten syllables only by a more drastic
use of elision than Donne allowed himself elsewhere, except in the
Satires; and others, if we are to trust the best manuscripts, are a
syllable short and fill out the line by a pause.[1] This dramatic lan-
guage has a magic that is unanalysable: words, movement, and
feeling have a unity in which no element outweighs the other.

The effect of completely natural speech is achieved by exploiting
to the full the potentialities of the sonnet.[2] The formal distinction
of octave and sestet becomes a dramatic contrast. The openings of
Donne's sestets are as dramatic as the openings of the sonnets
themselves: impatient as in

> Why doth the devill then usurpe in mee?

or gentle as in

> Yet grace, if thou repent, thou canst not lacke;

or imploring as in

> But let them sleepe, Lord, and mee mourne a space.

Though the *turn* in each of these is different, in all three there is
that sudden difference in tension that makes a change dramatic.
Donne avoids also the main danger of the couplet ending: that it
may seem an afterthought, or an addition, or a mere summary.
His final couplets, whether separate or running on from the preced-
ing line, are true rhetorical climaxes, with the weight of the poem
behind them. Except for Hopkins, no poet has crammed more into

---

[1] See note on Versification, p. 54, and notes to 'Holy Sonnets' (1633), 3.4, 12.4,
and 11.

[2] Donne keeps to two rhymes in the octave. Eight sonnets rhyme the sestet
cddcee; eleven have *cdcdee*. No clear pattern governing the choice emerges in any
of the differing orders in the manuscripts and editions.

the sonnet than Donne. In spite of all the liberties he takes with
his line, he succeeds in the one essential of the sonnet: he appears
to need exactly fourteen lines to say exactly what he has to say.
Donne possibly chose the sonnet form as appropriate for a set of
formal meditations, but both in meditation and in the writing of
his sonnets he converts traditional material to his own use. He was
not, I believe, aiming at originality, and therefore the originality
of the 'Holy Sonnets' is the more profound.

With the exception of 'The Lamentations of Jeremy', in which
Donne, like so many of his contemporaries, but with more success
than most, attempted the unrewarding task of paraphrasing the
Scriptures, the remainder of the *Divine Poems* are occasional. The
poem 'Upon the Annunciation and Passion' is very near in mood
and style to '*La Corona*'. As there, Donne writes with strict objec-
tivity. He contemplates two mysteries which are facets of one
supreme mystery, and tries to express what any Christian might
feel.[1] On the other hand, 'Good Friday, Riding Westward' is a
highly personal poem: a free, discursive meditation arising out of
a particular situation. The elaborate preliminary conceit of the con-
trary motions of the heavenly bodies extends itself into astronomical
images, until the recollection of the Passion sweeps away all
thoughts but penitence. As in some of the finest of the *Songs and
Sonnets*, Donne draws out an initial conceit to its limit in order, as
it seems, to throw it away when 'to brave clearnesse all things are
reduc'd'. What he first sees as an incongruity—his turning his back
on his crucified Saviour—he comes to see as perhaps the better
posture, and finally as congruous for a sinner. The poem hinges on
the sudden apostrophe:

> and thou look'st towards mee,
> O Saviour, as thou hang'st upon the tree.

After this, discursive meditation contracts itself to penitent prayer.
The mounting tension of the poem—from leisurely speculation,

---

[1] F. E. Hutchinson told me that he once had the experience of being invited
to preach a Lady Day Sermon in a year when Good Friday fell on the same day,
and when, having written his sermon, he looked up Donne's poem, he found that
he had done little but expand Donne's couplet:

> Or 'twas in him the same humility,
> That he would be a man, and leave to be.

through the imagination kindled by 'that spectacle of too much weight for mee', to passionate humility—makes it a dramatic monologue. So also does the sense it gives us of a second person present—the silent figure whose eyes the poet feels watching him as he rides away to the west.

'Good Friday' is the last divine poem Donne wrote before his ordination and it points forward to the Hymns. They also arise from particular situations, are free, not formal meditations, and have the same unforced feeling. They are the only lyrics among the *Divine Poems*, and it is not only in their use of the pun and conceit that they remind us of the *Songs and Sonnets*. They have the spontaneity which '*La Corona*' and 'A Litany' lack, without the overemphasis of the 'Holy Sonnets'. In them Donne's imagination has room for play. Each sprang from a moment of crisis. The 'Hymn to Christ' was written on the eve of his journey overseas with Doncaster, a journey from which, as his Valediction Sermon shows, he felt he might not return. It is a finer treatment of the subject of the sonnet written after his wife's death in the Westmoreland manuscript. While the sonnet is general and reflective, in the Hymn his imagination is fired by his immediate circumstances and he translates his thoughts into striking and moving symbols. The 'Hymn to God the Father' was written, according to Walton, during Donne's grave illness of 1623, and the 'Hymn to God my God, in my sickness', whether it should be dated during the same illness or in 1631, was written when he thought himself at the point of death. In both the conclusion is the same: 'So, in his purple wrapp'd receive mee Lord', and 'Sweare by thy selfe'. Donne's earliest poem on religion, the third Satire, ended with the words 'God himselfe to trust', and it is fitting that what is possibly his last divine poem, and certainly one of his best known, should end with the memory of the promise to Abraham, the type of the faithful.[1] For the *Divine*

---

[1] Cf. Gen. xxii. 16: 'By myself have I sworn, saith the Lord'; and Heb. vi. 13–18: 'For when God made promise to Abraham, because he could swear by no greater, he sware by himself.... For men verily swear by the greater: and an oath for confirmation is to them an end of all strife. Wherein God, willing more abundantly to shew unto the heirs of promise the immutability of his counsel, confirmed it by an oath: that by two immutable things, in which it was impossible for God to lie, we might have a strong consolation, who have fled for refuge to lay hold upon the hope set before us.'

Poems are poems of faith, not of vision. Donne goes by a road which is not lit by any flashes of ecstasy, and in the words he had carved on his tomb 'aspicit Eum cujus nomen est Oriens'. The absence of ecstasy makes his divine poems so different from his love poems. There is an ecstasy of joy and an ecstasy of grief in his love poetry; in his divine poetry we are conscious almost always of an effort of will. In the 'Holy Sonnets' there is passion and longing, and in the Hymns some of the 'modest assurance' which Walton attributed to Donne's last hours, but there is no rapture.

If Donne's spiritual and moral achievement are to be assessed, we must go to the sermons rather than to the *Divine Poems*. Their moral wisdom, their power to admonish or console, their faith in God's mercy, and their constant thankfulness for his bounty are the testimony of 'a clear knowing soul, and of a Conscience at peace with it self'.[1] What raises Donne as a preacher above the level of his contemporaries is his Evangelical fervour, the Pauline note which is everywhere in his sermons.[2] He speaks to sinners, as a sinner who has found mercy. The generous and affectionate side of his nature found its outlet here. As he said in a sermon:

Till we come to that joy, which the heart cannot conceive, it is, I thinke, the greatest joy that the soule of man is capable of in this life, (especially where a man hath been any occasion of sinne to others) to assist the salvation of others.[3]

We should not expect to find in the religious poetry of a man who speaks like this a foretaste of bliss, or even the expectation of it.

Donne was a man of strong passions, in whom an appetite for life was crossed by a deep distaste for it. He is satirist and elegist at the same period, and even in the same poem. The scorn of the satirist invades the world of amorous elegy; his gayest poems have a note of bitterness, his most passionate lyrics are rarely free from a note of contempt, even if it is only a sardonic aside or illustration. In his love poetry he set the ecstasy of lovers over against the dull, foolish,

[1] Walton, *Lives*, p. 83.

[2] 'The cross of Christ is dimly seen in Taylor's works. Compare him in this respect with Donne, and you will feel the difference in a moment' (Coleridge, *Table Talk* (1835), i. 168, quoted Simpson, *Prose Works*, p. 76). Coleridge might well have mentioned Andrewes with Taylor.

[3] *Sermons*, v. 384.

or sordid business of the world, or exalted one member of her sex by depreciating all the rest, or, in revulsion from the 'queasie pain of being belov'd, and loving', turned on his partner with savagery or mockery. But he was also a man of strong and loyal affections: a good son, a devoted husband, a loving father, and a warm and constant friend. From the beginning there is this other side to Donne. In moral and psychological terms, Donne's problem was to come to terms with a world which alternately enthralled and disgusted him, to be the master and not the slave of his temperament. Like Wordsworth in his middle years, he came to long for 'a repose that ever is the same'. He did not look to religion for an ecstasy of the spirit which would efface the memory of the ecstasy of the flesh; but for an 'evennesse' of piety which would preserve him from despair. In the boldest of the 'Holy Sonnets' it is in order that he may 'rise and stand' that he prays to be overthrown, and in order that he may be ever chaste that he prays God to ravish him. The struggles and conflicts to which the *Divine Poems* witness did not lead to the secret heights and depths of the contemplative life, but to the public life of duty and charity which Walton describes. That Donne had to wrestle to the end is clear. Like Dr. Johnson, with whom, in his natural melancholy and as a practical moralist, he has much in common, he remained burdened by the consciousness of his sins and aware of his need for mercy at the judgement.

Donne's divine poems are the product of conflict between his will and his temperament. They lack, therefore, the greatness of his love poetry, whose power lies in its 'unchartered freedom': in the energy of will with which he explores and expresses the range of his temperament. In his love poetry he is not concerned with what he ought or ought not to feel, but with the expression of feeling itself. Passion is there its own justification, and so is disgust, or hatred or grief. In his divine poetry feeling and thought are judged by the standard of what a Christian should feel or think. As a love poet he seems to owe nothing to what any other man in love had ever felt or said before him; his language is all his own. As a divine poet he cannot escape using the language of the Bible, and of hymns and prayers, or remembering the words of Christian writers. Christianity is a revealed religion, contained in the Scriptures and the experience of Christian souls: the Christian poet cannot voyage alone. The truths of Donne's love poetry are truths of the imagination, which freely transmutes personal experience. They are his own discoveries. The truths of revelation are the accepted basis of his religious poetry, and imagination has here another task. It is, to some extent, fettered. Donne anticipated Johnson's criticism of 'poetical devotion', and was perhaps his own best critic, when he wrote to Sir Robert Carr, apologizing for his poem on Hamilton:

You know my uttermost when it was best, and even then I did best when I had least truth for my subject. In this present case there is so much truth as it defeats all Poetry. . . . If you had commanded mee to have waited on his body to Scotland and preached there, I would have embraced the obligation with more alacrity.[1]

But although the *Divine Poems* are not the record of discoveries, but of struggles to appropriate a truth which has been revealed, that truth does not 'defeat all Poetry', but gives us a poetry whose intensity is a moral intensity. Some religious poetry, Herbert's perhaps, can be regarded as a species of love poetry; but Donne's is not of that kind. The image of Christ as Lover appears in only two of his poems—both written soon after the death of his wife. The image which dominates his divine poetry is the image of Christ as Saviour, the victor over sin and death. The strength with which his imagination presents this figure is the measure of his need, and that need is the subject of the finest of his religious poems.

II. THE DATE, ORDER, AND INTERPRETATION OF THE 'HOLY SONNETS'

The problem of the date of the 'Holy Sonnets' is a complicated one, since it has to be treated together with two related problems: the problem of their right order and the problem of their artistic intention.

The only external evidence for a date after Donne's ordination is Walton's statement, that Donne 'was not so falne out with heavenly

[1] Milgate, *Anniversaries etc.*, p. 209.

Poetry, as to forsake it, no not in his declining age, witnessed then by many divine Sonnets, and other high, holy, and harmonious composures'.[1] Walton goes on to quote 'A Hymn to God the Father' in full, and refers to Donne's having written his 'Hymn to God my God, in my sickness' on his death-bed, though he does not quote from this until the edition of 1670. He is precise in dating the two Hymns, though possibly wrong in the date he gives to the second; but his other references are too vague to be convincing, and they fit the picture he is drawing so well that he may have been mistaking probability for fact.[2] Walton sees Donne as a second St. Augustine: the idea that Jack Donne wrote secular poetry, but Dr. Donne wrote 'divine sonnets' and Hymns, is only too consistent with his whole conception of his subject. One would never guess from Walton that Donne wrote any divine poetry at all before his ordination. Grierson did not, however, use Walton's testimony in support for a late date for the 'Holy Sonnets'. He regarded the question as settled by Gosse's discovery in the Westmoreland manuscript of three additional sonnets, the first of which, 'Since she whome I lovd, hath payd her last debt', must have been written after 1617 when Anne Donne died, accepting Gosse's argument that this dated the 'Holy Sonnets' as a whole. This argument rests on the assumption that the nineteen poems we call the 'Holy Sonnets' were all written at the same time, and that to date one is consequently to date all. An examination of the transmission of the poems in manuscript does not support this assumption. It further enables us to see that the nineteen sonnets fall into distinct groups.

In the manuscripts of Group I and Group II[3] only twelve of the sonnets are found.[4] These same twelve in the same order were printed under the title 'Holy Sonnets' in the first edition of 1633,

---

[1] *Life of Donne* (1640); unchanged subsequently.

[2] See Appendix E, for a discussion of Walton's dating of the second Hymn. It is suggested there that his dating is less acceptable than Sir Julius Caesar's because of its very plausibility.

[3] For the manuscript groups, see the classified list of manuscripts on p. xcvii.

[4] In Group II they appear without title, following '*La Corona*'. In Group I they also follow '*La Corona*' and the heading 'Holy Sonnets' is given to both sets. *1633* follows Group I in giving the heading to both sets, but it repeats it for the second set. It is, of course, a description, not a title; but it has to be treated as a title to distinguish these sonnets from '*La Corona*'.

and can be found as they appear there in the present edition, under the heading 'Holy Sonnets (1633)', numbered 1–12. The manuscripts of Group III also contain only twelve sonnets, but not the same twelve. They omit four (7–10), they place the last (12) as their fourth, and they interpolate four other sonnets as their first, third, seventh, and tenth.[1] They give this set of twelve the title 'Divine Meditations'. Two manuscripts of Group III, *Luttrell* and *O'Flaherty*, add after their set of 'Divine-Meditations' the four sonnets (7–10 of *1633*) which are not found in the other members of the group, under the heading 'Other Meditations'. The Westmoreland manuscript has the twelve 'Divine Meditations' of Group III, the four 'Other Meditations' of *Luttrell* and *O'Flaherty*, and three sonnets which it alone preserves, written out as a continuous series of nineteen sonnets under the heading 'Holy Sonnets'. In the second and fuller edition of Donne's poems in 1635, sixteen sonnets were printed. The editor had access to a Group III manuscript, from which he supplemented the edition of 1633. The order of the sixteen sonnets of *1635*, which is the order of all subsequent editions, is not found in any manuscript, and plainly arose from a conflation of the order of *1633* and Group III. Tabular form can make the relation of the different witnesses clear, if we employ **1–12** for 'Holy Sonnets (*1633*)', 1, 2, 3, 4, for 'Holy Sonnets (added in *1635*)', and *1, 2, 3,* for 'Holy Sonnets (Westmoreland MS.)'.

```
I, II, 1633  1, 2, 3,   4, 5, 6, 7, 8, 9, 10, 11, 12
III          1, 1, 3,  12, 2, 3,  2, 4, 5,   4,  6, 11
Lut, O'F     1, 1, 3,  12, 2, 3,  2, 4, 5,   4,  6, 11, and 7, 8, 9, 10
W            1, 1, 3,  12, 2, 3,  2, 4, 5,   4,  6, 11, 7, 8, 9, 10, 1, 2, 3
1635         1, 1, 3,   2, 2, 3, 4,  4, 5,   6,  7,  8, 9, 10, 11, 12
(Grierson I–XVI)
```

[1] These four additional sonnets, which were first printed in *1635*, appear in the present edition as 'Holy Sonnets (added in 1635)', numbered 1–4. (For reasons which are given later, the order in which the second and third occur in Group III and *1635* has been reversed.)

Although, for reference, consecutive numbering would be convenient, to re-number the 'Holy Sonnets' 1–19 would disguise what I hope to establish: that they are not a single set of poems, but a set of twelve, a set of four, and three separate poems. There is also possibility of confusion in complete renumbering. The method adopted makes it possible to continue to use the old Roman numbers, which are given at the foot of each sonnet, for reference.

The picture which the manuscripts present is of two distinct sets of 'Holy Sonnets' in circulation, each set containing eight in common with the other and four peculiar to itself. *Westmoreland* must be regarded as having the set in Group III, followed, as in *Luttrell* and *O'Flaherty*, by the four sonnets otherwise peculiar to Groups I and II and the three peculiar to itself.[1] The obvious conflation of the two sets in *1635* we can ignore.[2]

When we look at the two sets of twelve sonnets, we see at once that while the set in the Group III manuscripts presents no obvious sequence, the twelve sonnets of Groups I and II, printed in *1633*, form a coherent set of poems, and are by no means 'separate ejaculations'. The first six are quite clearly a short sequence on one of the most familiar themes for a meditation: death and judgement, or the Last Things. The first sonnet is a preparatory prayer before making a meditation, beginning with an act of recollection:

> As due by many titles I resigne
> My selfe to thee, O God, first I was made
> By thee, and for thee, and when I was decay'd
> Thy blood bought that, the which before was thine . . .;

the second vividly imagines extreme sickness:

> Oh my blacke Soule! now thou art summoned
> By sicknesse . . .;

the third, with equal vividness, imagines the very moment of death:

---

[1] The compilers of *Lut* and *O'F* (see pp. lxix–lxxi) raked together all the poems they could find. Their basis was a Group III manuscript, but they had access also to a manuscript of Group II, from which they took poems not found in other Group III manuscripts. Fortunately they made no attempt to conflate the two sets of 'Holy Sonnets', but simply added under a separate heading, at the close of their Group III set, the four extra sonnets they found in their Group II manuscript.

W (see pp. lxxviii–lxxxi) differs from time to time in '*La Corona*' as well as in the 'Holy Sonnets' from Group III. But, except for a reading in 'Holy Sonnets' (1633), 11 (see p. 72), the differences are trivial and seem likely to be due to errors in the archetype of Group III. The agreement in the order of the 'Holy Sonnets' now seems to me more significant than the variants and I do not now regard *W* as preserving in its first twelve sonnets a different version from the version in Group III.

[2] It will be seen that the editor of *1635*, finding that the sonnet fourth in order in his Group III manuscript was already in print as the twelfth of *1633*, did not move it. He seems to have meant, allowing for this, to have inserted his four new sonnets in the places where he found them in his Group III manuscript. The printer may have misunderstood his instructions, and placed the last two (2 and 4) before, instead of after, 3 and 5 of *1633*.

This is my playes last scene, here heavens appoint
My pilgrimages last mile;

the fourth brings before us the general judgement at the Last Day:

At the round earths imagin'd corners, blow
Your trumpets, Angells . . .;

the fifth is more discursive, but its subject is damnation; the sixth is on the death of Death at the resurrection of the just. The last six sonnets do not form a sequence; but they are on two aspects of a single theme, love. The first three (7–9) are concerned with the Atonement, and the mystery of the Creator's love for his creatures, for whom he was willing to suffer death. The last three (10–12) reverse the theme and are on the love man owes to God and to his neighbour. The progress is clear: 'We love him because he first loved us.' I suggest that it is impossible when one reads these twelve sonnets in the order in which they were printed in the first edition, and as they appear in the two groups of manuscripts which have the higher authority, to resist the conclusion that they were intended to be read as a consecutive set of twelve, made up of two contrasted sets of six. For this reason I have returned to the first edition and print them as they appear there.

The set of twelve in the Group III manuscripts has ruined this sequence and makes no sense as it stands. But, if we take out from it the four sonnets which are interpolated there and in 1635, we see again that these four are related. Scattered through the Group III set they seem merely 'separate ejaculations'. Read together, as I have printed them, they are seen to be, if not so obviously a sequence, at least four sonnets on a single subject. They are all penitential and are linked by their common emphasis on sin and tears for sin. They also handle, in the manner of a meditation, a traditional subject for meditation.

On the other hand, the three sonnets which *Westmoreland* alone preserves are entirely unconnected with each other. They really deserve to be called 'separate ejaculations'. But they are also quite distinct in their inspiration from the sixteen which precede them in the manuscript. They owe nothing in either subject or treatment to the tradition of formal meditation. The first is highly personal,

on the death of Donne's wife; the second is a prayer to Christ for
unity in his Church; the third is again purely personal, but is
analytic and not devotional. Both their transmission in a single
manuscript and their nature allow us to regard the *Westmoreland*
sonnets as quite independent of the other sixteen, and from this
point onwards they are excluded from the discussion.[1]

Before the question of the date of the 'Holy Sonnets' can be
argued, the existence of the two sets in the manuscripts, and par-
ticularly the confused order of the Group III set, must be accounted
for. Any explanation can only be hypothetical, and involves a hypo-
thetical reconstruction of how Donne came to write the sixteen
sonnets. The core of the two sets is the six sonnets on the Last
Things (1–6 of *1633*). These appear in the same order in each set,
although in Group III other sonnets are interspersed among them.
It seems as if the last two sonnets of the set in Groups I and II (11
and 12 of *1633*), which are also to be found in the set in Group III,
must have been Donne's original pendant to his six sonnets on the
Last Things. Such a meditation, designed to deepen religious fear,
needs to be followed by a meditation to awaken love. This is exactly
what Donne's 'wholsome meditation' in the eleventh sonnet is to
do, while the twelfth points to the duty laid on man to fulfil the
Law by love. These eight sonnets appear to have been given by
Donne to someone as a set of six, written out consecutively, and
two separate sonnets, and to have been accompanied, or followed,
by four quite distinct sonnets on a different topic, sin, also on loose
sheets. The two, which should have been added at the close of the
sequence on the Last Things, as well as the four penitential sonnets,
have been, in error, interpolated into the sequence, thus giving us
the Group III set.[2] Some time after he had written his two additional
sonnets on love—probably quite soon afterwards—Donne expanded
his eight sonnets to twelve, by developing the ideas in the last two.

---

[1] For discussion of their dates and of possible reasons for their non-circulation,
see Commentary, pp. 77–80. A full treatment of the sonnet on the Church will be
found in Appendix C.

[2] The striking fact is that the first six sonnets of Groups I and II appear in the
right order in the set in Group III. The error could have arisen from the sequence
having been written in a small 'book' to which two loose sonnets were attached
at the beginning and the end, with the four others slipped between the leaves. Or
the loose sonnets could have been copied on blanks at the feet or on versos.

He thus created a balance of six against six, which gives us the set we find in the manuscripts of Groups I and II.[1] On the basis of this hypothesis, we must begin by attempting to date the six sonnets on the Last Things.

Two quite different kinds of evidence lead to the same period: the earlier part of 1609. The first argument rests on a disputed question in theology, on which Donne at different times of his life appears to have held different views. Anyone who reads Donne's sermons in the folios, going steadily through them in their formidable bulk, must be struck by the persistence with which he recurs to certain themes. As a moral theologian he is much concerned with the sin of diffidence, or its extremer form, despair. This subject occurs again and again, frequently in not very obvious contexts, as if it were of great personal importance to him. We know from his letters and poems that it was. He was deeply infected with melancholy, which, like Dr. Johnson, he regarded as a sin. As a dogmatic theologian he has little to say on the whole on Christology, or the Atonement, or on such hotly contested topics as Election and Reprobation. He usually tells his congregation not to inquire too curiously into such matters.[2] But on one topic he is oddly insistent and dogmatic. He insists again and again, with a curious and sometimes hardly relevant exactitude, on the nature of the immortality of the soul, and particularly on precisely what happens to the soul at the moment of death. In the first place, he insists that the soul is immortal by preservation and not by its own nature; and, in the

---

[1] The Textual Introduction argues that the manuscripts of Group I descend from a collection made by Donne in 1614, and the manuscripts of Group II from papers Donne left with Sir Robert Ker in 1619. If this is so we should expect these manuscripts to preserve the sonnets in the order in which Donne wished them to be read. The arguments here and there support each other. The only premiss they have in common is that there is no evidence for dating these sonnets after Donne's ordination.

[2] 'I am not ordinarily bold in determining points . . . wherein I find the Fathers among themselves, and the School in it selfe, and the reverend Divines of the Reformation amongst themselves to differ' (*Sermons*, ii. 320). It will be remembered that, according to R.B., the 'doctrine men' called Donne 'a bad edifier'; see Grierson, i. 387. In abstaining from doctrinal controversy Donne was conforming to the instructions of both James and Charles, and with that general Anglican policy which Laud summed up in his statement to Fisher: that the Church does not require assent to particulars. It was the blend of theological vagueness with liturgical rigidity which made the Established Church so abhorrent to the Puritans.

second place, that at death the virtuous soul goes immediately to heaven to enjoy the full vision of God, and awaits in heaven the full consummation of its joy when it will be reunited with the body at the Last Day.[1]

The remarkable number of times Donne recurs to this second point suggests that it was, for some reason, a matter of importance to him. His dogmatism here is very unlike his usual theological caution, and is particularly striking since the greatest of the Doctors of the Reformation, Calvin, whom Donne regarded with great veneration, had expressly declared that the question of what happened to the soul at death was an indifferent matter, on which the truth had not been revealed. Donne himself owned, in his *Devotions*, that he would get different answers from different men if he were to ask 'what becomes of the *soules* of the *righteous*, at the *departing* thereof from the *body*'.[2] Later in the century, Jeremy Taylor is as emphatic as Donne, but on the opposite side; and, in general, Anglican opinion tended towards belief in an intermediate state of blessedness, rejecting both the Roman doctrine of purgatory and this other view, which is also Roman, that pure souls at once enjoy the Beatific Vision, and do not have to wait until the general judgement for full bliss. It is therefore interesting that in his six sonnets on death and judgement Donne's language is extremely imprecise on this very point on which he holds such precise and individual views as a preacher, and that some phrases suggest that when he wrote them he leaned rather to the contrary view.

The fourth sonnet of the sequence, the famous sonnet on the Last Day, opens with the lines:

> At the round earths imagin'd corners, blow
> Your trumpets, Angells, and arise, arise
> From death, you numberlesse infinities
> Of soules, and to your scattred bodies goe.

This picture is quite inconsistent with the view Donne puts forward in his sermons. There is no suggestion that the 'soules' have been waiting in bliss in heaven for their reunion with their bodies; on

---

[1] See Appendix A for a full discussion of Donne's views on these points, and for the history of the question at issue.
[2] Sparrow, *Devotions*, p. 103.

the contrary, they are bidden themselves to 'arise from death'.[1]
Even more interesting is a manuscript variant in the third sonnet
of the sequence, 'This is my playes last scene'. The editions, sup-
ported by the manuscripts of Group II alone, read

> And gluttonous death will instantly unjoynt
> My body, and soule, and I shall sleepe a space,
> But my'ever waking part shall see that face,
> Whose feare already shakes my every joynt.[2]

This is perfectly consistent with the doctrine of the sermons; and,
if no alternative reading had survived, only a theologically minded
reader might have wondered why Donne, in thinking of the body
asleep in the grave and the soul awake in heaven, should have said
'I shall sleepe'—thus equating the body rather than the soul with
'I'; and only a Warburton would have inquired how 'I' can sleep,
if a part of me is awake.[3] But the manuscripts of Groups I and III
and W read for the third line

> Or presently, I know not, see that Face.

Here we have a proper alternative to 'I shall sleepe', and in his
parenthesis Donne indicates that he does not know which alterna-
tive is the true one: 'I shall either sleep for a while, or I shall im-
mediately see the face of my Judge—I don't know which will
happen.' The deliberate expression of doubt is the more impressive,
in that the sestet assumes that the second alternative is the true
one, and makes the soul receive its final judgement at death: it
wings its flight to heaven, leaving its body in earth and its sins
fallen to hell. The reading of these manuscripts must be the original
reading, which Donne emended to the reading of Group II and the
editions some time after he had made up his mind on the point. But
for these two sonnets, which show a striking inconsistency with the
view put forward in the sermons, I would not mention the last son-
net of the sequence: 'Death be not proud'. The idea of death as a

---

[1] The picture is different from that in a macabre simile in 'The Storm' (ll.
45–48) where 'sin-burd'ned soules' creep out of the graves at the last day. Here they
rejoin their 'scattred bodies'.

[2] *1633* reads 'my soule', an error corrected in *1635*.

[3] There is, of course, precedent for this in the text beloved of mystical writers: 'I
sleep, but my heart waketh' (Song of Sol. v. 2).

sleep is so scriptural that the sonnet taken by itself seems perfectly natural. But with the other two sonnets in mind, one notices that here, also, there is no suggestion that the soul does not sleep with the body.

I am not suggesting that when Donne wrote these sonnets he was affected, as Sir Thomas Browne owns to have been in his 'greener studies', by the heresy of the Arabians, 'that the Souls of men perished with their Bodies, but should yet be raised at the last day'.[1] Although this view seems implied in the fourth sonnet, another view—that the soul sleeps—is implied in the sixth, and given as an alternative to the Roman view in the original version of the third. The truth would seem to be that when he wrote these sonnets Donne had given no serious thought to the matter at all. It may be objected that poetry need not be as precise in its expressions as theology; but there is one poem of Donne's, and a great one, which fortunately we can date exactly, which is built on the belief that at death the righteous soul is immediately in heaven. This doctrine is given long and splendid poetic expression at the heart of *The Second Anniversary* of 1612, and the language of the poem is echoed in the sermons. Donne's imagination here has been fired by the terror and rapture implicit in the statement that at the very moment of death the virtuous soul is at once before the face of God. *The Second Anniversary* derives its power from its juxtaposition of death and heaven: two contrary states meeting in a moment. I cannot believe that, after he had written with this full imaginative acceptance of the doctrine, Donne could have written these sonnets, in which there are no signs that it has made any impression on him at all, except as a doubtful hypothesis.

The Second Anniversary shows Donne making poetry out of a theological opinion accepted as a belief. It is possible to go farther and suggest when he decided that this disputed point was of crucial importance and made up his mind on it. *Pseudo-Martyr* is the earliest of his works in which he gives emphatic expression to the view we find in *The Second Anniversary* and again and again in the sermons. In writing *Pseudo-Martyr* he was driven to analyse the motives which led men to what he regarded as a false martyrdom; and he

[1] *Religio Medici*, i. 7.

naturally laid stress on the Roman doctrines of Indulgences and the Treasury of Merits. Both depended on the doctrine of purgatory, and discussion of purgatory brought him at once to this related question. But although he possibly came to a decision for polemical reasons,[1] it is clear that, once grasped, this doctrine seized his imagination. It appealed to his dramatic sense and to his extreme individualism. The notion of a personal final judgement at death, rather than a judgement delayed until the general judgement at the Last Day, makes more intense the drama of the individual soul's moral conflict. I would suggest that it was in the course of writing *Pseudo-Martyr*, in the latter half of 1609, that Donne first considered this question seriously, and that consequently his six sonnets on the Last Things cannot have been written later than the first half of that year.

A quite different argument leads to the same conclusion. On the death of Mrs. Bulstrode, who died at Lady Bedford's home, on 4 August 1609, Donne wrote an elegy beginning:

> Death I recant, and say, unsaid by mee
> What ere hath slip'd, that might diminish thee.

A second elegy on the same lady, which in some manuscripts follows immediately on this one, as a kind of answer to it, opens with the lines:

> Death be not proud, thy hand gave not this blow;
> Sinne was her captive, whence thy power doth flow;
> The executioner of wrath thou art,
> But to destroy the just is not thy part.

Grierson relegated this second elegy, which was printed as Donne's in *1635*, to his Appendix, rightly declaring that it was quite unlike Donne in its manner; and in his discussion of the canon, while accepting that it was intended as a reply to the first, suggested that it might be the work of Lady Bedford herself.[2] Many years ago, in his edition of Donne's poems in 1896, Sir Edmund Chambers suggested that Donne's unquestioned poem 'Death I

---

[1] See Appendix A, pp. 114–17.

[2] See Grierson, ii. cxliii–clxv. The suggestion is based on the ascription of the poem to 'C.L. of B.' in Harleian MS. 4064, and to 'L.C. of B.' in Rawlinson Poetical MS. 31. See Milgate, *Anniversaries etc.*, pp. 235–7.

recant' was a palinode for his bold defiance of death in the sonnet
'Death be not proud'.[1] This suggestion was disregarded, for in the
following year the additional sonnets from the Westmoreland manu-
scripts were published, and Gosse's assumption that they proved
all the 'Holy Sonnets' to be after 1617 was generally accepted. It can
now be brought forward again, and it is possible to explain what
Grierson could only comment on: the very curious fact that one of
Donne's finest openings is also the opening of a commonplace pious
poem not by him, and is indeed the only striking phrase in the
poem. We can imagine Donne writing his sequence, ending with
his denigration of death, and then, either to please Lady Bedford,
or even because he was genuinely moved by the death of a young
woman he knew, recanting and declaring that death's power was
real and terrible. We may then imagine someone else in the circle,
possibly the Countess herself, rebuking him with words out of his
own mouth, and expounding, in sincere if rather tepid verse, the
Christian hope. This would put the six sonnets before August 1609,
but not too long before. Both Donne's palinode and the unknown
elegist's retort would be apposite only if Donne had fairly recently
written his defiance of death.

There is another problem we can solve by regarding these six
sonnets as a distinct set. Its solution again connects them with the
Countess of Bedford's circle. Among the Verse-Letters in *1633* is
a sonnet headed 'To E. of D. with six holy Sonnets'. Grosart moved
it from there to stand before '*La Corona*' and Grierson followed him
in this. In the sonnet Donne says his poems were begotten by the
noble lord's own rhymes, and that there should have been seven,
but 'the seaventh hath still some maime'. Grierson rejected
Grosart's suggestion that 'E. of D.' was Doncaster, and proposed
instead the third Earl of Dorset, who succeeded to the title in
February 1609, two days after his marriage to the Lady Anne
Clifford, the Earl of Bedford's niece.[2] He accepted, however,

---

[1] See Chambers, i. 246, where, in a note on the sonnet, Chambers writes: 'This
sonnet is probably earlier than the palinode in the *Elegy on Mrs Boulstred* "Death
I recant".'

[2] Lord Hay became Viscount, not Earl of, Doncaster in 1618, and was made
Earl of Carlisle in 1622. As Grierson says, he is not known to have written verses.
Dorset came of a famous literary family and may well have written poems, which no
doubt merited Donne's eulogy as much or as little as the satiric vein of his great-

Grosart's other suggestion that the sonnets sent to the Earl were six out of the 'La Corona' set. Grierson, in the same note, also suggested 'La Corona' had been sent to Mrs. Herbert in 1607. It is difficult to believe that seven sonnets, perfect enough to go to her in 1607, were sent to Dorset some time after 1609, with one left out as imperfect and with a covering sonnet to say that they were newly begotten by his quickening genius. If, with David Novarr, we reject Grierson's date of 1607, it might be suggested that six of the set went to Dorset as inspired by him, and went later, when the seventh was perfected, to Mrs. Herbert. But there is a strong argument against the idea that the six sonnets sent to 'E. of D.' can have been six of the 'La Corona' set. The ingenuity of 'La Corona' lies in the seven poems making up an unbreakable circle. To send them with one left out would be to destroy their point. But we have here, in the sequence on the Last Things, 'six holy Sonnets' beautiful and complete enough as a set to be sent to a patron, but, if we consider their subject, incomplete. There ought to be a seventh sonnet; for a meditation on the Last Things should have as its climax a meditation on the joys of heaven.[1] Although the sequence comes to a fine climax with 'Death, thou shalt die', it lacks its proper religious climax. Donne appears not to have written his seventh sonnet; but perhaps his abortive attempt contributed to the splendour of *The Second Anniversary*, where the subject of the joys of heaven is treated with great power.

I would therefore date these six sonnets between February 1609, when Dorset succeeded to the title, and August 1609, when Mrs. Bulstrode died. The other six sonnets, which appear with these in the manuscripts of Groups I and II, and were printed with them in *1633*, afford us no clues to a date. But they are so closely linked to the first set in inspiration that we can, in the absence of any evidence to the contrary, presume them to have been written soon

nephew, the sixth Earl, deserved Dryden's praise. Dorset appears to have had some interest in pious literature: the 1620 edition of Southwell's poems was dedicated to him, and in Lent 1619 his wife was having read to her Thomas Sorocold's *Supplication of Saints* 'which my Lord gave me' (*Diary of Lady Anne Clifford*, ed. V. Sackville-West, 1923, p. 91). Sorocold's book of prayers and praises, first published in 1608, remained popular for well over a century. By 1754 there had been 'at least forty-five editions' (*D.N.B.*).

[1] It was also customary, in composing meditations, to compose sets of seven; see later, p. li, note 2.

afterwards. The four penitential sonnets, first printed from a Group III manuscript in *1635*, cannot be dated with certainty either; but, again, it seems probable that they were written about the same time as the other two sets. Like them they depend on the exercise of meditation; but the fact that they do not follow closely the method of a formal meditation suggests that they are rather later than the set on the Last Things, in which the direct influence of the meditation is much more apparent. I would date them tentatively between the second half of 1609 and the writing of *The First Anniversary*, in which Donne made extended and highly original use of the tradition of meditation.[1]

The meditation is a very old religious exercise. Its essence is an attempt to stimulate devotion by the use of the imagination. The method of meditation was systematized in the sixteenth century by St. Ignatius Loyola, whose *Exercitia Spiritualia* was printed with Papal approval in 1548. A meditation on the Ignatian pattern, employing the 'three powers of the soul', consists of a brief preparatory prayer, two 'preludes', a varying number of points, and a colloquy. The preparatory prayer is 'to ask God our Lord for grace that all my intentions, actions and operations may be ordered purely to the service and praise of His divine Majesty'.[2] The first prelude is what is called the *compositio loci*: the seeing 'with the eyes of the imagination' either a place 'such as the Temple or the mountain where Jesus Christ is found', or, if the meditation is of an invisible thing such as sin, a situation: 'that my soul is imprisoned in this corruptible body, and my whole compound self in this vale [of misery] as in exile amongst brute beasts.' The second prelude is a petition 'according to the subject matter'; thus, if the meditation is of the Passion, the petition will be for 'sorrow, tears, and fellowship with Christ in his sufferings'; if the meditation is of sin, the petition will be for 'shame'. The meditation proper follows, divided into points, usually three or five. Lastly, the memory, the storehouse of images, having been engaged in the preludes, and the reason in the points, the third power of the soul, the will, is em-

---

[1] This date is consistent with a possible reference to Galileo's discoveries in the second sonnet; see note, p. 75.

[2] Quotations are taken from *The Spiritual Exercises*, translated from the Spanish with a Commentary, by W. H. Longridge, S.S.J.E. (1930).

ployed in the colloquy, which is a free outpouring of the devotion aroused.

The Ignatian method can be applied to any topic and was widely popular.[1] Donne, with his Jesuit uncles, his pious mother, and his tutors who were of her faith, must have been familiar as a boy and young man with systematic meditation. His teachers probably took the advice of St. Peter of Alcantara, who taught that beginners should specially practice two kinds of meditation: on the Last Things, 'which like sharpe prickes doe spurre us on to the love and feare of God', and on the life and Passion of our Lord, 'which is the springe and fountaine of all our good'.[2] Donne begins his set of sonnets on the Last Things in the proper manner with a preparatory prayer. In the octave of the first sonnet he recollects himself, remembers his creation and redemption and that he has received the gift of the Holy Spirit; in the sestet he laments the power of the devil upon him and asks for grace. The next three sonnets show very clearly the two preludes of a meditation, which correspond neatly to the two parts of a sonnet: the *compositio loci* occupying the octave, and the 'petition according to the subject' the sestet. In his second sonnet, where he imagines himself dangerously ill, Donne uses a pair of vivid images to make himself realize the situation.

[1] In a Bodleian manuscript (Tanner MS. 118, f. 54) there is a good example of a meditation on death, formally written out in the Ignatian manner, presumably for personal use, by an Elizabethan Catholic layman, Sir Alexander Culpepper of Bedgebury, Kent. He begins with 'The prayer preparatiue', followed by 'The first prelude': 'Make accoumpte y^t ere long you shall lye so sicke & weake in yor bedde, y^t ye phisitions will geue you ouer, and all about you from hower to hower expecte your departure.' There follows 'The second prelude', beginning 'Good Lorde, geeue me grace to conceaue aright, and fullie apprehend ye conflictes, agonyes & distresses of death: graunt mee to feele now by imagination what I shall feele in deede at that instant: y^t, forewarned, I make through thie assistance due preparation. . . .' The meditation then proceeds with five points and a long colloquy. Sir Alexander probably wrote it out some time near 1588, since his account later in the manuscript of the troubles 'I Sr Alexander Colepeper of Bedgeburie haue had for the Catholike Religion' ends with that year.

[2] See *A Golden Treatise of Mental Prayer*, translated by G. W. (Brussels, 1632), pp. 6–8. The original was written about 1558. St. Peter provides two sets of seven meditations to be used either on the mornings and evenings of one week, or in successive weeks. The first set are on Sin, the Miseries of Life, Death, the Judgement, Hell, Heaven, the Blessings of God; the second on the events of the Passion, the Resurrection, and Ascension. Similar sets can be found in another popular book of devotion: *The Exercise of a Christian Life*, by the Italian Jesuit, Gaspar Loarte, written in 1569 and translated into English in 1584.

He is here doing what St. Ignatius advised in the 'Additions for the purpose of helping the exercitant to make the Exercises better':

setting before myself examples, e.g. as if a knight were to find himself in the presence of his king and all his court, covered with shame and confusion because he has grievously offended him from whom he has first received many gifts and favours. Likewise in the second Exercise, considering myself a great sinner, bound with chains, and about to appear before the supreme eternal Judge, taking as an example how prisoners in chains, and worthy of death, appear before their temporal judge.

These examples, or 'congruous thoughts' as they are sometimes called, were regarded as an important element in meditation. Donne's pilgrim, who has done treason abroad, and his thief, who on the way to execution longs for the prison from which he had wished to be delivered, are excellent examples of 'congruous thoughts'. These brief, vivid, realistic images from human life are very characteristic of the 'Holy Sonnets', which show none of that elaboration of a simile or an analogy into a conceit which is characteristic of the *Songs and Sonnets*. After imagining the sick man's predicament, Donne in the sestet draws out the moral: that grace will follow repentance, and that grace is needed to repent. This is hardly a petition, though it comes near to one; but in the third and fourth sonnets a true 'petition according to the subject' follows a brilliant first prelude. In the third sonnet, the actual moment of death is imagined and the prayer is for a 'safe issue' from death. In the fourth, the *compositio loci* is a picture of the Last Judgement, when those who have met death in such diverse ways and distant ages rise together at the Trump; this is followed by the petition to the Lord to delay the summons and teach a present repentance. The fifth sonnet, on the other hand, has no *compositio loci*—its octave is more like a 'point' drawn out from a meditation on hell—though its sestet contains a striking petition; while the sixth, the sonnet to Death, is only linked to the others by its subject; in manner and temper it is quite undevotional. This is what we should expect with Donne, who always as he writes develops his material in his own way. He is a poet using for his own purposes various elements from a familiar tradition; not a pious versifier, turning common material into rhyme.

The last six sonnets of the twelve printed in *1633* depend less on the preludes of the Ignatian meditation than on the colloquy. They serve the purpose of the second set of meditations suggested by St. Peter of Alcantara and others, in that they fix the mind on the saving love of God in Christ; but they handle the subject with the discursive freedom of a colloquy. The eleventh sonnet, the 'wholsome meditation', which along with the twelfth appears to have been Donne's original pendant to his set on the Last Things, recalls the colloquy with which St. Ignatius concludes the first exercise, on sins:

Imagining Christ our Lord present before me on the Cross, to make a colloquy with Him, asking Him how it is that being the Creator, He has come to make Himself man, and from eternal life has come to temporal death, and in this manner to die for my sins. Again, reflecting on myself, to ask what have I done for Christ, what am I doing for Christ, what ought I to do for Christ. Then beholding Him in such a condition, and thus hanging upon the Cross, to make the reflections which may present themselves.

In these last sonnets, the influence of the meditation is felt, not in the structure of the sonnets, but in such things as the vivid sense of the actualities of the Passion in 'Spit in my face', the imagining of the face of Christ on the Cross in 'What if this present were the worlds last night', and the use of 'congruous thoughts' in this last sonnet and in the one that follows it, 'Batter my heart'.

The four penitential sonnets are less obviously meditations, because their subject is an invisible thing, sin. There is, therefore, less scope for a recognizable *compositio loci*. In the order in which they are printed here they form a brief sequence, beginning with the regular preparatory prayer. The sonnet which I have placed second, 'I am a little world', is a general meditation, with a very short *compositio loci*, in which Donne reminds himself, as St. Ignatius advised in meditating on sin, that both body and soul are given over to sin.[1] This is followed by a long second prelude asking for

[1] Cf. the passage quoted on p. l: 'the composition will be to see . . . my whole compound self in this vale [of misery] . . . I say my whole self, composed of soul and body.

repentance. The sonnet which I have placed third, 'O might those sighes and teares', specifies a particular sin, 'sufferance', in the sense of indulgence, particularly indulgence in excessive and misdirected grief. Its particularity makes it more suitably follow than precede the sonnet on sin in general. It also leads on to the last, 'If faithfull soules be alike glorifi'd', which develops a subsidiary point, arising out of the likeness and contrast between the tears he shed as a lover and the tears he sheds as a penitent: tears may be the signs of many kinds of grief, and only God, the giver of true grief, can know if grief is true. The four sonnets are closely linked together. It is the sin in his 'feebled flesh' that weighs him down in the opening prayer; 'lust and envie' that have burned his little world in the second sonnet: indulgence which has caused him mourning that he mourns in the third. The meditation on sin is the opening exercise of the *Spiritual Exercises* and Donne develops the subject on the lines suggested there. But here again he writes with the freedom of a poet whose imagination is not tied to an initial plan. The second sonnet has only a very short *compositio loci*; the third expands the *compositio* to fill the whole sonnet, which is wholly given up to the imagining of his predicament and contains no petition; while the fourth has no relation to the form of a meditation, but is an individual moralization, containing neither *compositio* nor petition.

The influence of the formal meditation lies behind the 'Holy Sonnets', not as a literary source, but as a way of thinking, a method of prayer. Louis Martz has convincingly shown that the Ignatian method of meditating by points and the use of parallel sets of meditations for mornings and evenings of a week provided Donne with the structure of the two *Anniversaries*.[1] That such different works as the 'Holy Sonnets' and the *Anniversaries* can be shown to depend on the same exercise points to real familiarity with the method. When we are genuinely familiar with something we can use it with freedom for our own purposes. There is no need to feel surprise that Donne, at a time when he was engaged in bitter con-

[1] See Louis L. Martz, 'John Donne in Meditation: the *Anniversaries*' (*E.L.H.* December 1947), developed into chapter 6 of *The Poetry of Meditation* (Yale University Press, New Haven, 1954, 2nd edn. revised, 1962). It was after I had come to my own conclusions on the 'Holy Sonnets' that I read the article. It was encouraging to find we had independently arrived at similar conclusions.

troversy with the Jesuits, should be drawing on Jesuit spirituality in his poetry, and presumably had continued to use a Jesuit method of prayer. He would be making a distinction here which Protestants made without difficulty—taking the corn and leaving the chaff. At the close of the sixteenth century perfectly orthodox Protestant works of devotion made use of contemporary Catholic devotional works, inspired by the Jesuit revival. Many Protestants felt that, in the bitter theological controversies of the time, the Christian life of prayer and devotion was in danger of perishing. They could not recommend the great medieval works of devotion, for these were almost all written for members of religious communities, and Protestants rejected the life of the cloister. But books such as Loarte's *The Exercise of a Christian Life*, which in its Protestant English dress converted Robert Greene, were, with judicious pruning, easily made suitable for devout Protestants.[1]

As in '*La Corona*' and 'A Litany', so in the 'Holy Sonnets', Donne is using as the material of his poetry ways of devotion he had learnt as a child. We have not accounted for the 'Holy Sonnets' if we say that he wanted to write sets of meditations in sonnet form, any more than we have accounted for *Paradise Lost* if we say that Milton wished to write a classical epic on a Christian subject. But recognition of a poet's conscious intentions takes us some way towards appreciation of his achievement, and can save us from too simple a correlation between the experience of the poet and his translation of it into poetry.

[1] See Helen C. White, 'Some Continuing Traditions in English Devotional Literature' (*P.M.L.A.* lxvii, 1942, pp. 966–80). The one medieval work which never lost its hold was the *Imitation of Christ*, which as Helen White rightly pointed out is the most deeply Scriptural of devotional works. This, for Protestants, outweighed the fact that it is impregnated with the spirit of the cloister.

TEXTUAL INTRODUCTION

Donne's text was first investigated fully by Sir Herbert Grierson in his edition of 1912. After collating all the seventeenth-century editions and then accessible manuscripts, he declared that to adopt readings by taste from editions subsequent to the first was as inadmissible as to adopt readings from the later Folios of Shakespeare, and that no single manuscript provided a basis for a text. He argued for the authority of the edition of 1633, and discussed the relations of the manuscripts to each other and to the editions.

In 1929 Grierson produced a one-volume edition without commentary and with a much reduced critical apparatus. A few alterations were made in the text, but in the main it is the same as the text of 1912. John Hayward made a fresh examination of the editions and of some manuscripts for the Nonesuch Press edition of the *Complete Poems and Selected Prose* in 1929. Allowing for occasional differences on a few disputed readings, his text was substantially Grierson's. R. E. Bennett, in *Complete Poems of John Donne* (Chicago, 1942), made radical departures from Grierson by modernizing the accidents, by using manuscripts for the basis of the text in some poems, and by adopting manuscript readings into texts based on the edition of 1633 solely on grounds of taste.

In setting out to edit the *Divine Poems* in 1952 my aim was to build on Grierson's work, carrying his analysis further, and taking into account manuscripts that had come to light since he worked. Since then new material has been discovered and much fresh information, some incorporated in my own and Milgate's editions of the remainder of Donne's poems. This textual introduction has now been corrected and revised in the light of the work done in the last twenty-five years, and information on manuscripts that need fuller treatment is given in supplementary notes. None of the new material or new information has necessitated any substantial alteration in the arguments put forward in 1952.

Alan MacColl in 'The Circulation of Donne's Poems in Manuscript', *John Donne: Essays in Celebration*, ed. A. J. Smith (1972), provides a general survey of what may be deduced about Donne's habits in allowing his poems to be copied. Evelyn Simpson in 'The Text of Donne's "Divine Poems"', *Essays and Studies*, xxvi, 1940 (1941), first argued the case for regarding the manuscript variations in the 'Holy Sonnets' as having arisen from authorial revision.

I. THE MANUSCRIPTS

Since Donne's poems, with the exception of the two *Anniversaries*, the 'Elegy on Prince Henry', and the lines 'Upon Mr. Thomas Coryat's Crudities', were first published after his death, the discussion of the text must begin with a study of the manuscript copies which antedate the editions, in order to discover their relations to the first edition of 1633 and the fuller edition of 1635.[1] The manuscripts fall into three main classes: those which aim at being collections of Donne's poems, those which contain a single poem or set of poems (e.g. the *Satires*), and those in which Donne's poems appear scattered among poems by various authors. The first class is the most important. Within it Grierson distinguished three groups.

i

Group I contains five manuscripts[2]: *D* (Dowden), *H 49* (Harley 4955),[3] and *Lec* (Leconfield),[4] with two which have come to light

[1] When I have not been able to examine a manuscript, but have had to rely on descriptions supplied and on photostats, this is recorded in a note. For present whereabouts and shelf-marks see list on pp. xcvii–xcviii.

[2] The acquisition of the Dowden manuscript by the Bodleian Library in 1960 enabled Margaret Crum to make a bibliographical examination of the manuscripts of Group I; see *The Library*, xvi (1961), pp. 127–32.

[3] *H 49* is mainly a Jonson manuscript. It was made for the Newcastle family. The Donne collection occupies ff. 88–144ᵛ, and follows poems by Dr. Francis Andrewes, which contain the date 'August 14. 1629'.

[4] *Lec* was in the library of Lord Leconfield at Petworth House, and was sold at Sotheby's, April 1928. Many of the manuscripts in this library had belonged to Henry, ninth Earl of Northumberland, who communicated the news of Donne's marriage to his father-in-law.

since 1912: *C 57* (Cambridge University Library, Add. MS. 5778) and *SP* (St. Paul's Cathedral Library).[1]

Of the two new manuscripts *SP* is almost a replica of *D*, and *C 57* is very closely related to *Lec*. *SP* and *D* have the same poems in the same order; and they even agree in leaving blank leaves in the same places. It is possible that both were very carefully copied from the same original, but their remarkable closeness suggests direct dependence of one on the other, and since *SP* has a few errors not found in *D*, we can assume *D* is the original.[2] *C 57* opens with 'The Progress of the Soul', which is not found in the other manuscripts of the group, followed by '*La Corona*' and the 'Holy Sonnets'.[3] Both these last are missing in *Lec*. Otherwise, *C 57* and *Lec* have the same poems in the same order. They share small variations in the text, both omit the last ten lines of the Verse-Letter to Sir Edward Herbert, and they have a version of the *Satires* which differs from the version found in the other three manuscripts of the group and which is the version found in the manuscripts of Group II. If one is copied from the other, then *Lec* must depend on *C 57*, which has both sets of sonnets and does not commit *Lec*'s error of omitting by an eye-slip lines 31–33 of 'Good Friday'.[4] It seems rather more likely that they both depend on a common original, which combined a separate text of the *Satires* with some rearrangement of the other poems in the collection, and that *C 57* added to this 'The Progress of the Soul'. *C 57* is, then, either the original of *Lec* or, more probably, the better representative of their common original.

---

[1] Both these manuscripts were first described by H. J. L. Robbie in 'An Undescribed MS. of Donne's Poems' (*R.E.S.* iii, 1927). Mabel Potter has established that *C 57* belonged to Dr. William Balam (1651–1726), who also owned the Dobell manuscript. He used both manuscripts as commonplace books, as well as commenting on the poems and correcting the text by reference to the editions; see p. lxxiv, n. 1.

[2] This is confirmed by the fact that one blank leaf in *D* has the heading 'An Elegie on Prince Henry' where *SP* has only a blank. The writer of *D* no doubt intended to copy in the poem from *Lachrymae Lachrymarum* (1613), while *SP*, finding the title but no poem following, omitted the title.

[3] The 'Holy Sonnets' in manuscripts of Group I and Group II consist of the twelve printed in *1633*.

[4] The scribe has been misled by the fact that both line 30 and line 33 end with 'mine eye'.

The five manuscripts of the group can thus be reduced to three: *D*, *H 49*, and *C 57*. These contain slightly different arrangements of the same collection.[1] *H 49* is the least logical in its arrangement. It opens with four Satires, omitting 'Satire V', followed by thirteen Elegies (one Funeral Elegy, 'Sorrow, who to this house scarce knew the way', and twelve Love Elegies). Then comes a short collection mainly of Verse-Letters: 'The Storm', 'The Calm', 'To Sir Henry Wotton' ('Sir, more then kisses'), 'The Cross', 'Elegy on Lady Markham', 'Elegy on Mrs. Bulstrode' ('Death I recant'), 'To Sir Henry Goodyer', 'To Mr. Rowland Woodward' ('Like one who'in her third widdowhood'), 'To Sir Henry Wotton' ('Here's no more newes'), 'To the Countess of Bedford' ('Reason is our Soules left hand'), 'To the Countess of Bedford' ('You have refin'd mee'), 'To Sir Edward Herbert', 'Annunciation and Passion', and 'Good Friday'. After this come the *Songs and Sonnets*, followed by 'To Lady Carey and Mrs. Rich' and the Palatine Epithalamium. Then, slipped in as an afterthought, comes 'To Mr. T.W.' ('At once, from hence, my lines and I depart'), called here 'An Old Letter', and four more of the *Songs and Sonnets*. The Somerset Epithalamium appears next, followed by 'A Litany', '*La Corona*', and the 'Holy Sonnets'. The manuscript ends with 'To the Countess of Salisbury' and 'Obsequies to the Lord Harington'. In *C 57* the last part of this collection has been rearranged. '*La Corona*' and the 'Holy Sonnets' are at the beginning, after 'The Progress of the Soul'. Then come five Satires and the thirteen Elegies, followed by the same poems as in *H 49* up to 'Good Friday'. This is followed by the letters to Lady Carey and to the Countess of Salisbury, and 'A Litany'. Then come the *Songs and Sonnets*, arranged as in *H 49*, except that 'The Prohibition' and 'Epitaph: On Himself' are omitted, and the four which occur separately in *H 49* are added to the end of the set. The manuscript concludes with the two Epithalamiums and the 'Obsequies'. In the rearrangement the short Verse-Letter 'At once, from hence' has

---

[1] Apart from *C 57*'s inclusion of 'The Progress of the Soul', the only differences in the poems included in the three manuscripts are that *H 49* has only four Satires instead of five; while *C 57* lacks the short Verse-Letter 'At once from hence' (headed 'An Old Letter' in *D* and *H 49*), the 'Epitaph: On Himself', and 'The Prohibition'. I give short titles, with spelling modernized, from the editions listed on p. xiii, and first lines as they appear there and not *literatim* from the manuscript.

disappeared. In D the grouping by kind, carried out rather half-heartedly by C 57, is fully achieved. After the Satires and Elegies D puts the two Funeral Elegies (Lady Markham and Mrs. Bulstrode) and intended to add the Elegy on Prince Henry. It then sorts the Verse-Letters into those addressed to men and those to women. After this the Divine Poems appear as a set, beginning with 'La Corona' and the 'Holy Sonnets', followed by 'The Cross', 'Annunciation and Passion', 'A Litany', and 'Good Friday'. The manuscript ends with the *Songs and Sonnets* (including 'The Prohibition' and 'Epitaph') followed by the two Epithalamiums and the 'Obsequies'.

The order alone might suggest that H 49 is the original of the group, with C 57 depending on it and D depending on C 57; but examination of the text shows that the relationship is not so simple. A fortunate series of omissions makes it clear that no one of the three can be the source of the other two; but that their common errors must be due to their dependence on a common source.[1] H 49 omits the end of line 10 and the beginning of line 11 in the first of the 'La Corona' sonnets. Since C 57 and D do not commit this error they cannot depend directly on H 49. They could hardly do so, for H 49 cannot have been written earlier than 1629, the date given in the collection of poems preceding the Donne collection, and the text has far too many careless blunders to be thought of as near the root of the tradition. It is much inferior to the text in D. The scribe of H 49 was plainly copying into his fine large folio material from various sources. He probably took his Donne collection from a small manuscript devoted solely to Donne's poems, like the other manuscripts of this group. But even if we are willing to ascribe his many errors to his own carelessness and acquit the

---

[1] As well as agreeing in a large number of patently wrong readings, they all omit lines in the 'Obsequies' (end of l. 159 to middle of l. 161), in the letter to the Countess of Salisbury (ll. 77–78), and in 'The Perfume' (ll. 7–8), though in this last they agree with *1633*. The existence of such a body of errors uncorrected in all the manuscripts of the group shows that this tradition was unaffected by contamination from the other groups; while the fact that each of them has additional errors peculiar to itself suggests that we can properly here construct an hypothetical pedigree. I have found nothing to suggest contamination within the group.

manuscript he was copying from any blame, it would seem that that manuscript could not have been the direct source of either *C 57* or *D*. *H 49* has a complete text of 'Good Friday', where *D* omits two lines (ll. 24-25) and *C 57* omits four (ll. 22-25).[1] The larger omission, in *C 57*, can only be explained if the copyist had before him a text which, like *D*, omitted lines 24 and 25. The text in *1633* runs:

> Could I behold those hands which span the Poles,
> And tune all spheares at once peirc'd with those holes?
> Could I behold that endlesse height which is
> Zenith to us, and our Antipodes,
> Humbled below us? or that blood which is   25
> The seat of all our Soules, if not of his . . .

D, misled by the recurrence of 'which is' at the close of line 25, has:

> Colde I beholde those hands, wch span the Poles,
> And tune all Spheares at Once, peirc'd wth those holes?
> Cold I behold that Endless Heighth, wch is
> The Seate of all our Soules, if not of hys . . .

C 57 has:

> Cold I behould those hands, wch Span the Poles
> The Seate of all our Soules, Yf not of hys . . .

This can be explained as an eye-slip from the repeated initial 'Could I behold', if the copyist had before him the version in *D*. It is difficult to see how the error could have arisen if he was working from the full text. But *C 57* cannot be dependent on *D*, which is so much better arranged. It is impossible to imagine *C 57* undoing the excellent arrangement of *D*, and by coincidence hitting on exactly the same muddle of Funeral Poems, Divine Poems, and Verse-Letters as we find in *H 49*. We must then postulate a common source for *D* and the manuscript from which *C57* and *Lec* are descended.[2]

---

[1] This confirms what we should assume from a study of the order of the poems: that the descent of *H 49* from the common original cannot be through either *C 57* or *D*.

[2] This is supported by the occurrence of a few minor errors in *C 57* and *D*, which are not in *H 49*, as well as their freedom from its blunders. Also, *D*, unlike *H 49*, omits the first line of the second verse of 'Break of Day'. In *C 57* the line has been written in, in the space the copyist originally left between verses 1 and 2. This suggests again that *C 57* and *D* descend from the same manuscript in which the line

The relations of the five manuscripts of Group I can then be summarized as follows. They all depend on a manuscript we may call *X*, to which their common errors and omissions are due. From *X* is derived, probably through more than one intermediary, *H 49*, and a manuscript in which lines 24 and 25 of 'Good Friday' were omitted, which we may call X_2. Both may have made some adjustments in the order of *X*. From X_2 came *D*, which made a full rearrangement of the poems and was copied by *SP*. From X_2 came also the original of *C 57* and *Lec*, which combined a different text of the *Satires* with the other poems of the collection. This we may call X_3. To this original *C 57* added 'The Progress of the Soul'.

Manuscripts of Group I

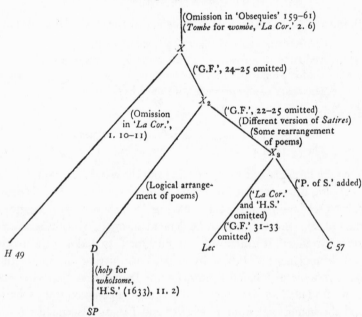

Margaret Crum's bibliographical examination of the manuscripts of Group I demonstrated that it was unlikely that *X* was a single manuscript. The treatment of the material by the scribes points to was omitted. Dr. William Balam, the late seventeenth-century owner of *C 57*, supplied the missing line very neatly between the two stanzas. His attempt to imitate the hand of the scribe misled me into thinking this an unique case of a scribe of one of the Group I manuscripts recognizing an error and correcting by reference to another manuscript.

its having consisted of separable parts: on the one hand poems on loose papers, on the other of 'books' containing sets of poems or one long poem. Thus, the Elegies, the main series of *Songs and Sonnets* (excepting the four found separately in *H 49*), '*La Corona*' with the twelve 'Holy Sonnets', and the 'Obsequies' would seem to have been in books, while the miscellaneous collection of Funeral Elegies, Verse-Letters, and Divine Poems, which appear in a medley in *H 49*, were partially sorted in X_2, and logically arranged in *D*, would seem to have been on loose papers.[1] The Satires present a problem. *H 49* lacks 'Satire V' and *C 57/Lec* have the text of Group II. It would seem that *X* contained only four Satires, to which *D* added the fifth, while X_3 may either have been defective at the beginning or the scribe may have already had a copy of the five Satires to which he added the other poems. If we can take the order of *H 49* as resembling the order in which the compiler of *X* put his poems together, he began with the Satires and Elegies and ended with the 'Obsequies'.

X was a collection of poems only. The manuscripts of Group I, unlike those of Group II and the fullest collections in Group III, contain no prose Paradoxes and Problems. It was also canonical. All the poems in these manuscripts are accepted as Donne's without question.[2] But it had some very interesting omissions. It included no poems which can be dated with certainty after Donne's ordination in 1615.[3] Its other deficiency was in the Verse-Letters, for the love poetry, except for the Lincoln's Inn Epithalamium, was well represented. It lacked almost all the short letters to Donne's male friends, and many of the letters to noble ladies. It had, for instance, only two of those to Lady Bedford. What letters there were—

---

[1] *The Library*, xvi (1961), 127–32.

[2] The only qualification to this statement is that there is some doubt about Donne's authorship of the final stanza of 'The Prohibition'. The significance of this is discussed in a note on p. lxxxiv.

[3] It lacked all three Hymns, 'To Mr. Tilman', 'Upon the Translation of the Psalms', 'Hymn to the Saints, and to Marquis Hamilton', which are all datable, and 'The Lamentations of Jeremy', which, though its date cannot be fixed, is usually put after 1615. It is true it contained the twelve 'Holy Sonnets' of *1633*, but, as I have said, there is no solid evidence that these were written after 1615. Even if my arguments for dating them in 1609 are not accepted, the statement above that *X* 'included no poems which can be dated with certainty after Donne's ordination' holds good.

lengthy ones, serious epistles—are such as might well seem
worthy of publication when other short, purely occasional pieces
did not seem so. Finally, *X* probably ended with the 'Obsequies to
the Lord Harington', the last poem Donne wrote before his ordina-
tion, declaring in it that his Muse had 'spoke her last'.[1]

The nature of the collection in *X* is now clear. It was a selection
from the poems Donne had written before his ordination, made by
someone who, since he included no spurious pieces, knew very well
how to distinguish Donne's poems from those of other wits. We
know that Donne himself was collecting his poems together at the
close of 1614, and I believe that *X* derives from Donne's own
collection, which he speaks of in a long letter to Goodyer, dated
'*Vigilia St. Tho.* [20 December] 1614', just over a month before he
took orders.

One thing more I must tell you; but so softly, that I am loath to hear
my self: and so softly, that if that good Lady were in the room, with
you and this Letter, she might not hear. It is, that I am brought to a
necessity of printing my Poems, and addressing them to my L. Cham-
berlain. This I mean to do forthwith; not for much publique view, but
at mine own cost, a few Copies. I apprehend some incongruities in the
resolution; and I know what I shall suffer from many interpretations:
but I·am at an end, of much considering that; and, if I were as startling
in that kinde, as ever I was, yet in this particular, I am under an unescap-
able necessity, as I shall let you perceive, when I see you. By this
occasion I am made a Rhapsoder of mine own rags, and that cost me
more diligence, to seek them, then it did to make them. This made me
aske to borrow that old book of you, which it will be too late to see,
for that use, when I see you: for I must do this, as a valediction to the
world, before I take Orders.[2]

Donne's uneasiness and embarrassment are obvious, and he must
have been under very strong pressure from Somerset, whom he
dared not offend, to consider such a scheme at all. A more unsuit-

---

[1] Harington died in February 1614, but the 'Obsequies' cannot have been written
before August, for the long Verse-Letter to the Countess of Salisbury is dated
August 1614 in these manuscripts as in *1633*. In his letter to Goodyer of 20 December
1614 Donne wrote: 'I would be just to my written words to my L. *Harrington*,
to write nothing after that '(*Letters*, p. 197). He could not have said this if he had
already broken his promise, by writing the letter to the Countess after the 'Ob-
sequies'. He apologizes at the close of the 'Obsequies' for being 'behind hand'.

[2] *Letters*, pp. 196-7.

able method of bidding farewell to the world on taking holy orders it would be hard to imagine. Presumably the poems were to have been printed with some kind of prefatory palinode or retractation for the follies of his youth, but even so their publication at this moment could hardly be regarded as edifying.[1] If, as I have argued, the compiler of X concluded with a poem which ended with a solemn promise to write no more, we may see in this an effort to soften the probable 'interpretations' which Donne expected to suffer through publishing on the eve of his ordination 'love-song weeds, and Satyrique thornes'. The request Donne goes on to make to Goodyer would suggest an explanation of the paucity of Verse-Letters in the collection: 'But this is it, I am to aske you; whether you ever made any such use of the letter in verse, *A nostre Countesse chez vous*, as that I may not put it in, amongst the rest to persons of that rank.' With the exception of 'The Storm' and 'The Calm', which are hardly Verse-Letters, and had anyhow so great a reputation that Donne could hardly have omitted them from a collection of his poems, and the serious and beautiful letter to Rowland Woodward, the Verse-Letters of the collection are all addressed to persons of rank and importance: Wotton, Goodyer, the Countesses of Bedford and Salisbury, and Lady Carey. There was point in publishing these letters in a volume dedicated to Somerset and including the Palatine and Somerset Epithalamiums and the 'Obsequies to the Lord Harington'. The familiar letters addressed to the less distinguished circle of his youth Donne might well have thought not worthy of inclusion in a volume designed to win the favour of the great. Donne's question to Goodyer also suggests that he felt some diffidence in including in a printed volume letters he had sent to noble ladies in the attempt to win their patronage by flattery. This might account for the absence of the letters to Mrs. Herbert and the Countess of Huntingdon, as well as of the rest of those to Lady Bedford.

[1] It is not necessary to suppose that, had Donne proceeded with his plan, he would have printed all the poems in the collection. On the other hand, if one were to remove all that contained matter likely to offend, one would be left with a very slim volume indeed. Although some poems may seem to modern taste more improper than others, any representative collection of Donne's poems published at this time would necessarily be a cause of scandal. Both Walton and Jonson, as reported by Drummond, say that later he wished them destroyed.

If this suggested origin for *X* is accepted, we can then regard the Group I manuscripts as preserving 'the text of the "edition" of 1614'. It is important to establish the relations of these manuscripts and their origin, since, as Grierson showed, a large portion of *1633* was taken from a manuscript of this group.

ii

No new manuscript has come to light in Grierson's second group, although the Dolau Cothi manuscript has affinities with it. Group II consists of four manuscripts: *A 18* (British Library, Add. MS. 18647),[1] *N* (Norton), *TCC* (Trinity College, Cambridge),[2] and *TCD* (Trinity College, Dublin).[3] *A 18* has the same poems in the same order as *TCC*, and the collation of the Divine Poems fully bears out Grierson's suggestion that it is a copy of *TCC*. It shares the bad readings which distinguish *TCC* from *N* and *TCD*, and adds a fair number of its own. Similarly *N*, according to Grierson, has 'the same poems, arranged in the same order' as *TCD*, and its many small careless slips in the Divine Poems justify us in regarding it as a copy of *TCD*. The group can thus be reduced to *TCC* and *TCD*.

TCD is the larger collection. It opens with six Satires,[4] 'The Bracelet', 'The Storm', and 'The Calm'. Then comes the Elegy 'The Anagram', with which *TCC* opens. From this point until about two-thirds of the way through *TCC* the two manuscripts continue together with a haphazardly arranged collection of Elegies, Lyrics, Verse-Letters, and Funeral Poems, except that *TCD* has a few scattered poems and a set of eight Verse-Letters to ladies which are not in *TCC*. Towards the close *TCD* has not only added poems, but has

---

[1] The manuscript was bought from the Earl of Denbigh in 1851. On f. 108, under the title of the Hamilton Elegy, a late seventeenth-century hand has written 'The Lady Desmond'. The Earls of Denbigh had the second title of Desmond from 1628.

[2] The manuscript came to Trinity in 1691 among the books of Sir Henry Newton, afterwards Puckering (1618–1701). It has 'E. Puckering' on the first page. Sir Henry's wife was named Elizabeth, but so was the wife of his maternal uncle, Sir Thomas Puckering, whose name he took on succeeding to the estates. Sir Thomas, son of Lord Keeper Puckering, was companion to Prince Henry.

[3] I have not seen *N* and *TCD*. For *N*, I rely on Grierson's account and that in the Grolier Club edition (New York, 1895), and on photostats of the Divine Poems. For *TCD*, I have worked from a contents list supplied to me, and on photostats of the Divine Poems and the Index.

[4] It adds 'Sleep, next Society', ascribed by Grierson to Sir John Roe, to the accepted five, but it appends to it the initials J. R.

also a better arrangement. *TCD* thus seems to represent a later stage of the collection found in *TCC*; but it cannot depend upon *TCC*, since it has a much better text. It would seem to be an expansion of a collection of Donne's works which we may call *Υ*.

Manuscripts of Group II

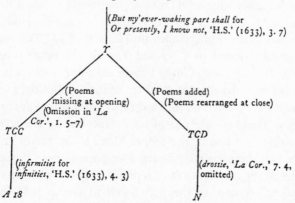

Υ cannot have reached final form before 1623, the date of the 'Hymn to God the Father', included in both *TCC* and *TCD*.[1] It differed from the collection *X*, preserved in Group I, in having, as well as some of the poems Donne wrote after his ordination, some short Verse-Letters and the Paradoxes and Problems. Its compiler had a clear idea of what he was doing: he was making as large a collection as he could of Donne's unpublished work in poetry and prose. In the poems they have in common, *TCC* and *TCD* are, except for one short lyric, canonical. It seems likely that the compiler of *Υ* had access to Donne's papers, for he included an unfinished poem: 'Resurrection: imperfect'.[2] Unfinished poems are not usually circulated by their authors, but may be found among their papers. *TCC*

[1] See supplementary notes, pp. 149–50, for a more detailed discussion of *Υ* and a description of the Dolau Cothi manuscript (*DC*), which is related to Group II but not descended from *Υ*.

[2] Apart from Group II and *DC*, and a miscellany (MS. Grey), which has in its Donne poems a corrupt version of the text of *TCC*, this poem is only found in *Lut* and its dependent *O'F*. The compiler of *Lut* had access to a Group II manuscript from which he took a certain number of Verse-Letters, otherwise only extant in Group II and *W*, and the four Holy Sonnets not found in other manuscripts of Group III.

and *TCD* are closely related to a smaller collection of Donne's poems in a composite manuscript, Lansdowne 740 (*L 74*), in which the latest datable poems are two elegies on Mrs. Bulstrode (1609). This collection would seem to be the nucleus of *Y* to which the compiler added poems that came to him later. Alan MacColl has very plausibly suggested that the compiler of *Y* was Sir Robert Ker, to whom Donne sent his poems before leaving England in 1619.

In the *Satires* (not included in *TCC* and *A 18*) *TCD* and *N* have the version found in *C 57* and *Lec*. In the other poems which Group II shares with Group I there are a few readings in Group II which cannot be accounted for by scribal corruption, but must, as Grierson suggested, be ascribed to Donne's own corrections of his poems. There is only one of importance in the *Divine Poems*: the rewriting of a line in the sonnet 'This is my playes last scene'.[1] Although there are more in the love poems, there are not enough for us to regard Group II as representing anything that could be called a 'revision' of the text found in Group I. In considering differences between texts in Group I and Group II which may be judged to be possibly due to authorial revision, it cannot be assumed that the Group II text is always the later. In those poems that *TCC* and *TCD* share with *L 74* it may well be that the Group II text is earlier than the text of Group I.[2]

The interest and value of Group II lies in the poems which are not to be found in Group I. It seems very likely, as Grierson says, that the editor of *1633* took the poems he did not find in his Group I manuscript from a manuscript of Group II. Almost all the poems in *1633* not in the Group I collection are in *TCD*. More significant, the poems which were not printed in 1633, and which first appeared in the edition of 1635, are also missing in *TCD*. The portion of *1633* which is based on a Group II manuscript is textually much inferior to the rest, and the Group II manuscripts are of use both in establishing the text and in explaining some of the errors of *1633*.

---

[1] See the discussion on p. xlv, which shows that the Group II reading is a rewriting of the line as it appears in Groups I and III and *W*.

[2] This *caveat* is not necessary in the *Divine Poems*, none of which are included in *L 74*.

iii

The remaining manuscript collections containing Divine Poems are not a group in the sense that behind them is a single collection from which, with additions and rearrangement, they all descend. They can, however, be called a group because they agree in preserving, in certain poems, a text which is not the same as the text we find in Group I. The differences are not occasional, as are the differences between Group I and Group II, but occur in poem after poem. The Group III manuscripts vary greatly in the number of poems included, and almost always they contain a good many poems which are not Donne's. Sometimes these are marked as not his, or queried; at other times they are definitely ascribed to him or tacitly included as his. A study of these manuscripts shows us a process of accretion, with fresh poems, genuine and spurious, being added by the various compilers as they came by them. There is much evidence of contamination within the group, and it is impossible even to hazard a line of descent; but the process of collecting together Donne's poems from various sources appears to culminate in the O'Flaherty manuscript, dated, after its table of contents, '12 Oct. 1632'. This is the largest manuscript collection of Donne's poems.[1]

For an editor of the *Divine Poems* six of these manuscripts are important: *B* (Bridgewater), *Dob* (Dobell), *Lut* (Luttrell), *O'F* (O'Flaherty), *S 96* (Stowe 961), and *W* (Westmoreland). Of these Westmoreland stands apart from the others and must be considered separately.[2]

Lut and *O'F* are very closely related. *Lut* formerly belonged to

[1] O'Flaherty belonged to the Rev. T. R. O'Flaherty, of Capel, near Dorking, a nineteenth-century collector of Donne's works. His collection included the John Cave manuscript, and a copy of *An Anatomie of the World* (*1611*) which is now in the library of Sir Geoffrey Keynes. Before Sir Geoffrey acquired this in 1948, the only recorded copy was that in the Huntington Library. The O'Flaherty manuscript was described by R. Warwick Bond in catalogue no. 93 of Ellis and Elvey (1899), and was sold by them to the Houghton Library. Grierson repeats a suggestion of Warwick Bond's, that the collection in *O'F* was made by the younger Donne (Grierson, ii. 268). I have found no evidence to support this suggestion. The fact that *O'F* was used by the editor of *1635* makes it highly unlikely, since the first edition over which the younger Donne had control was that of 1650.

[2] I have worked from photostats of *B*, *Dob*, *O'F*, and *W*.

Narcissus Luttrell, whose signature with the date 1680 appears characteristically on the recto of the first blank leaf. There is nothing to show how it came into his hands. It was written after Donne's death, since it contains his epitaph on his wife, with the statement that he was not buried beside her, as he there expressed the wish to be, but in St. Paul's. It is a well-arranged collection, obviously aiming at completeness. It opens with 'A Litany', 'Good Friday', and 'The Cross', followed by seven Satires.[1] After three blank pages there is a collection of Elegies. The first is headed 'Elegye 2', so presumably 'Elegye 1' should occupy the blank pages. There are twenty-four poems with the title of 'Elegye' and two six-line epigrams. Seventeen of the poems were included by Grierson among his twenty Elegies;[2] the remaining seven and the two epigrams he rejected. A section headed 'Epicedes and Obsequies Upon the Deathes of severall Personages' follows. Apart from 'Death be not proud, thy hand gave not this blow', which follows on 'Death I recant', and two short pieces on Mrs. Bulstrode, all the poems in this section are authentic. The next section is headed 'Letters to severall personages', and contains four pieces now excluded from the canon. Then come the three Epithalamiums and, with no fresh heading, the remainder of the Divine Poems: 'Resurrection', 'Annunciation and Passion', '*La Corona*' (under the title 'The Crowne'), the Hymn 'Wilt thou forgive' (under the title 'Christo Salvatori'), twelve 'Holy Sonnets' (under the title 'Divine Meditations'), four more 'Holy Sonnets' (under the title 'Other Meditations'), and the 'Hymn to Christ' of 1619.[3] The only unauthentic poem in this section is a poem on the Incarnation, which follows, after a line drawn, 'Annunciation and Passion'; but the scribe has written 'Quaere if Donne's' at the close. The final section is headed 'Sonnets and Songes', and opens with the four 'Valedictions'. Apart from four short pieces at the end, all the poems here are accepted as authentic.

[1] The first is 'Sleep, next Society' headed 'A Satyricall letter to Sᵣ Nich: Smith. Quere if Donnes or Sᵣ Th: Rowes'. The seventh is 'Men write that love and reason disagree'. Both are printed by Grierson in his Appendix B.

[2] For an examination of the canon of the *Elegies*, see Gardner, *Elegies etc.*, pp. xxxi–xlvi.

[3] The 'Divine Meditations' consist of eight of the 'Holy Sonnets' of the Group I and Group II manuscripts with four others interspersed; the four 'Other Meditations' are the remaining four of the Group I set. For the order of the 'Holy Sonnets' in Group III and *W* see pp. xxxix–xl.

O'F has added to this collection and carried its plan farther. It puts all the Divine Poems together at the beginning, preserving the order in which they appear in *Lut* but inserting a sonnet 'On the Blessed Virgin Mary' after 'The Cross', and adding at the end 'The Lamentations of Jeremy', 'To Mr. Tilman', the Ode 'Vengeance will sit', and 'Upon the Translation of the Psalms'.[1] It then has the same seven Satires, but it puts the queried 'Sleep next Society' last and adds 'The Progress of the Soul'. It has exactly the same poems under the heading 'Elegies', except that it has the missing 'Elegie I', and it has the same poems in the section headed 'Epicedes and Obsequies'. The order of the Verse-Letters is slightly different at the close, and two short ones are added, as well as some missing lines in the letter to the Countess of Salisbury. The *Songs and Sonnets* come next. A few poems are added here. Of these, Grierson accepted only 'Farewell to Love' and 'The Token'. I regard the latter as doubtful. The Epithalamiums follow and *O'F* then adds the Epigrams and the prose Paradoxes and Problems. The collation of the Divine Poems supports the conclusion to be drawn from a comparison of the contents of the two manuscripts: that *O'F* is an expansion of *Lut*. They constantly agree in minor details against the other manuscripts of the group.

Lut and, even more, *O'F* suggest at once that someone, soon after Donne's death, was collecting his poems together with a view to publication. On f. 55 in *Lut* the heading 'Elegye on Prince Henry' goes on, in the scribe's hand, 'since in print but out of print', an obvious defence of its inclusion in a volume that would no doubt bear on its title-page the boast 'never before imprinted'. The scribe of *Lut* has also frequently rewritten in the margin a word which was smudged or ill-written in the text, as if for the benefit of a compositor or someone who was going to prepare copy for the press. The completeness of *O'F* and its beautifully logical arrangement, with its table of contents headed 'The Poems of D. J. Donne (not yet imprinted)' give an even stronger impression of a projected edition. Whoever he was, the compiler of *O'F* was forestalled by the edition of 1633, but he had no reason to be discouraged in

---

[1] 'On the Blessed Virgin Mary' is almost certainly by Constable, and 'Vengeance will sit' is by Herbert of Cherbury.

his enterprise, since he had many more poems in his manuscript than the editor of *1633* had printed. Someone, possibly not the original scribe, went through *O'F*, and corrected many, though by no means all, of its characteristic Group III readings to the readings of *1633*. A second person, with a quite distinct hand, has made some further corrections.[1] That the corrections of the first corrector were made from the edition of 1633 and not from a Group I or Group II manuscript is seen by the alteration of 'Make' to 'Made' in 'Good Friday' (l. 27). All the manuscripts, with the exception of one manuscript of Group III, read 'Make'.[2] The corrector appears to have used his judgement and emended, one supposes, when he thought *1633* gave better sense or a better metrical line.

The other three manuscripts do not seem closely connected with each other or with *Lut* and *O'F*. *B* would seem to have been written about 1620, since, although it obviously aims at completeness, it contains only the first of Donne's Hymns, written in 1619, and does not contain the Hamilton Elegy of 1625. Since both the 1623 Hymn 'Wilt thou forgive' and the Hamilton Elegy were 'published', to judge by Walton's account of the setting of the one and John Chamberlain's reference to the other,[3] it seems probable that *B* was compiled before they were available. *B* has a good many spurious poems and little attempt at arrangement has been made; but the five accepted Satires occur together in the middle and the Divine Poems, except for 'The Cross' with which the manuscript opens, are collected together at the end. These consist of 'The Lamentations of Jeremy', the 'Holy Sonnets', called 'Devine Meditations',[4] 'Annunciation and Passion', 'On the Blessed Virgin Mary', 'A Litany', 'Good Friday',

---

[1] The first corrector either altered a word, or wrote the correction above, in this case usually scoring through the word to be corrected. It is impossible to say whether he was the original scribe writing rather differently because he was cramped for space, or a second writer, and I do not feel absolutely certain that all the corrections made in this way are in the same hand. The second corrector, who has an easily recognizable hand, employed the method of underlining a word and writing the correction in the margin. His corrections can be easily overlooked, while the first set cannot be missed. R. W. Hunt kindly examined my photostats with me.

[2] The sole manuscript to agree with *1633* in reading 'Made' is *Dob*, a Group III manuscript which often 'improves' its text.

[3] Quoted on p. 78.

[4] *B*, like *Dob* and *S 96*, has the same twelve 'Holy Sonnets' under this title as are found so named in *Lut* and *O'F*.

'*La Corona*', called 'The Crowne', and the Hymn of 1619. Although *B* bears on its first leaf the signature of the first Earl of Bridgewater, son of Donne's patron the Lord Keeper Egerton, it is weak in its canon, though it does at times query spurious poems, and its text is poor. On the other hand, the copyist, since he was quite content to write absolute nonsense, is less misleading than the more sophisticated writers of *Lut*, *O'F*, and *Dob*. Although *B* is too erratic to be used as a representative of the group, it is often helpful in establishing the genuine group reading and its errors are at times instructive.

S 96 is, as Grierson says, 'very neatly and prettily transcribed'. It contains fewer poems than *B*, but it has some which are only rarely found in manuscript. It is the only collection to contain the 'Hymn to God my God, in my sickness' and the only one, besides *O'F* and *S 962*, to have 'Farewell to Love'. It opens with three Satires (II, I, IV), and continues with a mixed collection of secular poems. The Elegies occur in small groups and the three Epithalamiums are brought together, but on the whole *S 96*, like *B*, appears to be a clean copy made from a collection of loose papers, or from a book into which someone had copied poems as he came by them. The Divine Poems, however, are put together at the close and consist of the 'Holy Sonnets' ('Divine Meditations'), 'Good Friday', 'On the Blessed Virgin Mary', '*La Corona*' ('The Crowne), 'Annunciation and Passion', 'A Litany', and all three Hymns. Grierson stated that the text of *S 96* is poor. I do not agree generally, and particularly not in its Divine Poems, where it is free from the gross blunders of *B*, and seems to represent the Group III tradition very fairly. It usually agrees with *B* and *Dob* against *Lut* and *O'F*, or with *B*, *Lut*, and *O'F* against *Dob* alone. If we accept Walton's story that the 'Hymn to God my God, in my sickness' was written by Donne on his death-bed, then *S 96* must, like *Lut* and *O'F*, have been written after 1631. But if, as is argued in Appendix E, it seems more likely that Sir Julius Caesar was right and that the Hymn was written in Donne's severe illness of 1623, then we can regard *S 96* as a collection made in the middle twenties.

Finally, there is *Dob*, a manuscript unknown to Grierson, discussed by Evelyn Simpson in her article on 'The Text of Donne's

"Divine Poems"'. It has been fully studied by Mabel Potter.[1] It is the only collection of Donne's poems to contain some of his sermons. It opens with three, followed by a number of blank pages on which we may imagine further sermons were to be transcribed as the writer of the manuscript came across them.[2] The Divine Poems come next: '*La Corona*' ('The Crowne'), the 'Holy Sonnets' ('Devine Meditations'), 'A Litany', 'Good Friday', 'Annunciation and Passion', 'The Cross', the 1619 Hymn, 'To Mr. Tilman', and the Hymn 'Wilt thou forgive' (called 'To Christ'). After this come the Paradoxes and Problems, followed by a collection of Donne's secular poems, with some included that are not his. *Dob* is a beautiful and carefully written manuscript, but although it is free from obvious errors it is a rather dangerous guide. In the text of its Divine Poems it has a certain number of independent readings. These are often attractive at first sight, but prove less satisfactory on examination.

Each of these five manuscripts contains a substantial number of Divine Poems, which appear as a set even in the otherwise chaotic collections of *B* and *S 96*. Two more manuscripts, *S* (Stephens)[2] and

---

[1] See *Essays and Studies*, xxvi (1941) and 'A Seventeenth-Century Literary Critic of John Donne: the Dobell Manuscript Re-examined', *Harvard Library Bulletin*, xxiii. 1 (Jan. 1975). Mabel Potter was continuing the work done by her husband, G. R. Potter, the first scholar to study the manuscript. She is unable to suggest who was the original owner; but she gives an account of a late seventeenth-century owner, Dr. William Balam (1651–1726), an ecclesiastical lawyer of Ely, who also owned *C 57*. He used the manuscript as a personal commonplace book, covering the margins with 'personal comments, quotations, emotional outbursts, poems and transcripts of letters', of which Mabel Potter gives an entertaining account. In addition he corrected some titles to the titles of the editions, supplied titles from the editions to untitled poems, and made frequent critical comments.

[2] The Stephens MS. was so named by Grosart, who used it for his edition of 1873, because it has the book-plate of Thomas Stephens of the Inner Temple. My knowledge of it is derived from photostats. For a full account of it, see C. E. Norton, 'The Text of Donne's Poems' (*Studies and Notes in Philology and Literature*, vol. v, Boston, 1897). Grosart assumed that Stephens was the compiler, but Norton states that the book-plate is much later than the manuscript, which is dated at the close '19th July 1620'. There are three Thomas Stephens indexed as at the Inner Temple: one in 1609, another in 1717, and his son in 1725. It seems likely from Norton's statement that the manuscript belonged to one of these last two.

S consists of 343 pages, with many leaves left blank, presumably for the insertion of more poems. It contains an ambitious collection, in which some attempt at classification has been made. It opens with the Paradoxes and Problems, followed by Satires, Elegies, and a mixed collection of Lyrics, Verse-Letters, Funeral Poems, and Divine Poems. Like other members of its group, *S* contains some poems which are not Donne's.

O1 (Osborn 1),[1] have a smaller number of Divine Poems. For this reason, and because their texts are extremely poor, I am unwilling to group them with the important manuscripts described above. *S* contains 'A Litany', '*La Corona*' (under that title and not under its usual Group III title 'The Crowne'), 'The Cross', and 'Annunciation and Passion' as a set, and 'Good Friday' at the end. Grierson stigmatized it as the worst manuscript he had examined. It is indeed too poor in the Divine Poems to be of much use beyond bearing a general witness to the Group III tradition. *O1* has 'Annunciation and Passion', '*La Corona*' (again under that title), 'On the blessed Virgin Mary', and 'A Litany'. Its text is even worse than that in *S*. It has many of the blunders peculiar to *S* and adds others of its own.[2]

Other manuscripts of Group III contain either no Divine Poems or a few odd ones scattered among the secular poems. Thus, the interesting composite manuscript *L 74* (Lansdowne 740), in which we can see a collection formed from various sources, has no Divine Poems, and *A 25* (British Library, Add. MS. 25707), another composite manuscript,[3] has only 'Good Friday' and 'The Cross'; *JC* (John Cave), compiled by John Cave in 1620, and *D 17* (Dyce), which depends on it,[4] have only 'A Litany' and 'The Cross'; *P*

---

[1] *O1*, formerly *K* (King), was sold at Hodgson's, 27 April 1950 and bought by Raphael King, Museum Street. See King, catalogue no. 51 (1950), Item 73.

[2] *O1* is a small, neatly written manuscript in its original vellum binding (8°, approx. 4″ × 6″), with pagination and signatures. Pp. 1–336. It opens with eight 'Satires' (Satires I–V, 'Sleep next Society', 'Men write that love and reason disagree', and the Verse-Letter to Herbert 'Man is a lumpe'). After a single epigram 'Upon Mercurius Gallo-Belgicus', nineteen poems are collected under the heading 'Elegies'. These are made up of eleven Love Elegies and 'Sorrow who to this house', three Funeral Poems: 'Man is the World', 'Death I recant', 'Language thou art too narrow', and four spurious poems: 'Shall I goe force an Elegie', 'Tell her if she to hired servants shew', 'True Love finds witt', and 'Come Fates; I feare you not' (Grierson, i. 410, 416, 412, 407). After the two epistles to Ben Jonson often found in Group III manuscripts, 'The State and mens affaires' and 'If great men wrong me' (Grierson, i. 414, 415), come the four Divine Poems and then, after 'The Will' (complete in six stanzas), there are six Problems. Seven Verse-Letters, one spurious, are followed by some of the *Songs and Sonnets*, headed 'Canzons / Amourenses par le mesne Author'. There are twenty-five lyrics, all authentic. The manuscript concludes with the 'Obsequies', the last page being missing.

[3] See the description of this manuscript given by Grierson, ii. clii. *L 74* and *A 25* show well the bringing together of poems separately transcribed, which must lie behind such 'fair copies' as we find in the Group III collections.

[4] *JC* opens with a poem 'Upon Mr Donn's Satires' with 'Jo. Ca. June 3. 1620'

(Phillipps) has the 1619 Hymn, 'Annunciation and Passion', and 'The Cross'; *O2*, a manuscript collateral with *P*, adds to these 'A Litany' and 'The Lamentations of Jeremy'; *Cy* (Carnaby) has only 'Good Friday'. These are fairly full collections. The large collection in *S 962* (Stowe 962), which, though strictly speaking a miscellany, contains so many of Donne's poems that it deserves inclusion here, has, of the *Divine Poems*, only 'The Cross', 'A Litany', and 'Wilt thou forgive', with the two spurious poems 'Vengeance will sit' and 'On the Blessed Virgin Mary'.[1] The Group III manuscripts contain collections made by lovers of poetry who had come by copies of poems Donne had handed at times to his friends. None of those so far described suggests any direct contact with Donne, in the sense that we can imagine the actual source of the manuscript to be a collection Donne had himself handed to a friend who wished to take a copy. They all seem far remote from the author. Those soundest in canon, such as *JC*, are often weak in their text and have far too many blunders for us to regard them as copied from Donne's

---

written at the foot. For John Cave, see *D.N.B.* Dyce 25 F 17 is, as Grierson says, 'practically a duplicate of *JC*'. It is dated 1625 by the writer 'Johannes Nedham e Collegio Lincolniense'. The name John Nedham occurs among others scribbled in *JC* and John Cave was at Lincoln College; he took his M.A. from there in 1619.

1 This interesting manuscript opens with Paradoxes and Problems, followed by 'Characters of Johē Done', the first two of which are Donne's, the rest being from Earle's *Microcosmography*. These occupy ff. 1–31^r, which include an index. There follows a large collection of poems by various authors. The original foliation runs from f. 37 (numbered 2) to f. 243 (numbered 208). The few poems and a prose letter on ff. 31^v–39^v are in a different hand from the rest of the poetry, and were perhaps written in on leaves originally left blank. The collection of poems that follows may be the work of more than one writer, or more probably of a single writer who at times wrote rather carelessly. It ends on f. 242^v with a poem on the death of John Pulteney 'who died 15° May A° 1637'. (Another poem on his death occurs on the originally unnumbered blank leaves at the beginning.) The Divine Poems occur as follows: f. 114, 'Sonnet. On the blessed Virgine Marie' and 'A Letanie of J.D.', followed by (f. 118^v) 'Of the Crosse'; f. 209, 'Vengance will sitt', without title and unascribed, and f. 220, 'Wilt thou forgive', without title, but initialled 'J.D.' at the close. As will be seen from this, an effort has been made to distinguish Donne's poems from those of others; but, since many of Donne's genuine poems occur without initials, anyone searching through this manuscript might be excused for adopting with genuine though unascribed poems some that were not genuine. *S 962* looks like a degenerate descendant—for it is late and its texts are poor—of the kind of manuscript the compilers of *Lut* and *O'F* quarried in. It contains, for instance, the rarely found 'Farewell to Love' and 'The Token', which *O'F* added to the lyrics it found in *Lut*.

originals. Most of these manuscripts were written after 1620, and have brought together poems of very varied provenance, some of which had been circulating in 'books', some in small collections, some as single poems. It is only very occasionally, as in Sir Julius Caesar's Letter-Book (British Library, Add. MS. 34324), where we find Donne's 'Hymn to God my God, in my sickness' written on a sheet of paper, endorsed by Caesar on the back, or in *A 23* (British Library, Add. MS. 23229),[1] that we find examples of single poems that Donne had handed to a friend to copy. Study of the manuscripts suggests he usually gave poems to be copied in sets.

The collation of the Divine Poems contained in the five main manuscripts described above makes clear that no single manuscript is by itself a safe witness to the tradition they represent. Although *Dob* has some readings that are in themselves not unplausible, a comparison with other members of the group shows that it agrees in the main with *S 96*, and that its independent readings are almost certainly sophistications, which usually reveal on examination a misunderstanding of Donne's meaning. Similarly, *Lut* and *O'F* do not suggest in their variation from the general tradition any contact with a more authentic manuscript, but only an intelligent resolution of minor difficulties, probably made with an eye to publication. These manuscripts must be treated as a group, and unique readings in any one of them should be regarded with great suspicion.

The interest of the group is very great. It preserves, as has been said, in many poems, a text which differs substantially from the text in Group I. Grierson thought that in some poems it preserved earlier versions of poems found in a revised form in Groups I and II, and I have no doubt that he was right. The evidence his collations provided was fully discussed in relation to the *Divine Poems* by

---

[1] *A 23* is a miscellaneous collection of fragments (Conway Papers). It contains an autograph of Jonson's Epigram xci. The remains of a copy of the Somerset Epithalamium in the hand of Sir Henry Goodyer are on ff. 10–14; 'Good Friday' occurs on a folded sheet (ff. 76–77); and the end of what was once a finely written 'book' of the *Satires* on ff. 95–98. F. 132, containing a set of early Verse-Letters, is of interest in relation to the Westmoreland MS. On the back of one rather unedifying little song the writer has written 'Pray my Lord tell nobody from whom this Song comes, for I am ashamed to owne it' (f. 44ᵛ). This cry from the heart explains the difficulties of ascription the compilers of the Group III manuscripts had to confront in attempting to collect privately circulated poems.

Evelyn Simpson, who accepted his view. If, as is suggested, the Group I manuscripts descend from a copy of Donne's own collection of 1614 and the Group II manuscripts, which preserve substantially the same version, descend from a collection made by someone who had access to Donne's papers after 1623, this would confirm the view of the relation of the versions which Evelyn Simpson came to by comparing readings. The version of 1614 and 1623 must be the final version.[1] The differences between Groups I and II and Group III throw light on Donne the craftsman, since, though some of the revisions affect the sense, the great majority appear to have been made for the sake of euphony or greater clarity. Again, in the poems which are not included in Group I,[2] the witness of these manuscripts has to be weighed against Group II and the weaker portion of *1633* and often helps to decide the true text. Finally, a number of poems are preserved by the Group III manuscripts alone, and it was from one of them that the editor of the second edition of 1635 supplemented and corrected the edition of 1633.

iv

The Westmoreland manuscript, although it shares many of the Group III readings, stands by itself. It was bought by Gosse when the library of the Earl of Westmorland was sold in 1892. It is peculiarly rich in early Verse-Letters, including some not found elsewhere and first printed by Gosse. So many of these are to Rowland Woodward that Gosse conjectured that it had belonged to him. It is now established that the manuscript is in his hand.[3] Gosse acquired at the same sale a fine copy of *Pseudo-Martyr* inscribed by Donne 'ex dono authoris: Row: Woodward'.[4] Towards the end of his life

---

[1] There are no Divine Poems among those shared by the early collection in *L* 74 and Group II.

[2] This means, if my theory of the origins of Group I is correct, poems not revised in 1614 or not written by that date.

[3] The identification was made by Alan MacColl and has been confirmed by R. E. Alton and P. J. Croft. R. E. Alton has pointed out to me that throughout the manuscript Woodward uses the same very distinctive form of cursive 'k', with a loop below the line, as Donne uses, a form that does not occur in Woodward's letters in the P.R.O. This suggests he was copying from papers in Donne's hand and was influenced by his model.

[4] Now in the library of John Sparrow.

Woodward was a client of the Earl of Westmorland and is buried in the church at Apethorpe, the Earl's seat.[1] He probably gave his patron the presentation copy of *Pseudo-Martyr* and copied out for him into a fine large book poems by Donne in his possession. Extrinsically the authority of the manuscript is very high. Its text is excellent.

W opens with the five Satires, followed after a blank page by thirteen Elegies, the last being the Funeral Elegy of the set of Elegies in Group I.[2] Then comes the Lincoln's Inn Epithalamium, headed simply 'Epithalamium', and a collection of Verse-Letters, beginning with 'The Storm' headed 'To Mr. C. B.'. As Grierson pointed out, the letters to Wotton are headed 'To Mr. H. W.', which suggests the copyist had before him a manuscript written before 1603 when Wotton was knighted,[3] just as the undistinguished Epithalamium suggests that the two later ones had not been written. It is notable that the letter to Wotton on his appointment to Venice in 1604 is not included, nor the letter to Goodyer, written during the Mitcham period, nor any of the letters to Lady Bedford and other ladies. Except for the sonnet 'To E. of D.', headed 'To L. of D.' all the letters belong to the time before Donne's marriage and are addressed to his men friends when he was at the Inns of Court. Up to this point *W* appears to be copied from a collection antedating 1600. A remarkable feature is the absence of any lyrics. After the Verse-Letters come the 'Holy Sonnets', under that title and not the Group III title 'Divine Meditations'. There are nineteen sonnets, made up of the twelve 'Divine Meditations' of Group III, the four others found in Groups I and II and *1633*, which appear in *Lut* and *O'F* as 'Other Meditations', and three final sonnets not

---

[1] Woodward (1573–1636/7) was with Wotton in Venice in 1605 and probably accompanied him there in 1604. In 1607, bringing home dispatches, he was robbed and wounded and did not return to Venice. He was in the service of the Bishop of London in 1608. Later he was employed by Windebank. See M. C. Deas, 'A Note on Rowland Woodward, the friend of Donne' (*R.E.S.* vii, 1931).

[2] *A 25* and *JC* have the same Elegies in the same order, except that *A 25* has dropped the Funeral Elegy. The order differs from that of the thirteen in the Group I manuscripts and each set has one Elegy that the other set lacks.

[3] As Woodward was perfectly aware that Wotton had been knighted, the fact that he has not altered the title gives us confidence that he copied what was before him and did not 'improve' his text.

preserved elsewhere, and first printed by Gosse from this manuscript. Since one of these is the sonnet on the death of Donne's wife, the manuscript cannot have been written before 1617. 'La Corona' follows, under that title, not the Group III title 'The Crowne'. The manuscript ends with the Paradoxes and a single lyric 'A Jet Ring Sent'.

It is obvious that *W* falls into two parts: an early collection and the two sets of Holy Sonnets.[1] The gift of a copy of *Pseudo-Martyr* shows that Donne and Woodward took up their friendship on Woodward's return to England. It was probably about the same time that Donne gave him copies of '*La Corona*' and those of the 'Holy Sonnets' which I date 1609–10.[2] In '*La Corona*' *W* agrees strikingly with Group III. Where it reads with Groups I and II against Group III the differences are trivial and could have arisen from errors in the archetype of the text in Group III. In the eight 'Holy Sonnets' common to the three Groups, *W* agrees strikingly with Group III on two occasions, and where it reads with Groups I and II the differences are again trivial, with one exception.[3] In the four sonnets of *1635* (only extant in Group III and *W*) *W* reads with *Dob* against *O'F*, and on the four occasions on which it reads independently the Group III readings could be scribal in origin.

We can either regard *W* as preserving Donne's first version and the Group III manuscripts as descending from a corrupt copy of it, or, if we think the differences between *W* and Group III, though trivial, are sufficiently numerous to be impressive, we could regard *W* as having a slightly different version from the version in Group III, containing minor alterations that Donne retained in the revision that gives us the Group I text. This second view does not account for the coincidence in order between the sonnets in Group III and

[1] Donne's Verse-Letter to Woodward declaring that his Muse was now affecting 'a chast fallownesse' was probably written soon after Donne took service with Egerton and wanted a reputation for 'gravity'; see Milgate, *Satires etc.*, p. 223. It suggests why Woodward's collection of secular poems contains none we would date after 1597.

[2] The presence of the sonnet 'To E. of D.' among Verse-Letters addressed to the friends of Donne's youth suggests that Woodward did not obtain his sonnets as a single set. It is difficult to account for its coming into Woodward's hands, unless it came with the 'six Holy Sonnets' it was written to introduce. I suggest (pp. xlviii–xlix) that these were the first six of *1633*.

[3] See the discussion on p. 72 of the reading 'steede' for 'stuffe'.

the first twelve in *W*. On balance this seems to me of greater significance than the differences in readings.

v

The manuscript miscellanies, in which Donne's poems occur among those of other wits, rarely contain any Divine Poems. Their texts inspire little confidence, and an editor would be rash to adopt a reading from them without external evidence of reliability. They are of little value in an attempt to establish the text.[1]

vi

The theory of the transmission of the *Divine Poems* in manuscript put forward here can be summarized by a *stemma* for the two sets of Holy Sonnets: '*La Corona*' and 'Holy Sonnets' (1633).

Original Versions ?1608 and 1609

(*begotten*, '*La C*.', 2. 9)
(*easyer*, 'H.S.', 6. 12)
(*Or presently, I know not*, 'H.S.', 3. 7)

————*W*————('H.S.' 7–10 not included)———— { *Dob, Lut, O'F* / *S 96, B* }   III

(*created*, '*La C*.', 2. 9)
(*better*, 'H.S.', 6. 12)

Version of 1614————————*X*———— *C 57* / *D*——*SP* / *H 49*   I

(*But my'ever waking part shall*, 'H.S.', 3. 7)

Version of 1619 ————————*Y*———— *TCD*——*N* / *TCC*——*A 18*   II

This *stemma* assumes the differences between Group III and *W* are scribal in origin. If the opposite view is held the *stemma* begins:

Original Versions ?1608 and 1609

(*steede*, 'H.S.', 11. 10)
(*begotten*, '*La C*.', 2. 9)
(*easyer*, 'H.S.', 6. 12)
(*Or presently, I know not*, 'H.S.', 3. 7)

———————— ('H.S.' 7–10 not included)———————— { *Dob, Lut, O'F* / *S 96, B* }   III

(*stuffe*, 'H.S.', 11. 10)

————————————————————————————*W*

If we omit *W*, this *stemma* holds for the remainder of the Divine

---

[1] If a poem occurs in one, this is noted at the beginning of the commentary on that poem, and any points of interest in the manuscript are noted there.

Poems included in the Group I manuscripts: 'A Litany', 'The Cross', 'Annunciation and Passion', and 'Good Friday'. The others are either extant in Groups II and III, or Group III only, or in separate manuscripts, and problems of transmission are dealt with in the Commentary.

II. THE EDITIONS

On 13 September 1632, eighteen months after Donne's death, the Clerk of the Stationers' Company entered to John Marriott 'under the handes of Sir Henry Herbert and both the Wardens *a booke of verses and Poems* (the five *satires*, the first, second, Tenth, Eleventh, and Thirteenth *Elegies* being excepted) and these before excepted to be his when he bringes lawfull authority . . . written by Doctor John Dunn'. On 31 October there was a further entry to Marriott: 'Entred for his Copy under the hands of Sir Henry Herbert and Master Aspley warden *The five Satires* written by Doctor J: Dun these being excepted in his last entrance'. The ban on the five Elegies was not lifted. The book was published in 1633, printed by MF. (Miles Fletcher). Two years later the same publisher and the same printer brought out the enlarged edition of 1635. Further editions appeared in 1639, 1649, 1650, 1654, and 1669.[1]

i

The first edition of 1633 appears at first sight to be a haphazardly assembled collection; but Grierson demonstrated that the order in which the poems appear can be explained by reference to the manuscripts of Group I and Group II. The printer followed as his main source a manuscript of Group I, which was supplemented by the addition of poems from a manuscript of Group II, and the reprinting of those already published.

The edition of 1633 opens, like *C 57*, with 'The Progress of the Soul' and two sets of Holy Sonnets. The *Satires* do not, as we should expect, come next, but are printed towards the end of the volume. This might be accounted for by the exception taken to them: the printer got on with his work while their fate was being decided. In their place we have the Epigrams, not in the Group I manuscripts.

[1] See Keynes, for descriptions of these editions.

Eight Elegies follow. As Grierson pointed out, these eight, in this order, are what would be left if we took out from the thirteen which appear in Group I the first, second, tenth, eleventh, and thirteenth: the Elegies 'excepted' in the entry in the Stationers' Register. After the Elegies comes the same collection of poems as follows them in C 57, H 49, and Lec[1] as far as the letter to Sir Edward Herbert. Here 1633 deserts its Group I manuscript to include a long series of additional Verse-Letters from a Group II manuscript.[2] It returns to it for the letters to Lady Carey and the Countess of Salisbury, the Epithalamiums (to which it adds the early Lincoln's Inn one from its Group II manuscript), and the 'Obsequies'. An odd assortment of poems, taken from various sources, comes next: an Elegy 'The Comparison' (in Group II), 'The Autumnal' and 'Image of her whom I love, more then she' (both of which appear among the Songs and Sonnets in Group I), the Elegy on Prince Henry (previously printed), 'Psalm 137' (not by Donne), 'Resurrection' and the Hamilton Elegy (both in Group II), Basse's Epitaph on Shakespeare (this and 'Psalm 137' are the only poems certainly not by Donne), and 'Sapho to Philaenis' (in Group II). The printer then went back to his Group I manuscript for 'Annunciation and Passion', 'Good Friday', 'A Litany', and the collection of Songs and Sonnets.[3] After the Songs and Sonnets come some miscellaneous poems (most of these occur in Group II) including the delayed Satires. The volume concludes with nine prose letters and the 'Elegies upon the Author'.

The relation of Marriott's Group I manuscript to the extant ones presents a problem. In the poems taken from it, 1633 gives us a better text than we could construct from the manuscripts of this

[1] The collection, as has been said, is differently arranged in D and SP.

[2] The series begins with two more letters to Lady Bedford and one to Lady Huntingdon ('Man to Gods Image'), which appear together in TCD and N, followed by a series of letters in the order in which they appear in TCC, A 18, and TCD, N, except that the sonnet 'To E. of D.' is included. Lastly, there are two more to Lady Bedford, the first of which is in TCD and N.

[3] He added two at the beginning and six at the close to the collection we find in Group I, and inserted the two Anniversaries (previously printed) in the middle of the set. The only differences from the Group I collection are: 'A Lecture upon the Shadow' is missing, and 'The Prohibition' (not in C 57 and Lec) is among the six added at the close; 'Epitaph: On Himself' (also not in C 57 and Lec) is missing and 'The Autumnal' and 'Image of Her' have been removed, as they appear earlier in the volume. The only difference in order is that 'The Undertaking', which follows 'The Exstasy' in Group I, occurs in place of 'Image of Her' in 1633.

group alone, and a much better one than any single manuscript provides. We have to account for its superiority. An answer that at first sight suggests itself is that, as the copy for *1633* was free from the errors that Group I derived from *X*, it must lie behind *X*. But there are resemblances between *1633* and *C 57* and *Lec* which make it impossible to argue that the copy for *1633* was anterior to *X*. Grierson noted that *1633* was nearer to *Lec* than to *D* and *H 49*. It is even closer to *C 57*. Both *C 57* and *1633* begin with 'The Progress of the Soul' and the two sets of Holy Sonnets, and both have the Group II text of the *Satires*. They both omit 'Epitaph: On Himself'; and 'The Prohibition' and the letter 'At once from hence', both of which are missing in *C 57*, occur in *1633* among the poems it took from its Group II manuscript. Even more striking than these facts are the resemblances in readings. *D* reads with *1633* against *C 57* and *H 49* four times, and *H 49* reads with *1633* against *C 57* and *D* nineteen times. In each case the single manuscript agrees with the edition in preserving the right reading where the two others have a slip. But *C 57* reads with *1633* against the other two manuscripts on fifty-five occasions, including five misreadings and one omission of a word. The trivial agreements are perhaps even more significant. It seems more than coincidence that on ten occasions *C 57* and *1633* make the same choice between singular and plural forms, and on six the same choice between 'these' and 'those'.

To demonstrate a close relation between *C 57* and Marriott's Group I manuscript leaves us with the problem of explaining the superiority of the copy for *1633* to the text in *C 57*, and the fact that in the portion of the edition which depends upon a Group I manuscript we find titles taken from Group II, readings from Group II, and some readings that have no support or only random support in the manuscripts. My work on the Love Poems has led me to reject the conjectural explanation that I put forward in 1952: that Marriott's Group I manuscript had been 'authoritatively corrected' before it came into his hands, and that, as Grierson had suggested, the manuscript came from Goodyer.[1] I was much more impressed

---

[1] In accepting Grierson's suggestion I omitted to recognize that it is highly unlikely that so close a friend as Goodyer would have a manuscript so far from one of Donne's own copies as a manuscript closely resembling *C 57* would be.

then by the 'excellence' of *1633* than I have come to be, and I was relying, outside the *Divine Poems*, on Grierson's collations. I had not then realized how much sporadic editorial work existed in some manuscripts and had not made the obvious comparison with the 'editorial' work done on the O'Flaherty manuscript by which many of its Group III readings have been corrected to the readings of *1633*. Also, in working on the *Divine Poems*, I was not confronted by any very striking examples of readings in *1633* which had no manuscript support.[1] It was the examination of these in the *Songs and Sonnets* that led me to the conclusion that Marriott's Group I manuscript had not been corrected by its owner consulting Donne's own copies but had been 'edited', both by collation with a manuscript of Group II and by attempts to emend where the text was thought by the reader to require it.[2] Whether more than one person was concerned it is not possible to say with certainty; but the evidence of the anomalous Dolau Cothi manuscript suggests that there were at least two stages in the transformation of a manuscript closely resembling *C 57* into the copy for this portion of *1633*.

DC is fundamentally a Group II manuscript in its text; but it has some striking affinities with the edition of 1633. In general it has the titles that *1633* adopted from Group II in the form in which they are found in manuscript; but on three occasions it has titles that are found only in the edition. It omits, with *1633*, ll. 53–54 of 'The Anagram', present in all other manuscripts, and ll. 7–8 of 'The Perfume', which *1633*, following Group I in error, also omits. Where there is a choice between a Group I and a Group II text of a poem, *DC* makes the same choice as *1633*. On the other hand, *DC* never reads with *1633* against both Groups I and II; that is, it has none of the unsupported readings of the edition. It also lacks the third stanza of 'The Prohibition' and the third stanza of 'The Will',

[1] Examples in the *Divine Poems* are 'Holy Sonnets' (1633), 9. 14, 'assumes' ('assures' *MSS.*) and 'The Cross', l. 61, 'faithfully' ('fruitfully' *MSS.*), both rejected by Grierson as well as by me.

[2] For examples of readings in *1633* which have no manuscript support and, although plausible at first sight, are demonstrably wrong, see Gardner, *Elegies etc.*, pp. lxxxvi–lxxxviii. See also Milgate, *Satires etc.*, p. lxix, where he states that whenever *1633* reads against the combined authority of the manuscripts containing its version of the *Satires* 'it is wrong, except for three obvious emendations not beyond the power of the editor'.

agreeing here with Group II against the edition. These last two points make it seem unlikely that *DC* derives from a manuscript of Group II which had been corrected from the edition. Its connexions must be with the manuscript that provided the copy for *1633* before some final corrections and improvements were made. These final sophistications may have been the work of the same person who conflated the manuscript of Group I with a manuscript of Group II, or there may have been two persons at work as we can see in *O'F*. But whether there was one person or two, the copy provided for that portion of *1633* that depends upon a Group I manuscript was an 'edited' text.

In the poems the edition took from a Group II manuscript, the *Divine Poems* provide a test-piece: 'The Lamentations of Jeremy'. Although it is not of very great interest poetically, this poem is of considerable interest textually, for we have an objective test of the merits of the variants in the Latin of Tremellius, which Donne was attempting to paraphrase as closely as possible. It is safe to assume that the reading which is nearest to Tremellius is the right reading. The results of applying this test are not very reassuring. They show that *1633* requires emendation on twenty-six occasions, at times from the manuscripts combined, most often from *O'F* and *B*, whose text here is markedly superior to that in *TCD*.[1] The text of this poem also supports the view that the volume as a whole was not 'edited' and that the Group I manuscript had been worked on before it came into Marriott's hands. Obvious error has not been emended, the most striking example being 'black as an Ocean' (l. 368) for 'black as an Oven', the reading of all the manuscripts, and, when the text is compared with the text of poems taken from the Group I manuscript, it conspicuously lacks contractions and elision marks. In 'The Lamentations of Jeremy' (390 lines) contractions and elision marks have had to be supplied on twenty-nine occasions, whereas in 'A Litany' (252 lines) they are needed on only ten occasions.

We must, therefore, in speaking of *1633* recognize that we are dealing with a book that is not textually homogeneous, but falls

---

[1] The inferiority of *TCD* in this poem does not cast doubt on the general reliability of the Group II tradition. It is one of the poems that *TCD/N* add to the poems they share with *TCC/A 18* and so was not included in *Y*.

into three parts. The printer reprinted poems already published, taking them from the current edition on sale. Thus he printed the two *Anniversaries* from the edition of 1625. The text was corrected, not as Grierson thought by reference to earlier editions, but by intelligent guess-work, some of the corrections being obvious ones, others erroneous. In the portion that depends on a Group I manuscript the printer was working on a manuscript that had been worked over by some person or persons whose authority we have no means of judging and on a manuscript that was at some remove from Donne's own papers. In the portion that depends upon a manuscript of Group II, the manuscript used seems to have been inferior to *TCD* and does not show signs of having been much worked upon. It yet remains true that, with the possible exception of the Westmoreland manuscript, no manuscript can replace *1633* as the copy-text. Although they provide some superior substantive readings, individual manuscripts have many terminal errors and the accidentals of their texts would require much supplementation and correction.

ii

The second edition of Donne's poems in 1635 differs from the first in three respects. Fresh poems were added, the contents were rearranged, and a considerable number of alterations were made in the text of the poems reprinted.[1]

Of the twenty-eight poems added,[2] twenty-three are to be found in *O'F*, more than any other single manuscript could provide.[3] One

---

[1] *1635* reprinted all the poems in *1633*, with the exception of Basse's 'Epitaph on Shakespeare', and one of the Elegies on Donne, Thomas Browne's.

[2] One of them 'Epitaph: On Himself' appears twice, so that there are actually twenty-nine additional items among the poems. I follow Keynes in counting the four additional 'Holy Sonnets' as a single item.

[3] The poems not in *O'F* are 'Come, Fates; I feare you not' (ascribed by Grierson to Sir John Roe); 'To the Countess of Huntington': 'That unripe side of earth' (formerly regarded as spurious, but now accepted in the canon); 'A Dialogue

of these, 'Upon the Translation of the Psalms', is extant in *O'F* only; others are poems which are only to be found elsewhere in one or two manuscripts. The rearrangement in *1635* is under the headings which *O'F* took over from *Lut*: it has their title 'Epicedes and Obsequies' for the Funeral Poems, and collects the lyrics under the heading 'Songs and Sonets', where they have 'Sonnets and Songes'. It appears as if the compiler of *O'F* came to terms with Marriott after the publication of *1633*, and that Marriott either acquired the manuscript or collaborated with him to produce *1635*. The assumption that *O'F* was a main source for the additions and alterations in *1635* is strongly supported by an examination of the text of the Divine Poems.

Seven Divine Poems were added in *1635*, of which two: 'On the Sacrament' and 'Hymn to God my God, in my sickness' are not in *O'F*. Two of the remaining five are spurious: 'On the Blessed Virgin Mary' and 'Ode: Of our Sense of Sin'.[1] There are no striking features in the text of these brief poems, except that in the first we find twice over 'ô' for 'O'. This is one of the characteristics of the *O'F* scribe. But in 'Upon the Translation of the Psalms' and the four additional 'Holy Sonnets' the resemblances between *O'F* and *1635* are most remarkable. In the first, which is only extant in *O'F*, there are only two verbal differences between *1635* and the manuscript, both of which are explicable as misreadings of the manuscript;[2] and in punctuation the two texts are very close. On six occasions *O'F* employs brackets for parentheses, and on all six *1635* has brackets too. Also, words, other than proper names, which are italicized in *1635* are distinguished by being within square brackets, or between two upright lines, in *O'F*. In the four 'Holy Sonnets', which are found in five other manuscripts as well as in *O'F*, there are only three verbal differences between *1635* and *O'F*. In each case *O'F* has the support of the other manuscripts against what is plainly an

between Sir Henry Wotton and Mr. Donne' (ascribed to Pembroke and Ruddier); the quatrain 'On the Sacrament' (ascribed to Queen Elizabeth); and 'Hymn to God my God, in my sickness'.

[1] The first is almost certainly by Henry Constable. It could not possibly be Donne's, since it celebrates the Immaculate Conception, a doctrine he explicitly rejects in 'A Litany' and shows no sign of ever having held. The second is now accepted as Lord Herbert of Cherbury's.

[2] *1635* has 'thy' for 'this' (l. 46) and 'those' for 'these' (l. 53).

error in *1635*.[1] Apart from supplying stops at the ends of lines, which *O'F*, like most of the manuscripts, tends to omit, *1635* differs from *O'F* in punctuation only six times. Although it does not reproduce all the capitals in *O'F*, all the capitals it has are to be found there, some of them having little logical justification. Details such as 'ô' for 'O' (2. 12) and the brackets in 'to (poore) me' (3. 12) and 'and (oh) both parts must die' (2. 4) are found in both. On the other hand in the lines 'To Mr. Tilman' the resemblance is far less close. There are eleven verbal differences between *1635* and *O'F*, and though some of the readings in *1635* may be ascribed to carelessness, and some appear to be sophistication, the support that *1635* receives at times from the version of the poem found in the Welbeck miscellany suggests that the text was derived from another manuscript than *O'F*.[2] The punctuation also does not suggest any dependence on *O'F*.

When we turn to the poems which *1635* reprinted from *1633*, we find that, as well as correcting misprints, revising the punctuation, and making a certain number of minor alterations in wording, *1635* has on a good many occasions a different reading from *1633*.[3] In one poem, 'A Hymn to Christ' (1619), *1635* has two readings for which no manuscript support exists, though it also inexplicably adopted the absurd Group III reading 'Face' for 'Fame' (l. 28). Outside this poem, there is only one *1635* reading which is not to be found in the manuscripts: 'On his distressed mother' for 'Upon his miserable mother' in 'Good Friday' (l. 30).[4] The rest are all to be found in *O'F*. In general they are readings common to the Group III manuscripts, but it will be remembered that *O'F* has had many of its Group III readings corrected to the readings of *1633*, and it is notable that Group III readings which have been corrected in *O'F* are not adopted in *1635*.[5] On one occasion, also, *1635* adopts a reading

---

[1] *1635* reads 'feeble' for 'feebled' of the MSS. (1. 7); omits the auxiliary 'hath/have' of the MSS. (2. 11); and reads 'stile' for 'vile/vild' of the MSS. (4. 10).

[2] See note to l. 30, p. 101.

[3] See Appendix A: 'Verbal Alterations in the *Divine Poems* in the edition of 1635' for a complete list of verbal variants between *1633* and *1635*.

[4] This is probably an editorial emendation to avoid the awkward elisions necessary in 'miserable'.

[5] There is one exception to this, but it is explicable. In 'A Litany' (l. 128) *1635* reads 'clouds' for 'clods'. The Group III reading 'clouds' was corrected

which is only to be found in *O'F* and is *O'F*'s attempt to make sense of an error in Group III.[1]

The study of the *Divine Poems*, therefore, does not give us grounds for regarding *1635* as an edition of any great authority. In the poems it reprinted from *1633* it presents us with a conflation of *1633* and *O'F*. Our judgement on it here depends on our judgement of *O'F*, and on whether we think that whoever corrected *O'F* by *1633* and whoever then corrected *1633* by *O'F* were guided in their choice of readings by anything but personal preference. In its treatment of the canon, *1635* showed some discrimination. It dropped one of the two spurious pieces in *1633* and, although among its twenty-eight new poems it included eleven which are not Donne's, it rejected a good many of the spurious pieces in *O'F* and the other Group III manuscripts. But I see no reason to believe that its treatment of the text was inspired by any other principle than taste. In its corrections of the punctuation of *1633*, however, *1635* is useful to a modern editor. Although the printer plainly preferred a heavier punctuation than we find in *1633*, he was, after all, punctuating on the same principles. Of the poems first printed in *1635*, some appear to have been taken directly from *O'F*, but in one of the poems which *1635* could have found there it appears to have followed another manuscript. It had at any rate some other source, either another manuscript, or possibly some loose poems. It has here the authority of a first edition, but it has little intrinsic authority. *O'F*, though in many respects a good manuscript, is a not altogether reliable representative of the Group III tradition, and we have no evidence at all as to the reliability of the other sources which *1635* drew upon.

iii

The subsequent editions of Donne's poetry do not concern an editor of the *Divine Poems*. The only poem in this category which

---

in *O'F*, but by the second corrector, who corrected it in his usual way by underlining 'clouds' and writing 'clods' in the margin. His correction might easily be overlooked.

[1] In '*La Corona*' (1. 2), *1633*, with Group I (except for *C 57*), Group II, and *W*, reads 'low/lowe'. *B, Lut, S*, and *C 57*, misreading 'we' as 'ue', read 'loue', which *Dob* and *S 96* have improved to 'loues'. *O'F*, however, has improved the *Lut* reading to 'lone', the reading found in *1635*.

was added was the Latin poem to Herbert with its translation. This appeared among some poems on inserted sheets in the edition of 1650. The text in these editions is the text of *1635* reprinted with minor alterations and corruptions. The only exception is the last seventeenth-century edition, that of 1669. This made additions of importance and as Grierson says 'bears evidence of recourse to manuscript sources'. This edition made a considerable number of alterations in the text, 'some of the changes showing a reversion to the text of *1633*, others a reference to manuscript sources, many editorial conjecture'. But although it is interesting that a serious attempt was made in 1669 to present a rather better text, the edition has no authority, except in those poems it printed for the first time.

III. CONCLUSIONS

i

The edition of 1633 provides the only possible basis for a critical edition. It was carefully printed and its accidentals are, in the main, consistent with good seventeenth-century usage. But it needs correction from the manuscripts beyond the correction of misprints and obvious misreadings. Although different portions of the text present special problems,[1] certain general rules apply. Readings in the edition which have no manuscript support should be rejected. (This should include readings in which *1633* has only the support of an odd manuscript and the consensus of the manuscripts is against it).[2]

In the poems taken from a Group I manuscript closely resembling *C 57*, readings in which *1633* follows *C 57* and its collateral *Lec* against all other manuscripts should be rejected. We should also,

---

[1] The text of the *Satires* presents special problems, since there are plainly distinct versions and the main manuscript groupings break down. The *Songs and Sonnets* also present problems. Although in some of the poems the variants suggest the existence of different versions, there is little in the variants themselves, as there is in the *Divine Poems*, to make us decide which is an earlier and which a later version.

[2] An example in the *Divine Poems* is 'Good Friday', l. 27, where only *Dob* out of all the manuscripts supports *1633* in reading 'Made' for 'Make'.

though not invariably, adopt the readings of Group II and Group
III when they agree against *1633* and Group I. The presumption
here is that Group I is in error, since Group II in general reads with
Group I against Group III. The occasions when *1633* has the support
of Group III only present more difficulty. On most of the occasions
on which this occurs in the *Divine Poems* the reading of the two
better groups of manuscripts seems to me preferable. But in both
these last cases an editor has to exercise judgement on the merit of
the readings. The reading of a single manuscript should never be
adopted unless the manuscript has very high authority or the
reading is unquestionably superior.[1]

In the poems it took from a Group II manuscript the readings of
1633 have to be weighed against those of Groups II and III. When
the manuscripts agree against the edition, their readings should
be accepted; but when the two Groups read against each other, the
readings can only be considered on their merits. When there are
three traditions independent of each other, the agreement of two
has weight against one. When there are only two traditions, each
has an equal right to consideration. The most important poem in
this class in the *Divine Poems* is 'The Lamentations of Jeremy'. This
poem is a rather special case. It is rarely found in manuscript, and
we can hardly speak of a 'Group II text' when it is not present in
TCC and *A 18*, or of a 'Group III text' when it only occurs in *B*, *O'F*,
and *O*. By the test of closeness to the Latin which Donne was
paraphrasing, *1633* was following a manuscript inferior to *TCD*; but,
by the same test, *TCD* needs correction from *B* and *O'F*.[2] The text
of the edition here has to be corrected by reference to all the avail-
able manuscripts.

In the poems first printed in the second edition of 1635, we are
dealing with poems that are, in the main, preserved in the Group
III manuscripts alone. The edition was carefully printed and, on
the whole, well punctuated, and can serve as a copy text. When, as
in the majority of cases, the source of the text is *O'F*, we must re-

---

[1] Thus, in 'Holy Sonnets' (1633), 4. 6, I accept the reading of Westmoreland,
because of its high authority, against *1633* and all other manuscripts, although it
cannot be said that 'dearth' is 'unquestionably superior' to 'death'; see pp. 67–8.

[2] For details, see the Commentary, p. 103.

member that *O'F*, although it has few 'obvious errors', can be seen
by reference to other Group III manuscripts to have a tendency to
'clean up' its text. Readings in *1635* that depend on unsupported
readings in *O'F* should be rejected for the readings of its group,
unless it is correcting an obvious error in the group reading. Where
the source of the text in *1635* is uncertain, as in 'To Mr. Tilman',
the text of the edition has to be weighed as an independent witness
along with the extant manuscripts.

ii

The text that follows is, therefore, that of the first edition of each
poem, except for the three sonnets which are printed from the
Westmoreland manuscript. The spelling and punctuation are that of
the basic text, but I have not preserved the long *ſ* or the ligatured
ct, and have modernized the treatment of *I* and *J* and *U* and *V*.[1]
I have also expanded printers' contractions: e.g. I print *and* for *&*,
and *when* for *whē*. The typography of the titles is standardized. The
holograph of the poem to Lady Carey shows that Donne, as we
might have assumed from the *Anniversaries*, used a heavier punctua-
tion than we find in *1633* and used it to bring out the syntax. This
justifies an editor in strengthening, as Grierson did, the punc-
tuation of the edition. Such emendations are made on my own
judgement; but when the sense is affected, the evidence of the
manuscripts is discussed in the commentary. The holograph also
shows that Donne used fewer elision marks than his modern editor,
Milgate, but more than we find in *1633*. When I first edited the
Divine Poems, influenced by Grierson's conservatism here, I supplied
such marks only when I thought the reader would find the line
unmetrical without them. In the Love Poems I attempted to make
the practice of *1633* consistent, thinking it confusing if on one
occasion where suppression of a syllable is necessary it is marked,
and on another, where it is equally necessary, it is left unmarked.
Milgate followed me, and in revising the *Divine Poems* I have fol-
lowed the same policy. As there is no means of deciding when

[1] *1633* follows modern usage in the lower case.

Donne thought an elision mark necessary and when he thought it was not, it seems better to err in supplying too many than too few.

The basis of the text for each poem is given at the beginning of the critical apparatus, followed by the list of manuscripts from which readings are given there. These have been selected to represent the main groups. *C 57* and *H 49* have been used to represent Group I; *TCD* to represent Group II; and *Dob* and *O'F* to represent Group III. Where the reading of *O'F* has been corrected, it is cited as having its original reading, but '(*b.c.*)', that is 'before correction', has been added to indicate that the reading has been corrected to that of *1633*. Usually the reading given is to be found in all the manuscripts of the group; when this is not so, it is either apparent from the divergence of *C 57* from *H 49*, or of *Dob* from *O'F*, or the fact is mentioned in the note on the passage. Apart from *W*, which is an independent manuscript, manuscripts outside the main groups have not been employed in the apparatus, except in 'To Mr. Tilman' and in the 'Hymn to God my God, in my sickness', where *Wel* (Welbeck) and *A 34* have been used. A list of the manuscripts in which a poem is to be found is given at the beginning of the commentary on each poem. In giving variants the spelling is that of the first manuscript cited and its usage with *i* and *j*, *u*, and *v*, is followed.[1] Variations in the spelling of the manuscripts are not noted, unless they help to explain errors.

The apparatus is strictly selective. Its first purpose is to record readings which deserve consideration, and particularly all those Group III readings which cannot be shown to be erroneous. Any readings which, in my opinion, cannot be Donne's, but have arisen through error or misunderstanding of his meaning, are considered in the note on the passage if they have surface plausibility, or have been approved by other critics or editors. They are not included in the apparatus, since this is designed to assist readers to a better appreciation of Donne's art by allowing them to study what are, I believe, his first thoughts. I had at first intended not to burden the apparatus with a few insignificant variants, which might as

---

[1] Exceptions to this are that when a reading from the manuscripts is adopted in the text, I have on one or two occasions made the spelling conform to the general usage of the printer, and I have not followed the scribe of *Dob* in his habit of not writing a capital at the beginning of a line.

probably be due to a copyist's error as to an author's change of mind, but the line between significance and insignificance cannot be firmly drawn, and I have felt it better to give all readings which cannot be shown to be wrong, and to let the reader draw the line himself. Readings from editions subsequent to the first are not recorded. They can be found, if wanted, in Grierson's edition. Although of interest in the history of Donne scholarship, they are of no value in establishing what he wrote. I have, however, given a list of the readings of *1635* in Appendix B; and the reading of Grierson's edition of 1912, which may be regarded as the *textus receptus*, is recorded when it differs from mine.

The order of the poems differs from Grierson's, which follows in general the order of *1635*. This was dictated by considerations of convenience in the printing house, and has no particular merit. I have followed *1633* in giving the general title of 'Holy Sonnets' to all the sonnets, though I have included under the title the two dedicatory sonnets, which I have placed before the sets they were written, I believe, to introduce. I have printed the 'Holy Sonnets' of *1633* as they appear there, the four which were interpolated among them in *1635* separately, followed by the three from the Westmoreland manuscript. I have placed 'A Litany', Donne's most considerable religious poem, next; and put the three Hymns together at the close, to follow the paraphrase of Lamentations. This brings together in the middle the Occasional Poems, and I have put them under that title. A grouping by kind seems more satisfactory than an attempt to arrange by date, though the Occasional Poems appear in what is probably their chronological order. I have placed at the end Donne's Latin verses to Herbert, and a line of Latin verse, which may be the last line he wrote: the Epigraph to the portrait of himself in his shroud, prefixed to *Deaths Duell*.

Note: I have to thank Alan MacColl for collating thirteen copies of *1633*[1] for press variants on the collating machine at the British Library and the librarians of the Oxford colleges concerned for making this possible by depositing their copies in the Bodleian Library. G. Blakemore Evans kindly collated the

[1] Bodleian Library (2), British Library (2), All Souls, Balliol, Brasenose, Christ Church, Corpus Christi, Queen's, St. John's, Wadham, and Worcester Colleges, Oxford.

two copies in the library of the University of Illinois at Urbana. The two
states of the outer forme of Aa have the only variants of interest. It needed
considerable correction and two misprints 'flame' for 'fame' and 'though' for
'through' ('A Litany', 153 and 167) remain uncorrected in the second state.
1635 has readings of the first state in 'A Litany', 164 and 231.

In revising, I have noted the readings of uncorrected formes in the critical
apparatus.

LIST OF SIGLA

Classified List of Manuscripts of the Divine Poems

(i) MSS. containing collections of Donne's poems

GROUP I

C 57	Cambridge University Library, Add. MS. 5778.
D	Dowden MS. Bodleian Library, MS. Eng. Poet. e 99 (formerly in the library of Wilfred Merton).
H 49	British Library, Harleian MS. 4955.
Lec	Leconfield MS. In the library of Sir Geoffrey Keynes.
SP	St. Paul's Cathedral Library, MS. 49 B 43.

GROUP II

A 18	British Library, Add. MS. 18647.
N	Norton MS. Harvard College Library, MS. Eng. 966/3 (formerly MS. Norton 4503).
TCC	Trinity College, Cambridge, MS. R 3 12.
TCD	Trinity College, Dublin, MS. 877 (formerly G 2 21).
DC[1]	National Library of Wales, Dolau Cothi MS.

GROUP III

(a) *MSS. containing a set of Divine Poems*

Dob	Dobell MS. Harvard College Library, MS. Eng. 966/4 (formerly MS. Norton 4506).
Lut	Luttrell MS. In the library of Sir Geoffrey Keynes.
O'F[2]	O'Flaherty MS. Harvard College Library, MS. Eng. 966/5 (formerly MS. Norton 4504).
S 96	British Library, Stowe MS. 961.
B[3]	Bridgewater MS. Huntington Library, MS. EL 6893.
O1	Osborn MS. 1 Osborn Collection, Yale University (formerly King MS. (*K*), Raphael King Catalogue, 51).
S	Stephens MS. Harvard College Library, MS. Eng. 966/6 (formerly MS. Norton 4500).

---

[1] *DC* reads with Group II but does not descend from the common exemplar of the group.

[2] *O'F* (*b.c.*): O'Flaherty, before correction. This indicates that the reading cited has been corrected to the reading of *1633*.

[3] *B*, *O 1*, and *S* read consistently with Group III in the *Divine Poems*, but read erratically elsewhere.

(b) MSS. containing only a few Divine Poems

A 25	British Library, Add. MS. 25707.
Cy	Carnaby MS. Harvard College Library, MS. Eng. 966/1 (formerly MS. Norton 4502).
D 17	Dyce Collection, Victoria and Albert Museum, MS. D 25 F 17.
JC	John Cave MS. George Arents Tobacco Collection, New York Public Library (formerly in the library of Richard Jennings).
O2	Osborn MS. 2 Osborn Collection, Yale University (sold at Hodgson's, 21 Nov. 1958, from the library of J. B. Whitmore).
P	Phillipps MS. Bodleian Library, MS. Eng. Poet. f 9.

IV

W	Westmoreland MS. Berg Collection, New York Public Library (formerly in the library of Edmund Gosse).

A 23	British Library, Add. MS. 23229 (Conway Papers).
A 34	British Library, Add. MS. 34324 (Sir Julius Caesar's Papers).
Ash	Bodleian Library, Ashmole MS. 38.
CCC	Corpus Christi College, Oxford, MS. 327.
E 20	British Library, Egerton MS. 2013.
Grey	S. African Public Library, Cape Town, MS. Grey 2 a 11.
Hd	Harvard College Library, MS. Eng. 966/17.
HK 2	Haslewood-Kingsborough MS., second part, Huntington Library, MS. HM 198.
La	Edinburgh University Library, Laing MS. iii. 493.
RP 117 (2)	Bodleian Library, Rawlinson Poetical MS. 117.
S 962	British Library, Stowe MS. 962.
Wed	Wedderburn MS. National Library of Scotland, MS. 6504.
Wel	Welbeck MS. In the library of the Duke of Portland, deposited in the library of the University of Nottingham.

The editions of Donne's poems from 1633 to 1669 are cited under their dates, as *1633*, *1635*, &c.

The Poems of John Donne, ed. H. J. C. Grierson, 2 vols. (Oxford, 1912) is cited as *Gr*.

DIVINE POEMS

HOLY SONNETS

To Mrs. Magdalen Herbert: of St. Mary Magdalen

HER of your name, whose fair inheritance
 Bethina was, and jointure *Magdalo*:
An active faith so highly did advance,
 That she once knew, more than the Church did know,
The *Resurrection*; so much good there is   5
 Deliver'd of her, that some Fathers be.
Loth to believe one Woman could do this;
 But, think these *Magdalens* were two or three.
Increase their number, *Lady*, and their fame:
 To their *Devotion*, add your *Innocence*;   10
Take so much of th'example,'as of the name;
 The latter half; and in some recompence
That they did harbour *Christ* himself, a Guest,
Harbour these *Hymns*, to his dear name addrest.   J.D.

La Corona

I

DEIGNE *at my hands this crown of prayer and praise,*
 Weav'd in my low devout melancholie,
Thou which of good, hast, yea art treasury,
All changing unchang'd Antient of dayes,

To Mrs. Magdalen Herbert: &c.   *Walton*, The Life of Mr. George Herbert
(*1670*)   To Mrs. Magdalen Herbert: *Ed.*: To the Lady Magdalen Herbert,
Walton.   4 know,] know *Walton*   11 'as] as *Walton*
La Corona 1633   MSS.: *C 57* and H *49*; *TCD*; *Dob* and *O'F*; *W*   *La Corona*]
The Crowne *Dob, O'F*   *C 57, H 49, Dob, O'F, W have no titles for separate*
sonnets.   1. 3 treasury] a Treasury *Dob, O'F*

But doe not, with a vile crowne of fraile bayes, 5
Reward my muses white sincerity,
But what thy thorny crowne gain'd, that give mee,
A crowne of Glory, which doth flower alwayes;
The ends crowne our workes, but thou crown'st our ends,
For, at our end begins our endlesse rest, 10
This first last end, now zealously possest,
With a strong sober thirst, my soule attends.
'Tis time that heart and voice be lifted high,
Salvation to all that will is nigh.

2. Annunciation

Salvation to all that will is nigh,
That All, which alwayes is All every where,
Which cannot sinne, and yet all sinnes must beare,
Which cannot die, yet cannot chuse but die,
Loe, faithfull Virgin, yeelds himselfe to lye 5
In prison, in thy wombe; and though he there
Can take no sinne, nor thou give, yet he'will weare
Taken from thence, flesh, which deaths force may trie.
Ere by the spheares time was created, thou
Wast in his minde, who is thy Sonne, and Brother, 10
Whom thou conceiv'st, conceiv'd; yea thou art now
Thy Makers maker, and thy Fathers mother,
Thou'hast light in darke; and shutst in little roome,
Immensity cloysterd in thy deare wombe.

9 ends crowne] end crownes *Dob, O'F* ends] dayes *Dob, O'F (b.c.)* 10
For] Soe *Dob, O'F (b.c.), W* 10-11 begins . . . end,] *Omit H 49* 11 This
TCD, Dob, O'F, W: The *1633, C 57, Gr* zealously] soberly *Dob, O'F (b.c.), W*
13 heart and voice] voyce and hart *Dob, O'F, W* 14 *nigh.] nigh, 1633*
2. Annunciation. 9 created] begotten *Dob, O'F (b.c.), W* 10 who] w^ch *Dob,*
W 11 conceiv'st] conceiu'dst *Dob, O'F, W*

3. Nativitie

Immensitie cloysterd in thy deare wombe,
Now leaves his welbelov'd imprisonment,
There he hath made himselfe to his intent
Weake enough, now into our world to come;
But Oh, for thee, for him, hath th'Inne no roome? 5
Yet lay him in this stall, and from th'Orient,
Starres, and wisemen will travell to prevent
Th'effect of *Herods* jealous generall doome.
Seest thou, my Soule, with thy faiths eyes, how he
Which fils all place, yet none holds him, doth lye? 10
Was not his pity towards thee wondrous high,
That would have need to be pittied by thee?
Kisse him, and with him into Egypt goe,
With his kinde mother, who partakes thy woe.

4. Temple

With his kinde mother who partakes thy woe,
Joseph turne backe; see where your child doth sit,
Blowing, yea blowing out those sparks of wit,
Which himselfe on those Doctors did bestow;
The Word but lately could not speake, and loe 5
It sodenly speakes wonders, whence comes it,
That all which was, and all which should be writ,
A shallow seeming child, should deeply know?
His Godhead was not soule to his manhood,
Nor had time mellow'd him to this ripenesse, 10
But as for one which hath a long taske, 'tis good,
With the Sunne to beginne his businesse,
He in his ages morning thus began
By miracles exceeding power of man.

3. Nativitie.   3 he hath] hath he *Dob, O'F*   4 our] the *Dob, O'F*
6 th'] the *1633*   7 will] shall *Dob, O'F, W*   8 effect *C 57, TCD, Dob,*
O'F, W: effects *1633, H49*   jealous] zealous *TCD*: dire and *Dob, O'F*
(b.c.), W   doome.] doome; *1633*   9 eyes] eye *TCD*   12 by] of *Dob, O'F,*
4. Temple.   2 your] thy *Dob, O'F*   4 those *H 49, TCD, Dob, O'F,*
W: the *1633, C 57, Gr*   10 mellow'd] mellowed *1633*   11 for one]
one *Dob*: some one *O'F*: to'one *W*   a long taske] long taskes *TCD, Dob, O'F, W*
'tis ('Tis *1633*)] thinkes it *Dob*: thinks *O'F, W*

5. Crucifying

By miracles exceeding power of man,
Hee faith in some, envie in some begat,
For, what weake spirits admire, ambitious, hate;
In both affections many to him ran,
But Oh! the worst are most, they will and can,   5
Alas, and do, unto th'immaculate,
Whose creature Fate is, now prescribe a Fate,
Measuring selfe-lifes infinity to'a span,
Nay to an inch. Loe, where condemned hee
Beares his owne crosse, with paine, yet by and by   10
When it beares him, he must beare more and die.
Now thou art lifted up, draw mee to thee,
And at thy death giving such liberall dole,
Moyst, with one drop of thy blood, my dry soule.

6. Resurrection

Moyst with one drop of thy blood, my dry soule
Shall (though she now be in extreme degree
Too stony hard, and yet too fleshly,) bee
Freed by that drop, from being starv'd, hard, or foule,
And life, by this death abled, shall controule   5
Death, whom thy death slue; nor shall to mee
Feare of first or last death, bring miserie,
If in thy little booke my name thou'enroule,
Flesh in that long sleep is not putrified,
But made that there, of which, and for which 'twas;   10
Nor can by other meanes be glorified.
May then sinnes sleep, and deaths soone from me passe,
That wak't from both, I againe risen may
Salute the last, and everlasting day.

5. Crucifying.   3 weake] meeke *Dob, O'F, W*   6 th'] the *1633*   8 to'a
span *TCD, Dob, O'F, W*: to span *1633, C 57, H 49*   9 inch. Loe] inch, loe
1633   11 die.] die; *1633*
6. Resurrection.   1 *soule] soule, 1633*   2 now be] bee now *TCD, Dob,*
O'F   5 this] thy *Dob, O'F, W*   6 shall] shall nowe *TCD, O'F*
8 little booke] litle Bookes *TCD*: life-booke *Dob, O'F, W: see note*   'enroule]
enroule *1633*   9 that long sleep] yᵗ sleepe *C 57*: that steep'd *H 49*: that
last longe sleepe *Dob, O'F, W*   11 glorified] puryfy'd *Dob, O'F (b.c.), W*
12 deaths *TCD, W*: death *1633, C 57, H 49, Dob, O'F*

7. Ascention

Salute the last and everlasting day,
Joy at th'uprising of this Sunne, and Sonne,
Yee whose just teares, or tribulation
Have purely washt, or burnt your drossie clay;
Behold the Highest, parting hence away, 5
Lightens the darke clouds, which hee treads upon,
Nor doth hee by ascending, show alone,
But first hee, and hee first enters the way.
O strong Ramme, which hast batter'd heaven for mee,
Mild lambe, which with thy blood, hast mark'd the path; 10
Bright torch, which shin'st, that I the way may see,
Oh, with thine owne blood quench thine owne just wrath,
And if thy holy Spirit, my Muse did raise,
Deigne at my hands this crowne of prayer and praise.

To E. of D. with six holy Sonnets

SEE Sir, how as the Suns hot Masculine flame
   Begets strange creatures on Niles durty slime,
   In me, your fatherly yet lusty Ryme
(For, these songs are their fruits) have wrought the same;
But though the ingendring force from whence they came 5
   Bee strong enough, and nature doe admit
   Seaven to be borne at once, I send as yet
But six, they say, the seaventh hath still some maime;

7. Ascention.   2 th'] the *1633*   3 just] true *Dob, O'F, W*   4 Have]
Hath *Dob, O'F, W*   8 way.] way, *1633*   10 lambe,] lambe *1633*
11 the way] thy wayes *Dob, O'F (b.c.), W*   12 thine . . . thine *TCD, Dob,
O'F, W*: thy . . . thy *1633, C 57, H 49, Gr*
To E. of D. &c. *1633   MSS.: O'F, W*   To E. of D. &c.] To L. of D. *W*
4 their fruits] the fruit *W*

I choose your judgement, which the same degree
  Doth with her sister, your invention, hold,   10
As fire these drossie Rymes to purifie,
  Or as Elixar, to change them to gold;
You are that Alchimist which alwaies had
Wit, whose one spark could make good things of bad.

Holy Sonnets
(1633)

Divine Meditations

I

As due by many titles I resigne
  My selfe to thee, O God, first I was made
By thee, and for thee, and when I was decay'd
Thy blood bought that, the which before was thine,
I am thy sonne, made with thy selfe to shine,   5
Thy servant, whose paines thou hast still repaid,
Thy sheepe, thine Image, and till I betray'd
My selfe, a temple of thy Spirit divine;
Why doth the devill then usurpe in mee?
Why doth he steale, nay ravish that's thy right?   10
Except thou rise and for thine owne worke fight,
Oh I shall soone despaire, when I doe see
That thou lov'st mankind well, yet wilt not chuse me,
And Satan hates mee, yet is loth to lose mee. (II)

---

9 choose] chose *W*
Holy Sonnets (1633) *1633*   MSS.: *C 57 and H 49; TCD; Dob and O'F; W*   Title:
see note
1. 2 I was] was I *Dob, O'F*   7 thine] thy *Dob, O'F*   9 then] thus *Dob,*
O'F   in *TCD, Dob, O'F (b.c.), W*: on *1633, C 57, H 49, Gr*   10 steale,] steale
1633   12 doe] shall *Dob, O'F*   13 wilt not] wilt'not *1633; see note*
me,] me. *1633*

2

Oh my blacke Soule! now thou art summoned
    By sicknesse, deaths herald, and champion;
Thou'art like a pilgrim, which abroad hath done
Treason, and durst not turne to whence hee's fled,
Or like a thiefe, which till deaths doome be read,   5
Wisheth himselfe delivered from prison;
But damn'd and hal'd to execution,
Wisheth that still he might be'imprisoned;
Yet grace, if thou repent, thou canst not lacke;
But who shall give thee that grace to beginne?   10
Oh make thy selfe with holy mourning blacke,
And red with blushing, as thou art with sinne;
Or wash thee in Christs blood, which hath this might
That being red, it dyes red soules to white. (IV)

3

This is my playes last scene, here heavens appoint
    My pilgrimages last mile; and my race
Idly, yet quickly runne, hath this last pace,
My spans last inch, my minutes last point,
And gluttonous death will instantly unjoynt   5
My body,'and soule, and I shall sleepe a space,
But my'ever-waking part shall see that face,
Whose feare already shakes my every joynt:
Then, as my soule, to'heaven her first seate, takes flight,
And earth-borne body, in the earth shall dwell,   10
So, fall my sinnes, that all may have their right,
To where they'are bred, and would presse me, to hell.
Impute me righteous, thus purg'd of evill,
For thus I leave the world, the flesh, and devill. (VI)

2. 3 'art] art *1633*   hath] had *TCD, O'F (b.c.), W*   4 to] from *Dob, O'F*
(b.c.)   hee's] hee is *1633*   8 be'] be *1633*
3. 4 last *C 57, H 49, TCD, W*: latest *Dob, O'F, Gr: see note*   5 death] death,
1633   6 'and] and *1633*   soule *C 57, H 49, TCD, O'F, W*: my soule *1633,*
Dob   7 Or presently, I know not, see yᵗ Face *C 57, H 49, Dob, O'F, W*
8 my] me *C 57, Dob, O'F*   10 earth-borne] earth borne *1633*   14 flesh,]
flesh *1633*   and *MSS.*: the *1633, Gr*

4

A T the round earths imagin'd corners, blow
  Your trumpets, Angells, and arise, arise
From death, you numberlesse infinities
Of soules, and to your scattred bodies goe,
All whom the flood did, and fire shall o'erthrow,   5
All whom warre, dearth, age, agues, tyrannies,
Despaire, law, chance, hath slaine, and you whose eyes,
Shall behold God, and never tast deaths woe.
But let them sleepe, Lord, and mee mourne a space,
For, if above all these, my sinnes abound,   10
'Tis late to aske abundance of thy grace,
When wee are there; here on this lowly ground,
Teach mee how to repent; for that's as good
As if thou'hadst seal'd my pardon, with thy blood. (VII)

5

I F poysonous mineralls, and if that tree,
  Whose fruit threw death on else immortall us,
If lecherous goats, if serpents envious
Cannot be damn'd; Alas; why should I bee?
Why should intent or reason, borne in mee,   5
Make sinnes, else equall, in mee, more heinous?
And mercy being easie,'and glorious
To God, in his sterne wrath, why threatens hee?
But who am I, that dare dispute with thee?
O God, Oh! of thine onely worthy blood,   10
And my teares, make a heavenly Lethean flood,
And drowne in it my sinnes blacke memorie.
That thou remember them, some claime as debt,
I thinke it mercy, if thou wilt forget. (IX)

---

4. 6 dearth *W*: death *1633*, *C 57*, *H 49*, *TCD*, *Dob*, *O'F: see note*   8 woe.] woe,
1633
5. 1 and if that] or yf the *Dob*, *O'F*   5 or] and *Dob*, *O'F*   7 'and] and
1633   9–10 thee ? O God,] thee O God ? *O'F*, *W*, *Gr*   10 thine] thy
Dob, *O'F*   12 memorie.] memorie, *1633*   13 some claime] no more
Dob, *O'F*   14 forget.] forget, *1633*

6

DEATH be not proud, though some have called thee
    Mighty and dreadfull, for, thou art not soe,
For, those, whom thou think'st, thou dost overthrow,
Die not, poore death, nor yet canst thou kill mee;
From rest and sleepe, which but thy pictures bee,   5
Much pleasure, then from thee, much more must flow,
And soonest our best men with thee doe goe,
Rest of their bones, and soules deliverie.
Thou'art slave to Fate, chance, kings, and desperate men,
And dost with poyson, warre, and sicknesse dwell,   10
And poppie,'or charmes can make us sleepe as well,
And better then thy stroake; why swell'st thou then?
One short sleepe past, wee wake eternally,
And death shall be no more, Death thou shalt die. (X)

7

SPIT in my face yee Jewes, and pierce my side,
    Buffet, and scoffe, scourge, and crucifie mee,
For I have sinn'd, and sinn'd, and onely hee,
Who could do no iniquitie, hath dyed:
But by my death can not be satisfied   5
My sinnes, which passe the Jewes impiety:
They kill'd once an inglorious man, but I
Crucifie him daily, being now glorified.
Oh let mee then, his strange love still admire:
Kings pardon, but he bore our punishment.   10
And *Jacob* came cloth'd in vile harsh attire
But to supplant, and with gainfull intent:
God cloth'd himselfe in vile mans flesh, that so
Hee might be weake enough to suffer woe. (XI)

6. 8 bones] bodyes *Dob, O'F (b.c.)*   deliverie.] deliverie *1633*   9 'art]
'art *1633*   10 dost *MSS.*: doth *1633*   dwell,] dwell. *1633*   11 'or] or
1633   12 better] easyer *Dob, O'F, W*   13 wake] liue *Dob, O'F (b.c.), W*
14 Death *MSS.*: death *1633*
7. *Dob omits.*   1 yee *TCD, O'F, W*: you *1633, C 57, H 49, Gr*   3 onely] humbly
W   4 Who] W^ch *W*   no] none *C 57, H 49, TCD*   8 glorified.] glorified;
1633   12 intent:] intent *1633*

8

WHY are wee by all creatures waited on?
   Why doe the prodigall elements supply
Life and food to mee, being more pure then I,
Simple, and further from corruption?
Why brook'st thou, ignorant horse, subjection?   5
Why dost thou bull, and bore so seelily
Dissemble weaknesse, and by'one mans stroke die,
Whose whole kinde, you might swallow'and feed upon?
Weaker I am, woe's mee, and worse then you,
You have not sinn'd, nor need be timorous.   10
But wonder at a greater wonder, for to us
Created nature doth these things subdue,
But their Creator, whom sin, nor nature tyed,
For us, his Creatures, and his foes, hath dyed.   (XII)

9

WHAT if this present were the worlds last night?
   Marke in my heart, O Soule, where thou dost dwell,
The picture of Christ crucified, and tell
Whether that countenance can thee affright,
Teares in his eyes quench the amasing light,   5
Blood fills his frownes, which from his pierc'd head fell,
And can that tongue adjudge thee unto hell,
Which pray'd forgivenesse for his foes fierce spight?
No, no; but as in my idolatrie
I said to all my profane mistresses,   10
Beauty, of pitty, foulnesse onely is
A signe of rigour: so I say to thee,
To wicked spirits are horrid shapes assign'd,
This beauteous forme assures a pitious minde.   (XIII)

8. *Dob omits*   1 are wee] ame I *W*   3 I,] I? *1633 uncorrected*
4 Simple] Simpler *TCD*   7 by'one . . . die,] by one . . . die? *1633 uncorrected*
8 'and] and *1633*   upon?] upon. *1633 uncorrected*   9 Alas I'ame weaker *W*
woe's] woe is *1633*   10 timorous.] timorous, *1633*   13 Creator . . .
sin,] creator . . . sinne *1633 uncorrected*
9. *Dob omits*   2 Marke] Looke *W*   4 that *TCD, O'F, W:* his *C 57, H 49*
5 eyes] eyes, *1633 uncorrected*   6 fell,] fell *1633*   8 fierce] ranck *W*
9 my] myne *W*   14 assures *MSS.:* assumes *1633*

10

BATTER my heart, three person'd God; for, you
  As yet but knocke, breathe, shine, and seeke to mend;
That I may rise, and stand, o'erthrow mee,'and bend
Your force, to breake, blowe, burn and make me new.
I, like an usurpt towne, to'another due,   5
Labour to'admit you, but Oh, to no end,
Reason your viceroy in mee, mee should defend,
But is captiv'd, and proves weake or untrue,
Yet dearely'I love you, and would be lov'd faine,
But am betroth'd unto your enemie,   10
Divorce mee,'untie, or breake that knot againe,
Take mee to you, imprison mee, for I
Except you'enthrall mee, never shall be free,
Nor ever chast, except you ravish mee. (XIV)

11

WILT thou love God, as he thee! then digest,
  My Soule, this wholsome meditation,
How God the Spirit, by Angels waited on
In heaven, doth make his Temple in thy brest,
The Father having begot a Sonne most blest,   5
And still begetting, (for he ne'r begonne)
Hath deign'd to chuse thee by adoption,
Coheire to'his glory,'and Sabbaths endlesse rest;
And as a robb'd man, which by search doth finde
His stolne stuffe sold, must lose or buy'it againe: 10
The Sonne of glory came downe, and was slaine,
Us whom he'had made, and Satan stolne, to unbinde.
'Twas much, that man was made like God before,
But, that God should be made like man, much more. (XV)

10. *Dob omits.*   9 and] 'and *1633, Gr.*   lov'd] loved *MSS., Gr: see note*
11. 10 stuffe] steede *Dob, O'F (b.c.): see note*   12 stolne] stole *O'F, W*

12

FATHER, part of his double interest
    Unto thy kingdome, thy Sonne gives to mee,
His joynture in the knottie Trinitie,
Hee keepes, and gives mee his deaths conquest.
This Lambe, whose death, with life the world hath blest,   5
Was from the worlds beginning slaine, and he
Hath made two Wills, which with the Legacie
Of his'and thy kingdome, doe thy Sonnes invest,
Yet such are those laws, that men argue yet
Whether a man those statutes can fulfill;   10
None doth, but all-healing grace and Spirit,
Revive againe what law and letter kill.
Thy lawes abridgement, and thy last command
Is all but love; Oh let that last Will stand! (XVI)

Holy Sonnets
(added in 1635)

Divine Meditations

I

THOU hast made me, And shall thy worke decay?
    Repaire me now, for now mine end doth haste,
I runne to death, and death meets me as fast,
And all my pleasures are like yesterday,
I dare not move my dimme eyes any way,   5
Despaire behind, and death before doth cast
Such terrour, and my feebled flesh doth waste
By sinne in it, which it t'wards hell doth weigh;

12. 4 mee *C 57, H 49, TCD, Dob, W*: to me *1633, O'F, Gr*   7–8 Wills, which
. . . doe] wills, w^ch . . . doth *C 57, H 49, TCD, W*: Wills; he . . . doth *Dob, O'F*
(*b.c.*)   8 'and] and *1633*   9 those *H 49, TCD*: thy *Dob, O'F, W, Gr*:
these *1633, C 57*   11 all-healing *C 57, H 49, TCD, W*: thy all-healing *1633, Dob,*
O'F   12 Revive againe] Reviue and quicken *Dob, O'F, W*   kill.] kill, *1633*
14 that *C 57, H 49, TCD, W*: thy *Dob, O'F*: this *1633, Gr*
Holy Sonnets (added in 1635) *1635   MSS.: Dob and O'F; W*
1. 1 decay ?] decay. *1635*   7 feebled *MSS.*: feeble *1635, Gr*

Onely thou art above, and when towards thee
By thy leave I can looke, I rise againe;   10
But our old subtle foe so tempteth me,
That not one houre I can my selfe sustaine;
Thy Grace may wing me to prevent his art
And thou like Adamant draw mine iron heart. (I)

2

I AM a little world made cunningly
  Of Elements, and an Angelike spright,
But black sinne hath betraid to endlesse night
My worlds both parts, and (oh) both parts must die.
You which beyond that heaven which was most high   5
Have found new sphears, and of new lands can write,
Powre new seas in mine eyes, that so I might
Drowne my world with my weeping earnestly,
Or wash it, if it must be drown'd no more:
But oh it must be burnt; alas the fire   10
Of lust and envie'have burnt it heretofore,
And made it fouler; Let their flames retire,
And burne me ô Lord, with a fiery zeale
Of thee'and thy house, which doth in eating heale. (V)

3

O MIGHT those sighes and teares returne againe
  Into my breast and eyes, which I have spent,
That I might in this holy discontent
Mourne with some fruit, as I have mourn'd in vaine;
In my Idolatry what showres of raine   5
Mine eyes did waste? what griefs my heart did rent?
That sufferance was my sinne, now I repent;
Because I did suffer'I must suffer paine.

12 I can my selfe *Dob, W*: my selfe I can *1635, O'F, Gr*   sustaine;] sustaine, *1635*
2. 6 lands *Dob, W*: land *1635, O'F*   9 it,] it *1635*   10 burnt;] burnt,
1635   11 'have burnt *Dob, W (elision mark supplied)*: hath burnt *O'F*: burnt
1635   12 fouler;] fouler *1635*   their] those *W*   13 Lord] God *W* ·
14 'and] and *1635*
3. 5 my *Dob, W*: mine *1635, O'F, Gr*   7 sinne, now I repent; *W*: sinne,
nowe I repent *Dob*: sinne I now repent, *1635, O'F*   8 Because *Dob, W*: 'Cause
1635, O'F, Gr: see note   suffer'I] suffer I *1635*

Th'hydroptique drunkard, and night-scouting thiefe,
The itchy Lecher, and selfe tickling proud   10
Have the remembrance of past joyes, for reliefe
Of comming ills. To (poore) me is allow'd
No ease; for, long, yet vehement griefe hath beene
Th'effect and cause, the punishment and sinne. (III)

                              4

I F faithfull soules be alike glorifi'd
  As Angels, then my fathers soule doth see,
And adds this even to full felicitie,
That valiantly I hels wide mouth o'rstride:
But if our mindes to these soules be descry'd   5
By circumstances, and by signes that be
Apparent in us, not immediately,
How shall my mindes white truth to them be try'd?
They see idolatrous lovers weepe and mourne,
And vile blasphemous Conjurers to call   10
On Jesus name, and Pharisaicall
Dissemblers feigne devotion. Then turne
O pensive soule, to God, for he knowes best
Thy true griefe, for he put it in my breast. (VIII)

Holy Sonnets
(from the Westmoreland MS.)

                              I

S INCE she whome I lovd, hath payd her last debt
  To Nature, and to hers, and my good is dead,
And her soule early'into heaven ravished,
Wholy in heavenly things my mind is sett.

4. 2 fathers] father W   7 us,] us 1635   8 to Dob, W: by 1635, O'F, Gr
10 vile Dob, W: vild O'F: stile 1635   14 Thy true griefe . . . in W: Thy
griefe . . . into 1635, Dob, O'F
Holy Sonnets (from the Westmoreland MS.) W   1. First printed Gosse,
Jacobean Poets (1894); 2. and 3. First printed Gosse, Life and Letters of John Donne
(1899).
1. 2 dead,] dead MS.   3 early'] early MS   4 in] on Gr

Here the admyring her my mind did whett   5
To seeke thee God; so streames do shew the head,
But though I'have found thee,'and thou my thirst hast fed,
A holy thirsty dropsy melts mee yett.
But why should I begg more love, when as thou
Dost wooe my soule, for hers offring all thine: 10
And dost not only feare least I allow
My love to saints and Angels, things divine,
But in thy tender jealosy dost doubt
Least the World, fleshe, yea Devill putt thee out. (XVII)

2

SHOW me deare Christ, thy spouse, so bright and cleare.
What, is it she, which on the other shore
Goes richly painted? or which rob'd and tore
Laments and mournes in Germany and here?
Sleepes she a thousand, then peepes up one yeare?   5
Is she selfe truth and errs? now new, now'outwore?
Doth she,'and did she, and shall she evermore
On one, on seaven, or on no hill appeare?
Dwells she with us, or like adventuring knights
First travaile we to seeke and then make love?   10
Betray kind husband thy spouse to our sights,
And let myne amorous soule court thy mild Dove,
Who is most trew, and pleasing to thee, then
When she'is embrac'd and open to most men. (XVIII)

3

OH, to vex me, contraryes meete in one:
Inconstancy unnaturally hath begott
A constant habit; that when I would not
I change in vowes, and in devotione.

6 the] their *Gr:*   7 'have . . .'and] have . . . and *MS.*   10 wooe] woe
MS.   soule, for hers] soule for hers; *MS., Gr: see note*   12 Angels, . . . divine,]
Angels . . . divine *MS.*
2. 2 What,] What *MS.*   6 now'] now *MS.*

As humorous is my contritione   5
As my prophane love, and as soone forgott:
As ridlingly distemperd, cold and hott,
As praying, as mute; as infinite, as none.
I durst not view heaven yesterday; and to day
In prayers, and flattering speaches I court God: 10
To morrow'I quake with true feare of his rod.
So my devout fitts come and go away
Like a fantastique Ague: save that here
Those are my best dayes, when I shake with feare. (XIX)

A Litanie

I

The Father

FATHER of Heaven, and him, by whom
    It, and us for it, and all else, for us
    Thou mad'st, and govern'st ever, come
And re-create mee, now growne ruinous:
        My heart is by dejection, clay,   5
        And by selfe-murder, red.
From this red earth, O Father, purge away
All vicious tinctures, that new fashioned
I may rise up from death, before I'am dead.

II

The Sonne

    O Sonne of God, who seeing two things,   10
Sinne, and death crept in, which were never made,
    By bearing one, tryed'st with what stings
    The other could thine heritage invade;

11 morrow'] morrow MS.
A Litanie 1633.   MSS.: C 57 and H 49; TCD; Dob and O'F   Title from
TCD, Dob, O'F: The Litanie 1633, C 57, H 49: see note   3 mad'st] madest
1633   9 before] ere Dob, O'F   13 could] did Dob: would O'F   thine]
thy Dob, O'F

O be thou nail'd unto my heart,
   And crucified againe,   15
Part not from it, though it from thee would part,
But let it be by'applying so thy paine,
Drown'd in thy blood, and in thy passion slaine.

III

The Holy Ghost

O Holy Ghost, whose temple I
Am, but of mudde walls, and condensed dust,   20
   And being sacrilegiously
Halfe wasted with youths fires, of pride and lust,
     Must with new stormes be weatherbeat;
     Double'in my heart thy flame,
Which let devout sad teares intend; and let   25
(Though this glasse lanthorne, flesh, do suffer maime)
Fire, Sacrifice, Priest, Altar be the same.

IV

The Trinity

O Blessed glorious Trinity,
Bones to Philosophy, but milke to faith,
   Which, as wise serpents, diversly   30
Most slipperinesse, yet most entanglings hath,
     As you distinguish'd undistinct
     By power, love, knowledge bee,
Give mee a such selfe different instinct,
Of these let all mee elemented bee,   35
Of power, to love, to know, you'unnumbred three.

17 by'] by *1633*   24 Double'] Double *1633*   26 glasse] darke *Dob*
30 serpents,] serpents *1633*   34 a such selfe] such a selfe *C 57, H 49, TCD*
instinct,] instinct *1633, Gr*   35 Of these] Of thee *TCD:* Of all these *Dob,*
O'F (b.c.): Of these; *Gr: see note*   36 you'] you *1633*

V

The Virgin Mary

For that faire blessed Mother-maid,
Whose flesh redeem'd us; That she-Cherubin,
  Which unlock'd Paradise, and made
One claime for innocence, and disseiz'd sinne,   40
    Whose wombe was a strange heav'n, for there
    God cloath'd himselfe, and grew,
Our zealous thankes wee poure. As her deeds were
Our helpes, so are her prayers; nor can she sue
In vaine, who hath such titles unto you.   45

VI

The Angels

And since this life our nonage is,
And wee in Wardship to thine Angels be,
  Native in heavens faire Palaces
Where we shall be but denizen'd by thee,
    As th'earth conceiving by the Sunne,   50
    Yeelds faire diversitie,
Yet never knowes which course that light doth run,
So let mee study, that mine actions bee
Worthy their sight, though blinde in how they see.

VII

The Patriarches

And let thy Patriarches Desire   55
(Those great Grandfathers, of thy Church, which saw
  More in the cloud, then wee in fire,
Whom Nature clear'd more, then us grace and law,
    And now in Heaven still pray, that wee
    May use our new helpes right,)   60
Be satisfied, and fructifie in mee;

V. The Virgin Mary] Our Lady *Dob*   47 thine] thy *Dob, O'F*   53 mee
... mine] vs ... our *Dob, O'F (b.c.)*   54 how] what *Dob, O'F (b.c.)*   58 and]
or *Dob, O'F*   61 satisfied *H 49, TCD, Dob, O'F*: sanctified *1633, C 57*

Let not my minde be blinder by more light
Nor Faith by Reason added, lose her sight.

VIII
The Prophets

   Thy Eagle-sighted Prophets too,
Which were thy Churches Organs, and did sound   65
   That harmony, which made of two
One law, and did unite, but not confound;
      Those heavenly Poëts which did see
      Thy will, and it expresse
In rythmique feet, in common pray for mee,   70
That I by them excuse not my excesse
In seeking secrets, or Poëtiquenesse.

IX
The Apostles

   And thy illustrious Zodiacke
Of twelve Apostles, which ingirt this All,
   (From whom whosoever do not take   75
Their light, to darke deep pits, throw downe, and fall,)
      As through their prayers, thou'hast let mee know
      That their bookes are divine;
May they pray still, and be heard, that I goe
Th'old broad way in applying; O decline   80
Mee, when my comment would make thy word mine.

X
The Martyrs

   And since thou so desirously
Did'st long to die, that long before thou could'st,
   And long since thou no more couldst dye,
Thou in thy scatter'd mystique body wouldst   85

---

72 In] Of *Dob, O'F*   or] in *Dob*   73 thy] the *Dob*   75–76 *Brackets
supplied*   75 whosoever] whoever *C 57, H 49, Dob, O'F*   78 bookes] workes
Dob, O'F

In Abel dye, and ever since
In thine, let their blood come
To begge for us, a discreet patience
Of death, or of worse life: for Oh, to some
Not to be Martyrs, is a martyrdome.   90

XI

The Confessors

Therefore with thee triumpheth there
A Virgin Squadron of white Confessors,
    Whose bloods betroth'd, not marryed were,
Tender'd, not taken by those Ravishers:
        They know, and pray, that wee may know,   95
        In every Christian
Hourly tempestuous persecutions grow,
Tentations martyr us alive; A man
Is to himselfe a Dioclesian.

XII

The Virgins

Thy cold white snowie Nunnery,   100
Which, as thy mother, their high Abbesse, sent
    Their bodies backe againe to thee,
As thou hadst lent them, cleane and innocent,
        Though they have not obtain'd of thee,
        That or thy Church, or I,   105
Should keep, as they, our first integrity;
Divorce thou sinne in us, or bid it die,
And call chast widowhead Virginitie.

XIII

The Doctors

Thy sacred Academe above
Of Doctors, whose paines have unclasp'd, and taught   110
    Both bookes of life to us (for love
To know thy Scriptures tells us, we are wrought

93 were,] were; *1633*   95 know,] know *1633 uncorrected*   100 Thy *H 49,*
TCD, Dob, O'F: The *1633, C 57, Gr*   105 That] That, *1633 uncorrected*
107 Divorce] Devorce *1633 uncorrected*   109 Academe *TCD, Dob, O'F*:
Academie *1633, C 57, H 49, Gr*

In thy'other booke) pray for us there
   That what they have misdone
Or mis-said, wee to that may not adhere;   115
Their zeale may be our sinne. Lord let us runne
Meane waies, and call them stars, but not the Sunne.

XIV

And whil'st this universall Quire,
That Church in triumph, this in warfare here,
   Warm'd with one all-partaking fire   120
Of love, that none be lost, which cost thee deare,
      Pray ceaslesly,'and thou hearken too,
      (Since to be gratious
Our taske is treble, to pray, beare, and doe)
Heare this prayer Lord, O Lord deliver us   125
From trusting in those prayers, though powr'd out thus.

XV

From being anxious, or secure,
Dead clods of sadnesse, or light squibs of mirth,
   From thinking, that great courts immure
All, or no happinesse, or that this earth   130
      Is only for our prison fram'd,
      Or that thou'art covetous
To them whom thou lov'st, or that they are maim'd
From reaching this worlds sweet, who seek thee thus,
With all their might, Good Lord deliver us.   135

XVI

From needing danger, to bee good,
From owing thee yesterdaies teares to day,
   From trusting so much to thy blood,
That in that hope, wee wound our soule away,

---

113 thy'] thy *1633*   115 adhere;] adhere, *1633*   122 Pray ceaslesly *C 57*,
H 49, *TCD*: Prayes ceaslesly *1633*, *Gr*: Ceaslesly prayes *Dob, O'F*   too,] too *1633*
132 'art] art *1633*   133 lov'st] lovest *1633*

From bribing thee with Almes, to'excuse 140
Some sinne more burdenous,
From light affecting, in religion, newes,
From thinking us all soule, neglecting thus
Our mutuall duties, Lord deliver us.

XVII

From tempting Satan to tempt us, 145
By our connivence, or slack companie,
From measuring ill by vitious,
Neglecting to choake sins spawne, Vanitie,
From indiscreet humilitie,
Which might be scandalous, 150
And cast reproach on Christianitie,
From being spies, or to spies pervious,
From thirst, or scorne of fame, deliver us.

XVIII

Deliver us for thy descent
Into the Virgin, whose wombe was a place 155
Of middle kind; and thou being sent
To'ungratious us, staid'st at her full of grace,
And through thy poore birth, where first thou
Glorifiedst Povertie,
And yet soone after riches didst allow, 160
By'accepting Kings gifts in th'Epiphanie,
Deliver, and make us, to both waies free.

XIX

And through that bitter agonie,
Which is still th'agonie of pious wits,
Disputing what distorted thee, 165
And interrupted evennesse, with fits,

---

140 to'] to *1633*   153 fame *MSS*.: flame *1633*   deliver us] good Lord
deliver vs *Dob, O'F*   154 for] through *Dob, O'F*   156 middle] midle
1633   159 Glorified'st] Glorifiest *1633 uncorrected*   161 By'...th'] By...
the *1633*   163 through *MSS*.: though *1633*   that] thy *Dob, O'F*
164 is still] still is *1633 uncorrected*   th'] the *1633*

And through thy free confession
Though thereby they were then
Made blind, so that thou might'st from them have gone,
Good Lord deliver us, and teach us when   170
Wee may not, and we may blinde unjust men.

XX

Through thy submitting all, to blowes
Thy face, thy clothes to spoile, thy fame to scorne,
   All waies, which rage, or Justice knowes,
And by which thou could'st shew, that thou wast born,   175
     And through thy gallant humblenesse
     Which thou in death did'st shew,
Dying before thy soule they could expresse,
Deliver us from death, by dying so,
To this world, ere this world doe bid us goe.   180

XXI

When senses, which thy souldiers are,
Wee arme against thee, and they fight for sinne,
   When want, sent but to tame, doth warre
And worke despaire a breach to enter in,
     When plenty, Gods image, and seale   185
     Makes us Idolatrous,
And love it, not him, whom it should reveale,
When wee are mov'd to seeme religious
Only to vent wit, Lord deliver us.

XXII

In Churches, when the'infirmitie   190
Of him that speakes, diminishes the Word,
   When Magistrates doe mis-apply
To us, as we judge, lay or ghostly sword,

168 thereby they were] they were thereby *Dob, O'F*   173 clothes] robes *Dob,*
O'F   spoile,] spoile; *1633*   175 And] Or *Dob, O'F*   178 soule . . .
expresse,] soule, . . . expresse *1633 uncorrected*   190 when] where *C 57, H 49,*
TCD   191 that *MSS.:* which *1633, Gr*

When plague, which is thine Angell, raignes,
 Or wars, thy Champions, swaie,   *195*
When Heresie, thy second deluge, gaines;
In th'houre of death, the'Eve of last judgement day,
Deliver us from the sinister way.

XXIII

Heare us, O heare us Lord; to thee
A sinner is more musique, when he prayes,   *200*
 Then spheares, or Angels praises bee,
In Panegyrique Allelujaes,
  Heare us, for till thou heare us, Lord
  We know not what to say.
Thine eare to'our sighes, teares, thoughts gives voice and word. *205*
O Thou who Satan heard'st in Jobs sicke day,
Heare thy selfe now, for thou in us dost pray.

XXIV

That wee may change to evennesse
This intermitting aguish Pietie,
 That snatching cramps of wickednesse   *210*
And Apoplexies of fast sin, may die;
  That musique of thy promises,
  Not threats in Thunder may
Awaken us to our just offices;
What in thy booke, thou dost, or creatures say,   *215*
That we may heare, Lord heare us, when wee pray.

XXV

That our eares sicknesse wee may cure,
And rectifie those Labyrinths aright,
 That wee by harkning, not procure
Our praise, nor others dispraise so invite,   *220*
  That wee get not a slipperinesse,
  And senslesly decline,

195 Or] When *Dob, O'F* 206 who] which *TCD, Dob, O'F* 214 offices;]
offices, *1633*

From hearing bold wits jeast at Kings excesse,
To'admit the like of majestie divine,
That we may locke our eares, Lord open thine.   225

XXVI

That living law, the Magistrate,
Which to give us, and make us physicke, doth
  Our vices often aggravate,
That Preachers taxing sinne, before her growth,
    That Satan, and invenom'd men   230
    Which well, if we starve, dine,
When they doe most accuse us, may see then
Us, to amendment, heare them; thee decline;
That we may open our eares, Lord lock thine.

XXVII

That learning, thine Ambassador,   235
From thine allegeance wee never tempt,
  That beauty, paradises flower
For physicke made, from poyson be exempt,
    That wit, borne apt, high good to doe,
    By dwelling lazily   240
On Natures nothing, be not nothing too,
That our affections kill us not, nor dye,
Heare us, weake ecchoes, O thou eare, and cry.

XXVIII

Sonne of God heare us, and since thou
By taking our blood, ow'st it us againe,   245
  Gaine to thy selfe, or us allow;
And let not both us and thy selfe be slaine;
    O lambe of God, which took'st our sinne
    Which could not stick to thee,

224 divine] divide *1633 uncorrected*   231 Which well] W^ch will *C 57*: That
will *Dob, O'F*: . . . will *1633 uncorrected*   233 heare them] hearken *Dob, O'F*
234 lock] stop *Dob, O'F*   236 thine] his *Dob*   239 doe,] doe *1633*
245 ow'st . . . againe,] owest . . . againe *1633*   246 or] and *Dob, O'F*

O let it not returne to us againe,   250
But Patient and Physition being free,
As sinne is nothing, let it no where be.

OCCASIONAL POEMS

The Crosse

SINCE Christ embrac'd the Crosse it selfe, dare I
    His image, th'image of his Crosse deny?
Would I have profit by the sacrifice,
And dare the chosen Altar to despise?
It bore all other sinnes, but is it fit   5
That it should beare the sinne of scorning it?
Who from the picture would avert his eye,
How would he flye his paines, who there did dye?
From mee, no Pulpit, nor misgrounded law,
Nor scandall taken, shall this Crosse withdraw,   10
It shall not, for it cannot; for, the losse
Of this Crosse, were to mee another Crosse;
Better were worse, for, no affliction,
No Crosse is so extreme, as to have none.
Who can blot out the Crosse, which th'instrument   15
Of God, dew'd on mee in the Sacrament?
Who can deny mee power, and liberty
To stretch mine armes, and mine owne Crosse to be?
Swimme, and at every stroake, thou art thy Crosse,
The Mast and yard make one, where seas do tosse.   20
Looke downe, thou spiest out Crosses in small things;
Looke up, thou seest birds rais'd on crossed wings;
All the Globes frame, and spheares, is nothing else
But the Meridians crossing Parallels.
Materiall Crosses then, good physicke bee,   25
And yet spirituall have chiefe dignity.

The Crosse *1633*   MSS.: *C 57 and H 49; TCD; Dob and O'F*   12 Crosse;]
Crosse. *1633*   13 affliction,] affliction *1633*   ·14 none.] none; *1633*   20
where] when *Dob, O'F*   26 And *C 57, H 49, TCD:* But *1633, Dob O'F, Gr*

These for extracted chimique medicine serve,
And cure much better, and as well preserve;
Then are you your own physicke, or need none,
When Still'd, or purg'd by tribulation.   30
For when that Crosse ungrudg'd, unto you stickes,
Then are you to your selfe, a Crucifixe.
As perchance, Carvers do not faces make,
But that away, which hid them there, do take:
Let Crosses, soe, take what hid Christ in thee,   35
And be his image, or not his, but hee.
But, as oft Alchimists doe coyners prove,
So may a selfe-dispising, get selfe-love.
And then as worst surfets, of best meates bee,
Soe is pride, issued from humility,   40
For, 'tis no child, but monster; therefore Crosse
Your joy in crosses, else, 'tis double losse.
And crosse thy senses, else, both they, and thou
Must perish soone, and to destruction bowe.
For if the'eye seeke good objects, and will take   45
No crosse from bad, wee cannot scape a snake.
So with harsh, hard, sowre, stinking, crosse the rest,
Make them indifferent; call nothing best.
But most the eye needs crossing, that can rome,
And move; To th'others th'objects must come home.   50
And crosse thy heart: for that in man alone
Points downewards, and hath palpitation.
Crosse those dejections, when it downeward tends,
And when it to forbidden heights pretends.
And as thy braine through bony walls doth vent   55
By sutures, which a Crosses forme present,
So when thy braine workes, ere thou utter it,
Crosse and correct concupiscence of witt.
Be covetous of Crosses, let none fall.

---

33 make,] make: *1633*   34 take:] take. *1633*   37 oft] oft, *1633*   42
losse.] losse, *1633*   44 destruction] corruption *Dob, O'F*   48 indifferent;]
indifferent all; *Gr*   50 others *MSS.*: other *1633, Gr*   52 Points *TCD,
Dob, O'F (b.c.)*: Pants *1633, C 57, H 49*   53 dejections] defections *Dob*:
detorsions *O'F*   55 thy *H 49, TCD, Dob, O'F*: the *1633, C 57, Gr*

Crosse no man else, but crosse thy selfe in all.   60
Then doth the Crosse of Christ worke fruitfully
Within our hearts, when wee love harmlesly
That Crosses pictures much, and with more care
That Crosses children, which our Crosses are.

Resurrection, imperfect

SLEEP sleep old Sun, thou canst not have repast
   As yet, the wound thou took'st on friday last;
Sleepe then, and rest; The world may beare thy stay,
A better Sun rose before thee to day,
Who, not content to'enlighten all that dwell   5
On the earths face, as thou, enlightned hell,
And made the darke fires languish in that vale,
As, at thy presence here, our fires grow pale.
Whose body having walk'd on earth, and now
Hasting to Heaven, would, that he might allow   10
Himselfe unto all stations, and fill all,
For these three daies become a minerall;
Hee was all gold when he lay downe, but rose
All tincture, and doth not alone dispose
Leaden and iron wills to good, but is   15
Of power to make even sinfull flesh like his.
Had one of those, whose credulous pietie
Thought, that a Soule one might discerne and see
Goe from a body,'at this sepulcher been,
And, issuing from the sheet, this body seen,   20
He would have justly thought this body'a soule,
If not of any man, yet of the whole.

Desunt cætera.

---

61 fruitfully *MSS.*: faithfully *1633*   63 That *MSS.*: The *1633*
Resurrection, imperfect *1633*   *MSS.: TCD; O'F*   21 'a] a *1633*   22 If]
If, *1633*

Upon the Annunciation and Passion falling upon one day. 1608

Tamely fraile body'abstaine to day; to day
My soule eates twice, Christ hither and away.
Shee sees him man, so like God made in this,
That of them both a circle embleme is,
Whose first and last concurre; this doubtfull day   5
Of feast or fast, Christ came, and went away;
Shee sees him nothing twice at once, who'is all;
Shee sees a Cedar plant it selfe, and fall,
Her Maker put to making, and the head
Of life, at once, not yet alive, and dead;   10
She sees at once the virgin mother stay
Reclus'd at home, Publique at Golgotha.
Sad and rejoyc'd shee's seen at once, and seen
At almost fiftie, and at scarce fifteene.
At once a Sonne is promis'd her, and gone,   15
Gabriell gives Christ to her, He her to John;
Not fully'a mother, Shee's in Orbitie,
At once receiver and the legacie;
All this, and all betweene, this day hath showne,
Th'Abridgement of Christs story, which makes one   20
(As in plaine Maps, the furthest West is East)
Of the'Angels *Ave*,'and *Consummatum est*.
How well the Church, Gods Court of faculties
Deales, in some times, and seldome joyning these;
As by the selfe-fix'd Pole wee never doe   25
Direct our course, but the next starre thereto,
Which showes where the'other is, and which we say
(Because it strayes not farre) doth never stray;
So God by'his Church, neerest to him, wee know,

Upon the Annunciation &c. *1633*   MSS.: *C 57 and H 49; TCD; Dob and O'F*
Title from Dob: The Annuntiation and Passion *1633*   1 body] flesh *Dob, O'F*
10 and *MSS.*: yet *1633, Gr*   13 Sad and rejoyc'd] Reioyc'd and sad *Dob,*
O'F   15 At once a Sonne] A Sonne at once *Dob, O'F*   17 'a] a *1633*
19 hath] is *Dob, O'F*   21 West is East] East is West *Dob, O'F*   29 by']
by *1633*

And stand firme, if wee by her motion goe;   30
His Spirit, as his fiery Pillar doth
Leade, and his Church, as cloud; to one end both:
This Church, by letting these daies joyne, hath shown
Death and conception in mankinde is one:
Or 'twas in him the same humility,   35
That he would be a man, and leave to be:
Or as creation he had made, as God,
With the last judgement, but one period,
His imitating Spouse would joyne in one
Manhoods extremes: He shall come, he is gone: 40
Or as though one blood drop, which thence did fall,
Accepted, would have serv'd, he yet shed all;
So though the least of his paines, deeds, or words,
Would busie'a life, she all this day affords;
This treasure then, in grosse, my Soule uplay,   45
And in my life retaile it every day.

Goodfriday, 1613. Riding Westward

LET mans Soule be a Spheare, and then, in this,
    Th'intelligence that moves, devotion is,
And as the other Spheares, by being growne
Subject to forraigne motions, lose their owne,
And being by others hurried every day,   5
Scarce in a yeare their naturall forme obey:
Pleasure or businesse, so, our Soules admit
For their first mover, and are whirld by it.
Hence is't, that I am carryed towards the West
This day, when my Soules forme bends toward the East.   10

33 these MSS.: those 1633   daies] feasts Dob, O'F   34 is] ar O'F   one:] one.
1633   35 Or 'twas in him the same] And/Or that in him 'twas one Dob, O'F
37 had TCD, Dob, O'F: hath 1633, C 57, H 49, Gr   38 the] his Dob, O'F
44 busie] buy Dob, O'F (b.c.)   'a] a 1633   46 my] thy Dob, O'F (b.c.)
Goodfriday &c. 1633   MSS.: C 57 and H49; TCD; Dob and O'F   2 Th']
The 1633   4 motions MSS.: motion 1633

There I should see a Sunne, by rising set,
And by that setting endlesse day beget;
But that Christ on this Crosse, did rise and fall,
Sinne had eternally benighted all.
Yet dare I'almost be glad, I do not see   15
That spectacle of too much weight for mee.
Who sees Gods face, that is selfe life, must dye;
What a death were it then to see God dye?
It made his owne Lieutenant Nature shrinke,
It made his footstoole crack, and the Sunne winke.   20
Could I behold those hands which span the Poles,
And tune all spheares at once, peirc'd with those holes?
Could I behold that endlesse height which is
Zenith to us, and to'our Antipodes,
Humbled below us? or that blood which is   25
The seat of all our Soules, if not of his,
Make durt of dust, or that flesh which was worne
By God, for his apparell, rag'd, and torne?
If on these things I durst not looke, durst I
Upon his miserable mother cast mine eye,   30
Who was Gods partner here, and furnish'd thus
Halfe of that Sacrifice, which ransom'd us?
Though these things, as I ride, be from mine eye,
They'are present yet unto my memory,
For that looks towards them; and thou look'st towards mee, 35
O Saviour, as thou hang'st upon the tree;
I turne my backe to thee, but to receive
Corrections, till thy mercies bid thee leave.
O thinke mee worth thine anger, punish mee,
Burne off my rusts, and my deformity,   40
Restore thine Image, so much, by thy grace,
That thou may'st know mee, and I'll turne my face.

22-25 Omit C 57   22 tune] turne TCD, Dob, Gr   once,] once 1633
24 and to' H 49, TCD Dob: and 1633, O'F, Gr   27 Make C 57, H 49, TCD,
O'F (b.c.): Made 1633, Dob, Gr

To Mr. Tilman after he had taken orders

THOU, whose diviner soule hath caus'd thee now
  To put thy hand unto the holy Plough,
Making Lay-scornings of the Ministry,
Not an impediment, but victory;
What bringst thou home with thee? how is thy mind   5
Affected in the vintage? Dost thou finde
New thoughts and stirrings in thee? and as Steele
Toucht with a Loadstone, dost new motions feele?
Or, as a Ship after much paine and care,
For Iron and Cloth brings home rich Indian ware,   10
Hast thou thus traffiqu'd, but with farre more gaine
Of noble goods, and with lesse time and paine?
Art thou the same materials, as before,
Onely the stampe is changed; but no more?
And as new crowned Kings alter the face,   15
But not the monies substance; so hath grace
Chang'd onely Gods old Image by Creation,
To Christs new stampe, at this thy Coronation?
Or, as we paint Angels with wings, because
They beare Gods message, and proclaime his lawes,   20
Since thou must doe the like, and so must move,
Art thou new feather'd with cœlestiall love?
Deare, tell me where thy purchase lies, and shew
What thy advantage is above, below.
But if thy gayning doe surmount expression,   25
Why doth the foolish world scorne that profession,
Whose joyes passe speech? Why do they think unfit
That Gentry should joyne families with it;
As if their day were onely to be spent
In dressing, Mistressing and complement?   30

To Mr. Tilman &c. *1635*   MSS.: *Dob, O'F, Wel*   6 in *Dob, O'F*: since *1635,*
Wel, Gr   13–14 Art thou . . . more? *MSS.*: Thou art . . . more. *1635, Gr*
18 Christs] Chists *1635*   Coronation? *MSS.*: Coronation; *1635, Gr*   25
gayning *Dob, O'F*: gainings *1635, Wel, Gr*   28 it;] it? *1635, MSS., Gr*
29 Would they thinke it well if the day . . . *Dob, O'F*: Would they thinke you that
the whole day . . . *Wel*   30 complement? *MSS.*: complement; *1635, Gr*

Alas poore joyes, but poorer men, whose trust
Seemes richly placed in refined dust;
(For, such are cloathes and beauties, which though gay,
Are, at the best, but as sublimed clay.)
Let then the world thy calling disrespect,   35
But goe thou on, and pitty their neglect.
What function is so noble, as to bee
Embassadour to God and destinie?
To open life, to give kingdomes to more
Than Kings give dignities; to keepe heavens doore?   40
Maries prerogative was to beare Christ, so
'Tis preachers to convey him, for they doe
As Angels out of clouds, from Pulpits speake;
And blesse the poore beneath, the lame, the weake.
If then th'Astronomers, whereas they spie   45
A new-found Starre, their Opticks magnifie,
How brave are those, who with their Engines, can
Bring man to heaven, and heaven againe to man?
These are thy titles and preheminences,
In whom must meet Gods graces, mens offences,   50
And so the heavens which beget all things here,
And th'earth our mother, which these things doth beare,
Both these in thee, are in thy Calling knit,
And make thee now a blest Hermaphrodite.

Upon the translation of the Psalmes
by Sir Philip Sydney,
and the Countesse of Pembroke his Sister

ETERNALL God, (for whom who ever dare
Seeke new expressions, doe the Circle square,
And thrust into strait corners of poore wit
Thee, who art cornerlesse and infinite)

32 refined *MSS.*: sublimed *1635*, *Gr*   33 beauties *Dob*, *O'F*: beauty *1635*,
Wel, *Gr*   34 as *MSS.*: of *1635*, *Gr*   clay.)] clay) *1635*   47 Engines
MSS.: Engine *1635*, *Gr*   52 th'] the *1633*
Upon the translation of the Psalms &c. *1635*   *MS.*: *O'F*

I would but blesse thy Name, not name thee now;   5
(And thy gifts are as infinite as thou:)
Fixe we our prayses therefore on this one,
That, as thy blessed Spirit fell upon
These Psalmes first Author in a cloven tongue;
(For 'twas a double power by which he sung   10
The highest matter in the noblest forme;)
So thou hast cleft that spirit, to performe
That worke againe, and shed it, here, upon
Two, by their bloods, and by thy Spirit one;
A Brother and a Sister, made by thee   15
The Organ, where thou art the Harmony.
Two that make one *John Baptists* holy voyce,
And who that Psalme, *Now let the Iles rejoyce*,
Have both translated, and apply'd it too,
Both told us what, and taught us how to doe.   20
They shew us Ilanders our joy, our King,
They tell us *why*, and teach us *how* to sing;
Make all this All, three Quires, heaven, earth, and sphears;
The first, Heaven, hath a song, but no man heares,
The Spheares have Musick, but they have no tongue,   25
Their harmony is rather danc'd than sung;
But our third Quire, to which the first gives eare,
(For, Angels learne by what the Church does here)
This Quire hath all. The Organist is hee
Who hath tun'd God and Man, the Organ we: 30
The songs are these, which heavens high holy Muse
Whisper'd to *David*, *David* to the Jewes:
And *Davids* Successors, in holy zeale,
In formes of joy and art doe re-reveale
To us so sweetly and sincerely too,   35
That I must not rejoyce as I would doe
When I behold that these Psalmes are become
So well attyr'd abroad, so ill at home,
So well in Chambers, in thy Church so ill,
As I can scarce call that reform'd untill   40

22 sing;] sing. *1635*   28 here] heare *1635, O'F*

This be reform'd; Would a whole State present
A lesser gift than some one man hath sent?
And shall our Church, unto our Spouse and King
More hoarse, more harsh than any other, sing?
For *that* we pray, we praise thy name for *this*,   45
Which, by this *Moses* and this *Miriam*, is
Already done; and as those Psalmes we call
(Though some have other Authors) *Davids* all:
So though some have, some may some Psalmes translate,
We thy Sydnean Psalmes shall celebrate,   50
And, till we come th'Extemporall song to sing,
(Learn'd the first hower, that we see the King,
Who hath translated these translators) may
These their sweet learned labours, all the way
Be as our tuning, that, when hence we part   55
We may fall in with them, and sing our part.

The Lamentations of Jeremy, for the most part according to Tremelius

CHAP. I

1 How sits this citie, late most populous,
    Thus solitary,'and like a widdow thus!
Amplest of Nations, Queene of Provinces
    She was, who now thus tributary is!

2 Still in the night shee weepes, and her teares fall   5
    Downe by her cheekes along, and none of all
Her lovers comfort her; Perfidiously
    Her friends have dealt, and now are enemie.

---

46 this *O'F*: thy *1635*.   53 these *O'F*: those *1635, Gr*
The Lamentations &c. *1633*   MSS.: *TCD; O'F and B.   Tr is for* Tremellius.
Biblical verse-numbers omitted or misplaced are supplied or corrected.   2–4
thus! . . . is!] thus ? . . . is ? *1633*   2 'and] and *1633*

3 Unto great bondage, and afflictions
   Juda is captive led; Those nations   10
With whom shee dwells, no place of rest afford,
   In streights shee meets her Persecutors sword.

4 Emptie'are the gates of Sion, and her waies
   Mourne, because none come to her solemne dayes.
Her Priests doe groane, her maides are comfortlesse,   15
   And shee's unto her selfe a bitternesse.

5 Her foes are growne her head, and live at Peace,
   Because when her transgressions did increase,
The Lord strooke her with sadnesse: Th'enemie
   Doth drive her children to captivitie.   20

6 From Sions daughter is all beauty gone,
   Like Harts, which seeke for Pasture, and find none,
Her Princes are, and now before the foe
   Which still pursues them, without strength they go.

7 Now in her daies of Teares, Jerusalem   25
   (Her men slaine by the foe, none succouring them)
Remembers what of old, shee'esteemed most,
   Whiles her foes laugh at her, for what she'hath lost.

8 Jerusalem hath sinn'd, therefore is shee
   Remov'd, as women in uncleannesse bee;   30
Who honor'd, scorne her, for her foulnesse they
   Have seene; her selfe doth groane, and turne away.

9 Her foulnesse in her skirts was seene, yet she
   Remembred not her end; Miraculously
Therefore shee fell, none comforting: Behold   35
   O Lord my'affliction, for the Foe growes bold.

10 Upon all things where her delight hath beene,
   The foe hath stretch'd his hand, for shee hath seene
Heathen, whom thou command'st, should not doe so,
   Into her holy Sanctuary goe.   40

13 'are] are *1633*   25 her *O'F*: the *B*: their *1633*, *TCD*: diebus afflictionis
suae *Tr*   26 them]] them *1633 uncorrected*   27 shee'] shee *1633*
28 Whiles] Whilest *O'F, B, Gr*   'hath] hath *1633*   32 seene;] seene, *1633*
36 my'] my *1633*

11 And all her people groane, and seeke for bread;
   And they have given, only to be fed,
All precious things, wherein their pleasure lay:
   How cheape I'am growne, O Lord, behold, and weigh.

12 All this concernes not you, who passe by mee,   45
   O see, and marke if any sorrow bee
Like to my sorrow, which Jehova hath
   Done to mee in the day of his fierce wrath?

13 That fire, which by himselfe is governed
   He'hath cast from heaven on my bones, and hath spred   50
A net before my feet, and mee o'rthrowne,
   And made me languish all the day alone.

14 His hand hath of my sinnes framed a yoake
   Which wreath'd, and cast upon my neck, hath broke
My strength. The Lord unto those enemies   55
   Hath given mee, from whom I cannot rise.

15 He underfoot hath troden in my sight
   My strong men; He did company invite
To breake my young men; he the winepresse hath
   Trod upon Juda's daughter in his wrath.   60

16 For these things doe I weepe, mine eye, mine eye
   Casts water out; For he which should be nigh
To comfort mee, is now departed farre,
   The foe prevailes, forlorne my children are.

17 There's none, though *Sion* do stretch out her hand,   65
   To comfort her, it is the Lords command
That *Jacobs* foes girt him. *Jerusalem*
   Is as an uncleane woman amongst them.

18 But yet the Lord is just, and righteous still,
   I have rebell'd against his holy will;   70
O heare all people, and my sorrow see,
   My maides, my young men in captivitie.

50 'hath] hath *1633*; *also in* ll. 181, 185, 219   hath spred *MSS.*: spred *1633, Gr*
56 whom *MSS.*: whence *1633*: in manus eorum a quibus *Tr*   58 invite] accite
O'F, B: convocat *Tr*   59 men;] men, *1633*   65 hand,] hand *1633*

19 I called for my *lovers* then, but they
 Deceiv'd mee, and my Priests, and Elders lay
Dead in the citie; for they sought for meat   75
 Which should refresh their soules, and none could get.

20 Because I am in streights, *Jehova* see
 My heart o'return'd, my bowells muddy bee,
Because I have rebell'd so much, as fast
 The sword without, as death within, doth wast.   80

21 Of all which heare I mourne, none comforts mee,
 My foes have heard my griefe, and glad they be,
That thou hast done it; But thy promis'd day
 Will come, when, as I suffer, so shall they.

22 Let all their wickednesse appeare to thee,   85
 Doe unto them, as thou hast done to mee,
For all my sinnes: The sighs which I have had
 Are very many, and my heart is sad.

Chap. II

1 How over Sions daughter hath God hung
 His wraths thicke cloud! and from the heaven hath flung
To earth the beauty'of *Israel*, and hath   91
 Forgot his foot-stoole in the day of wrath!

2 The Lord unsparingly hath swallowed
 All Jacobs dwellings, and demolished
To ground the strengths of *Juda*, and prophan'd 95
 The Princes of the Kingdome, and the land.

3 In heat of wrath, the horne of *Israel* hee
 Hath cleane cut off, and lest the enemie
Be hindred, his right hand he doth retire,
 But is towards *Jacob*, All-devouring fire.   100

---

76 and none could get *O'F*: they none could gett *B*: they could not get *1633, TCD,
Gr* 78 o'return'd] *O'F, B*: returned *1633, TCD*: versat se cor meum *Tr*
90 cloud!] cloud? *1633* the *MSS.*: omit *1633, Gr* flung] flung. *1633*
91 'of] of *1633* 92 wrath!] wrath? *1633*

4 Like to an enemie he bent his bow,
   His right hand was in posture of a foe,
To kill what *Sions* daughter did desire,
   'Gainst whom his wrath, he poured forth, like fire.

5 For like an enemie *Jehova* is,   105
   Devouring *Israel*, and his Palaces,
Destroying holds, giving additions
   To *Juda's* daughters lamentations.

6 Like to a garden hedge he hath cast downe
   The place where was his congregation,   110
And *Sions* feasts and sabbaths are forgot;
   Her King, her Priest, his wrath regardeth not.

7 The Lord forsakes his Altar, and detests
   His Sanctuary, and in the foes hand rests
His Palace, and the walls, in which their cries   115
   Are heard, as in the true solemnities.

8 The Lord hath cast a line, so to confound
   And levell *Sions* walls unto the ground;
He drawes not back his hand, which doth oreturne
   The wall, and Rampart, which together mourne. 120

9 Their gates are sunke into the ground, and hee
   Hath broke the barres; their King and Princes bee
Amongst the heathen, without law, nor there
   Unto their Prophets doth the Lord appeare.

10 There *Sions Elders* on the ground are plac'd, 125
   And silence keepe; Dust on their heads they cast,
In sackcloth have they girt themselves, and low
   The Virgins towards ground, their heads do throw.

11 My bowells are growne muddy, and mine eyes
   Are faint with weeping: and my liver lies   130
Pour'd out upon the ground, for miserie
   That sucking children in the streets doe die.

114 hand *MSS.*: hands *1633*: in manum inimici *Tr*   118 ground;] ground,
1633   119 hand,] hand; *1633*   122 barres *O'F, B*: barre *1633, TCD*:
vectes ejus *Tr*

12 When they had cryed unto their Mothers, where
   Shall we have bread, and drinke? they fainted there,
And in the streets like wounded persons lay   135
   Till 'twixt their mothers breasts they went away.

13 *Daughter Jerusalem*, Oh what may bee
   A witnesse, or comparison for thee?
Sion, to'ease thee, what shall I name like thee? ·
   Thy breach is like the sea, what help can bee?   140

14 For thee vaine foolish things thy Prophets sought,
   Thee, thine iniquities they have not taught,
Which might disturne thy bondage: but for thee
   False burthens, and false causes they would see.

15 The passengers doe clap their hands, and hisse,   145
   And wag their head at thee, and say, Is this
That citie, which so many men did call
   Joy of the earth, and perfectest of all?

16 Thy foes doe gape upon thee, and they hisse,
   And gnash their teeth, and say, Devoure wee this,   150
For this is certainly the day which wee
   Expected, and which now we finde, and see.

17 The Lord hath done that which he purposed,
   Fulfill'd his word of old determined;
He hath throwne downe, and not spar'd, and thy foe   155
   Made glad above thee, and advanc'd him so.

18 But now, their hearts against the Lord do call,
   Therefore, O walle of *Sion*, let teares fall
Downe like a river, day and night; take thee
   No rest, but let thine eye incessant be.   160

19 Arise, cry in the night, poure, for thy sinnes,
   Thy heart, like water, when the watch begins;
Lift up thy hands to God, lest children dye,
   Which, faint for hunger, in the streets doe lye.

134 there,] there *1633*   135 streetes *O'F, B*: street *1633, TCD*: in plateis
civitatis *Tr*   139 to'] to *1633*   141 For thee *O'F, B*: For, the *1633,*
TCD   145 hisse,] hisse *1633*   157 against] unto *O'F, B*: contra *Tr*
158 walle *O'F*: walls *1633, TCD, B, Gr*: mure *Tr*

20 Behold O Lord, consider unto whom   165
   Thou hast done thus; what, shall the women come
To eate their children of a spanne? shall thy
   Prophet and Priest be slaine in Sanctuary?

21 On ground in streets, the yong and old do lye,
   My virgins and yong men by sword do dye;   170
Them in the day of thy wrath thou hast slaine,
   Nothing did thee from killing them containe.

22 As to a solemne feast, all whom I fear'd
   Thou call'st about mee; when his wrath appear'd,
None did remaine or scape, for those which I   175
   Brought up, did perish by mine enemie.

CHAP. III

1 I AM the man which have affliction seene,
   Under the rod of Gods wrath having beene,
2 He hath led mee to darknesse, not to light,
   3 And against mee all day, his hand doth fight.   180

4 Hee'hath broke my bones, worne out my flesh and skinne,
   5 Built up against mee; and hath girt mee in
With hemlocke, and with labour; 6 and set mee
   In darke, as they who dead for ever bee.

7 Hee'hath hedg'd me lest I scape, and added more   185
   To my steele fetters, heavier then before,
8 When I crie out, he'out shuts my prayer: 9 And hath
   Stop'd with hewn stone my way, and turn'd my path.

10 And like a Lion hid in secrecie,
   Or Beare which lyes in wait, he was to mee,   190
11 He stops my way, teares me, made desolate,
   12 And hee makes mee the marke he shooteth at.

166 thus *TCD*, *B*: this *1633*, *O'F*, *Gr*: ita *Tr*   174 his] thy *O'F*, *B*: die irae
Jehovae *Tr*   181 skinne,] skinne , *1633 uncorrected*   182 girt] hemd
O'F, *B*   187 'out] out *1633*

13 Hee made the children of his quiver passe
  Into my reines, 14 I with my people was
All the day long, a song and mockery.   195
    15 Hee hath fill'd mee with bitternesse, and he

Hath made me drunke with wormewood. 16 He hath burst
  My teeth with stones, and cover'd mee with dust;
17 And thus my Soule farre off from peace was set,
  And my prosperity I did forget.   200

18 My strength, my hope (unto my selfe I said)
  Which from the Lord should come, is perished.
19 But when my mournings I do thinke upon,
  My wormwood, hemlocke, and affliction,

20 My Soule is humbled in remembring this;   205
    21 My heart considers, therefore, hope there is.
22 'Tis Gods great mercy we'are not utterly
  Consum'd, for his compassions do not die;

23 For every morning they renewed bee,
  For great, O Lord, is thy fidelity.   210
24 The Lord is, saith my Soule, my portion,
  And therefore in him will I hope alone.

25 The Lord is good to them, who'on him relie,
  And to the Soule that seeks him earnestly.
26 It is both good to trust, and to attend   215
  (The Lords salvation) unto the end:

27 'Tis good for one his yoake in youth to beare;
  28 He sits alone, and doth all speech forbeare,
Because he'hath borne it. 29 And his mouth he layes
  Deepe in the dust, yet there in hope he stayes.   220

30 He gives his cheekes to whosoever will
  Strike him, and so he is reproched still.
31 For, not for ever doth the Lord forsake,
    32 But when he'hath strucke with sadnes, hee doth take

198 cover'd] covered _1633_   213 'on] on _1633_   220 yet there O'F, B:
yet TCD: yet then _1633_, Gr

Compassion, as his mercy'is infinite;   225
 33 Nor is it with his heart, that he doth smite,
34 That underfoot the prisoners stamped bee,
 35 That a mans right the Judge himselfe doth see

To be wrunge from him, 36 That he subverted is
In his just cause; the Lord allowes not this: 230
37 Who then will say, that ought doth come to passe,
But that which by the Lord commanded was?

38 Both good and evill from his mouth proceeds;
 39 Why then grieves any man for his misdeeds?
40 Turne wee to God, by trying out our wayes;   235
 41 To him in heaven, our hands with hearts upraise.

42 Wee have rebell'd, and falne away from thee,
 Thou pardon'st not; 43 Usest no clemencie;
Pursu'st us, kill'st us, cover'st us with wrath,
 44 Cover'st thy selfe with clouds, that our prayer hath   240

No power to passe. 45 And thou hast made us fall
 As refuse, and off-scouring to them all.
46 All our foes gape at us. 47 Feare and a snare
 With ruine, and with waste, upon us are.

48 With water rivers doth mine eye oreflow   245
 For ruine of my peoples daughter so;
49 Mine eye doth drop downe teares incessantly,
 50 Untill the Lord looke downe from heaven to see.

51 And for my city daughters sake, mine eye
 Doth breake my heart. 52 Causles mine enemy,   250
Like a bird chac'd me. 53 In a dungeon
 They'have shut my life, and cast on mee a stone.

229 wrunge *MSS.*: wrong *1633* him,] him. *1633* 238 not;] not. *1633*
239 Pursu'st . . . cover'st] Pursuest . . . coverest *1633* 245 water] watry *O'F,*
B, Gr 246 daughter *MSS.*: daughters *1633*: propter contritionem filiae populi
mei *Tr* 249 city] cittyes *O'F, B, Gr* 250 my *MSS.*: mine *1633, Gr*
252 'have] have *1633* on mee *TCD, B*: me on *1633, O'F*: projiciunt lapides in
me *Tr*

54 Waters flow'd o'r my head, then thought I, I am
   Destroy'd; 55 I called Lord, upon thy name
Out of the pit. 56 And thou my voice didst heare;   255
   Oh from my sigh, and crye, stop not thine eare.

57 Then when I call'd upon thee, thou drew'st nere
   Unto mee,'and said'st unto mee, do not feare.
58 Thou Lord my Soules cause handled hast, and thou
   Rescud'st my life. 59 O Lord do thou judge now,   260

Thou heardst my wrong. 60 Their vengeance all they'have
   wrought;
   61 How they reproach'd, thou'hast heard, and what they
      thought,
62 What their lips utter'd, which against me rose,
   And what was ever whisper'd by my foes.

63 I am their song, whether they rise or sit,   265
   64 Give them rewards Lord, for their working fit,
65 Sorrow of heart, thy curse. 66 And with thy might
   Follow,'and from under heaven destroy them quite.

CHAP. IV

1 **H**OW is the gold become so dimme? How is
   Purest and finest gold thus chang'd to this?   270
The stones which were stones of the Sanctuary,
   Scattered in corners of each street do lye.

2 The pretious sonnes of Sion, which should bee
   Valued as purest gold, how do wee see
Low rated now, as earthen Pitchers, stand,   275
   Which are the worke of a poore Potters hand.

3 Even the Sea-calfes draw their brests, and give
   Sucke to their young; my peoples daughters live,
By reason of the foes great cruelnesse,
   As do the Owles in the vast Wildernesse.   280

258 'and] and *1633*   260 Rescud'st *O'F, B:* Rescuest *1633, TCD:* vindicabas
Tr   261 'have] have *1633*   262 'hast] hast *1633*   263 utter'd]
uttered *1633*   268 'and] and *1633*

4 And when the sucking child doth strive to draw,
   His tongue for thirst cleaves to his upper jaw.
And when for bread the little children crye,
   There is no man that doth them satisfie.

5 They which before were delicately fed, 285
   Now in the streets forlorne have perished,
And they which ever were in scarlet cloath'd,
   Sit and embrace the dunghills which they loath'd.

6 The daughters of my people have sinn'd more,
   Then did the towne of *Sodome* sinne before; 290
Which being at once destroy'd, there did remaine
   No hands amongst them, to vexe them againe.

7 But heretofore purer her Nazarite
   Was then the snow, and milke was not so white;
As carbuncles did their pure bodies shine, 295
   And all their polish'dnesse was Saphirine.

8 They'are darker now then blacknes, none can know
   Them by the face, as through the streetes they goe,
For now their skin doth cleave unto their bone,
   And withered, is like to dry wood growne. 300

9 Better by sword then famine 'tis to dye;
   And better through pierc'd, then by penury.
10 Women by nature pitifull, have eate
   Their children drest with their owne hands for meat.

11 *Jehova* here fully accomplish'd hath 305
   His indignation, and powr'd forth his wrath,
Kindled a fire in *Sion*, which hath power
   To eate, and her foundations to devour.

12 Nor would the Kings of th'earth, nor all which live
   In the inhabitable world beleeve, 310
That any adversary, any foe
   Into *Jerusalem* should enter so.

289 daughters] daughrers *1633 uncorrected*   sinn'd] sinned *1633*   296
Saphirine *O'F*: Sapherine *TCD, B*: Seraphine *1633*   297 'are] are *1633*
298 streetes *O'F, B*: street *1633, TCD*: in vicis *Tr*   299 their] the *O'F, B, Gr*
302 by] through *O'F, B, Gr*   302 penury.] penury, *1633*   304 hands *B*:
hand *1633, TCD, O'F*: manus . . . coquunt *Tr*   309 th'] the *1633*   312 so.]
so; *1633*

13 For the Priests sins, and Prophets, which have shed
   Blood in the streets, and the just murthered:
14 Which when those men, whom they made blinde, did
       stray   315
   Thorough the streets, defiled by the way

With blood, the which impossible it was
   Their garments should scape touching, as they passe,
15 Would cry aloud, depart defiled men,
   Depart, depart, and touch us not; and then   320

They fled, and strayd, and with the *Gentiles* were,
   Yet told their friends, they should not long dwell there;
16 For this they'are scatter'd by Jehovahs face
   Who never will regard them more; No grace

Unto their old men shall the foe afford,   325
   Nor, that they'are Priests, redeeme them from the sword.
17 And wee as yet, for all these miseries
   Desiring our vaine helpe, consume our eyes:

And such a nation as cannot save,
   We in desire and speculation have.   330
18 They hunt our steps, that in the streets wee feare
   To goe: our end is now approached neere,

Our dayes accomplish'd are, this the last day.
   19 Eagles of heaven are not so swift as they
Which follow us, o'r mountaine tops they flye   335
   At us, and for us in the desert lye.

20 Th'annointed Lord, breath of our nostrils, hee
   Of whom we said, under his shadow, wee
Shall with more ease under the Heathen dwell,
   Into the pit which these men digged, fell.   340

21 Rejoyce O *Edoms daughter*, joyfull bee
   Thou which inhabitst *Uz*, for unto thee
This cup shall passe, and thou with drunkennesse
   Shalt fill thy selfe, and shew thy nakednesse.

---

320 not;] not, *1633*   322 dwell there;] dwell; there. *1633*   323 'are
scatter'd] are scattered *1633*   326 'are] are *1633*   333 day.] day, *1633*
337 Th'] The *1633*   340 fell.] fell *1633*   342 Uz *O'F*: her *1633*: Hus
TCD: Huz *B*

22 And then thy sinnes O *Sion*, shall be spent,   345
   The Lord will not leave thee in banishment.
Thy sinnes O *Edoms daughter*, hee will see,
   And for them, pay thee with captivitie.

CHAP. V

1 REMEMBER, O Lord, what is fallen on us;
   See, and marke how we are reproached thus,   350
2 For unto strangers our possession
   Is turn'd, our houses unto Aliens gone,

3 Our mothers are become as widowes, wee
   As Orphans all, and without father be;
4 Waters which are our owne, wee drinke, and pay,   355
   And upon our owne wood a price they lay.

5 Our persecutors on our necks do sit,
   They make us travaile, and not intermit,
6 We stretch our hands unto th'*Egyptians*
   To get us bread; and to th'*Assyrians*.

7 Our Fathers did these sinnes, and are no more,
   But wee do beare the sinnes they did before.
8 They are but servants, which do rule us thus,
   Yet from their hands none would deliver us.

9 With danger of our life our bread wee gat;   365
   For in the wildernesse, the sword did wait.
10 The tempests of this famine wee liv'd in,
   Black as an Oven colour'd had our skinne:

11 In *Judaes* cities they the maids abus'd
   By force, and so women in *Sion* us'd.   370
12 The Princes with their hands they hung; no grace
   Nor honour gave they to the Elders face.

CHAP.] CAP. *1633*   349 us;] us *1633*   354 father *O'F*: fathers
1633, TCD, B: nullo patre *Tr*: absque patre *V*   355 drinke *O'F, B*: drunke
1633, TCD, Gr   360 th'] the *1633*   368 Oven *MSS*.: Ocean *1633*

13 Unto the mill our yong men carried are,
   And children fall under the wood they beare.
14 Elders, the gates; youth did their songs forbeare,   375
15   Gone was our joy; our dancings, mournings were.

16 Now is the crowne falne from our head; and woe
   Be unto us, because we'have sinned so.
17 For this our hearts do languish, and for this
   Over our eyes a cloudy dimnesse is.   380

18 Because mount *Sion* desolate doth lye,
   And foxes there do goe at libertie:
19 But thou O Lord art ever, and thy throne
   From generation, to generation.

20 Why should'st thou forget us eternally?   385
   Or leave us thus long in this misery?
21 Restore us Lord to thee, that so we may
   Returne, and as of old, renew our day.

22 For oughtest thou, O Lord, despise us thus,
   And to be utterly enrag'd at us?   390

HYMNS

A Hymne to Christ, at the Authors last going into Germany

IN what torne ship soever I embarke,
   That ship shall be my embleme of thy Arke;
What sea soever swallow mee, that flood
Shall be to mee an embleme of thy blood;

374 fall *O'F, B*: fell *1633, TCD, Gr*   beare *B*: bare *1633, TCD, O'F, Gr*: pueri ad
ligna corruunt *Tr*   389 thus,] thus *1633*
A Hymne to Christ *&c. 1633 MSS.: TCD; Dob and O'F Title*] A Hymne to
Christ *TCD*: At his departure with my L: of Doncaster. 1619. *Dob*: At the Sea-side
going over wth the Ld Doncaster. 1619 *O'F*   *Last line of each stanza as in*
MSS.: *divided into lines of eight and six syllables in* 1633   3 swallow mee]
swallowes me vp *Dob, O'F*

Though thou with clouds of anger do disguise   5
Thy face; yet through that maske I know those eyes,
Which, though they turne away sometimes, they never will
    despise.

I sacrifice this Iland unto thee,
And all whom I lov'd there, and who lov'd mee;
When I have put our seas twixt them and mee,   10
Put thou thy sea betwixt my sinnes and thee.
As the trees sap doth seeke the root below
In winter, in my winter now I goe,
Where none but thee, th'Eternall root of true love I may
    know.

Nor thou nor thy religion dost controule,   15
The amorousnesse of an harmonious Soule,
But thou would'st have that love thy selfe: As thou
Art jealous, Lord, so I am jealous now,
Thou lov'st not, till from loving more, thou free
My soule: Who ever gives, takes libertie: 20
O, if thou car'st not whom I love, alas, thou lov'st not mee.

Seale then this bill of my Divorce to All,
On whom those fainter beames of love did fall;
Marry those loves, which in youth scatter'd bee
On Fame, Wit, Hopes (false mistresses) to thee.   25
Churches are best for Prayer, that have least light:
To see God only, I goe out of sight:
And to scape stormy dayes, I chuse an Everlasting night.

---

5 with] in *Dob, O'F*   7 Which,] Which *1633 uncorrected*   9 lov'd ... lov'd]
loue . . . loue *Dob, O'F*   10 our] those *Dob, O'F*   11 thy sea *MSS.*:
thy seas *1633*   15 dost] doth *Dob, O'F*   16 Soule,] Soule *1633 uncor-
rected*   18 I am] am I *Dob, O'F*   21 love,] love *1633*   24 scat-
ter'd] scattered *1633*   26 Prayer] prayers *Dob, O'F*

Hymne to God my God, in my sicknesse

SINCE I am comming to that Holy roome,
   Where, with thy Quire of Saints for evermore,
I shall be made thy Musique; As I come
    I tune the Instrument here at the dore,
    And what I must doe then, thinke now before.   5

Whilst my Physitians by their love are growne
   Cosmographers, and I their Mapp, who lie
Flat on this bed, that by them may be showne
    That this is my South-west discoverie
    Per fretum febris, by these streights to die,   10

I joy, that in these straits, I see my West;
   For, though theire currants yeeld returne to none,
What shall my West hurt me? As West and East
    In all flatt Maps (and I am one) are one,
    So death doth touch the Resurrection.   15

Is the Pacifique Sea my home? Or are
   The Easterne riches? Is *Jerusalem*?
Anyan, and *Magellan*, and *Gibraltare*,
    All streights, and none but streights, are wayes to them,
    Whether where *Japhet* dwelt, or *Cham*, or *Sem*.   20

We thinke that *Paradise* and *Calvarie*,
   Christs Crosse, and *Adams* tree, stood in one place;
Looke Lord, and finde both *Adams* met in me;
    As the first *Adams* sweat surrounds my face,
    May the last *Adams* blood my soule embrace.   25

So, in his purple wrapp'd receive mee Lord,
   By these his thornes give me his other Crowne;
And as to others soules I preach'd thy word,
    Be this my Text, my Sermon to mine owne,
    Therfore that he may raise the Lord throws down.   30

Hymne to God my God &c. *1635*   *MSS.:* S 96, A 34   5 now *MSS.:* here
1635, Gr   12 theire S 96: theis A 34: those *1635*   19 streights,] streights
1635

A Hymne to God the Father

I

Wilt thou forgive that sinne where I begunne,
   Which is my sin, though it were done before?
Wilt thou forgive those sinnes through which I runne,
And doe them still: though still I doe deplore?
   When thou hast done, thou hast not done,   5
         For, I have more.

II

Wilt thou forgive that sinne by which I'have wonne
   Others to sinne? and, made my sinne their doore?
Wilt thou forgive that sinne which I did shunne
   A yeare, or two: but wallow'd in, a score?   10
   When thou hast done, thou hast not done,
         For, I have more.

III

I have a sinne of feare, that when I'have spunne
   My last thred, I shall perish on the shore;
Sweare by thy selfe, that at my death thy Sunne   15
   Shall shine as it shines now, and heretofore;
   And, having done that, Thou hast done,
         I have no more.

A Hymne to God the Father *1633*   MSS.: *TCD; Dob* and *O'F*   *Grierson prints two
texts: see note*   *Title*: A Hymne *&c. 1633*: To Christ *TCD, Dob*: Christo
Saluatori *O'F*: *see note*   2 is *MSS.*: was *1633*   were] was *Dob, O'F*   3 those
sinnes *MSS.*: that sinne; *1633*   4 doe them *MSS.*: do run *1633*   doe] do
1633   7 by which I have wonne *TCD*: by which I wonne *Dob, O'F*: which I
have wonne *1633*   10 wallow'd] wallowed *1633*   12 For,] For *1633*
13 'have] have *1633*   15 Sweare *MSS.*: But sweare *1633*   Sunne *MSS.*: sonne
1633   16 it *MSS.*: he *1633*   17 hast] haste *1633*   18 have *MSS.*:
feare *1633*

LATIN POEMS

To Mr. George Herbert, with my Seal, of the Anchor and Christ

Q VI *prius assuetus Serpentum fasce Tabellas*
　　Signare, (haec nostrae symbola parva Domus)
Adscitus domui Domini, patrióque relicto
　Stemmate, nanciscor stemmata jure nova.
Hinc mihi Crux primo quae fronti impressa lavacro,　　　　5
　Finibus extensis, anchora facta patet.
Anchorae in effigiem Crux tandem desinit ipsam,
　Anchora fit tandem Crux tolerata diu.
Hoc tamen ut fiat, Christo vegetatur ab ipso
　Crux, et ab Affixo, est Anchora facta, Iesu.　　　　　　10
Nec Natalitiis penitus serpentibus orbor,
　Non ita dat Deus, ut auferat ante data.
Quâ sapiens, Dos est; Quâ terram lambit et ambit,
　Pestis; At in nostra fit Medicina Cruce,
Serpens; fixa Cruci si sit Natura; Crucique　　　　　　15
　A fixo, nobis, Gratia tota fluat.
Omnia cum Crux sint, Crux Anchora facta, sigillum
　Non tam dicendum hoc, quam Catechismus erit.
Mitto nec exigua, exiguâ sub imagine, dona,
　Pignora amicitiae, et munera; Vota, preces.　　　　　　20
Plura tibi accumulet, sanctus cognominis, Ille
　Regia qui flavo Dona sigillat Equo.

A SHEAFE of Snakes used heretofore to be
　My Seal, The Crest of our poore Family.
Adopted in Gods Family, and so
Our old Coat lost, unto new armes I go.

To Mr. George Herbert &c. *1650*　　　*Title*: ... with my Seal] ... with one of my
Seal *1650*: *see note*　　5 fronti] fronte *1650*　　7 effigiem] effigiem, *1650*
17 facta] fixa *1650*　　19 Mitto] Mitto, *1650*
A sheafe of Shakes &c.　　1–2 *Printed as prose heading; see note on title and
setting*

The Crosse (my seal at Baptism) spred below,   5
Does, by that form, into an Anchor grow.
Crosses grow Anchors; Bear, as thou shouldst do
Thy Crosse, and that Crosse grows an Anchor too.
But he that makes our Crosses Anchors thus,
Is Christ, who there is crucifi'd for us.   10
Yet may I, with this, my first Serpents hold,
God gives new blessings, and yet leaves the old;
The Serpent, may, as wise, my pattern be;
My poison, as he feeds on dust, that's me.
And as he rounds the Earth to murder sure,   15
My death he is, but on the Crosse, my cure.
Crucifie nature then, and then implore
All Grace from him, crucified there before;
When all is Crosse, and that Crosse Anchor grown,
This Seal's a Catechism, not a Seal alone.   20
Under that little Seal great gifts I send,
⟨Wishes⟩, and prayers, pawns, and fruits of a friend.
And may that Saint which rides in our great Seal,
To you, who bear his name, great bounties deal.

22 ⟨Wishes⟩] Works *1650*

Epigraph to the Portrait of Donne in his Shroud, prefixed to *Deaths Duell* (1632)

Corporis haec Animae sit Syndon, Syndon Jesu.
                              Amen.

COMMENTARY

FOR the standard interpretation of passages from Scripture, I have gone to the *Biblia Sacra cum Glossa Ordinaria et Postilla Nicolai Lyrani*, in six volumes. Donne gave a copy of this Bible to the Library at Lincoln's Inn, when he resigned his office as Reader in 1622. All interpretations, when no reference is given, are from here. The term 'Gloss' is employed to cover both the original gloss and the additional matter in the margins and at the foot of the page.

Biblical quotations are from the Authorized Version, although most of the poems were written before its publication. All the texts quoted have been checked against the Vulgate, Genevan, Douai, and Rheims versions; if no alternative to the Authorized Version is given, it can be assumed that there are no substantial differences between it and the other versions.

In addition to the Gloss, I have used the ninth-century encyclopedist Rabanus Maurus, who gathered together the allegorical interpretations of the Fathers in his *De Universo* and *De Allegoriis in Sacram Scripturam*, and whose work was a foundation for later encyclopedists. The task of discovering in what form these commonplaces came to Donne is an impossible one; and it seemed pointless to attempt to trace their remote origin in one of the Fathers.

Versification

The majority of the *Divine Poems* present no metrical problems, but in the 'Holy Sonnets' the versification is very bold and original. Since the scansion of English verse is a matter of discussion and terms are not agreed upon, I give briefly the theory I hold and the conventions I have employed to mark the manner in which a line should be read. Donne's metrical base in the 'Holy Sonnets' is a decasyllabic line of five feet, each foot consisting of an unstressed and a stressed syllable, $^{\times}$ $^{\prime}$. He varies from this base with a boldness unprecedented in non-dramatic verse before Milton. Like Milton he makes great use of elisions and contractions to preserve an equal number of metrical syllables, although he allows himself an extra weak final syllable. (It should be noted that 'heaven' and 'spirit' are usually monosyllabic.) Elided syllables are not suppressed in reading, but are metrically worthless like grace-notes in music, giving a ripple without disturbing the time. Unlike Milton, however, Donne appears to have allowed himself the licence of occasional defective lines to achieve a particular rhythmical effect. This is not the Chaucerian licence of a syllable missing at the beginning of the line, but the licence of a defective medial foot. Such lines occur only rarely, but the evidence of the manuscripts points unmistakably to their existence. It is possible that Donne was impressed by Wyatt's bold handling of the long line in his sonnets, for it must be noted that he follows Wyatt and Sidney, rather than Surrey and Shakespeare, in the form of the sonnet he employs. More probably, his natural instinct for the dramatic led him to make use of this licence, which is common in the dramatic verse of his contemporaries.

In the arrangement of his stresses Donne again anticipates Milton, particularly in his fondness for using feet with level stress. It is this which gives his verse its peculiar weight and its extraordinary rhythmic variety. In marking the reading of a line, we have to allow for feet with normal stress ˣ ´, feet with inverted stress ´ ˣ, feet with level stress ´ ´, and feet with a very light stress ˣ ˊ. I mark this last, because I believe that the secret of reading the verse of poets who do not 'keep accent', such as Donne and Milton, is to be continually aware of the metrical stress supporting the rhythm of the line. In many lines, in which the speech stress seems at first sight to overwhelm the metrical stress, we need to give the metrical stress some value, in order to bring out not only the music but the full meaning of the line. In others, in which there are few speech stresses, it is our sense of the 'foot' as a metrical reality that enables us to accept the rhythmic variations as not inconsistent with the metrical norm. To read Donne we need a very keen sense of time, and the power to make use of *rubato* without destroying that sense. My scansion of the two lines quoted in the introduction would therefore be:

$$\overset{\times}{\text{From}} \overset{\prime}{\text{death,}} \mid \overset{\times}{\text{you}} \overset{\prime}{\text{num}} \mid \overset{\times}{\text{ber}} \overset{\prime}{\text{lesse}} \mid \overset{\times}{\text{infin}} \mid \overset{\prime}{\text{ities,}}$$

and

$$\overset{\prime}{\text{All}} \overset{\prime}{\text{whom}} \mid \overset{\prime}{\text{warre,}} \overset{\prime}{\text{dearth,}} \mid \overset{\prime}{\text{age,}} \overset{\prime}{\text{ag}} \mid \overset{\times}{\text{ues,}} \overset{\prime}{\text{tyr}} \mid \overset{\times}{\text{annies}}$$

To Mrs. Magdalen Herbert: of St. Mary Magdalen (*page 1*)

This sonnet, not elsewhere extant, was printed in Walton's *Life of Herbert* in 1670, after a letter to Mrs. Herbert, dated 'Micham, July 11. 1607', which ends:

By this Messenger, and on this good day, I commit the inclosed *Holy Hymns* and *Sonnets* . . . to your judgment, and to your protection too, if you think them worthy of it; and I have appointed this inclosed *Sonnet* to usher them to your happy hand.

Grierson was the first editor to place this sonnet before '*La Corona*', arguing that the 'inclosed *Holy Hymns* and *Sonnets*' or '*Hymns*, to his dear name addrest', which were sent with it to Mrs. Herbert, were the seven '*La Corona*' sonnets. His argument is plausible: the '*La Corona*' sonnets, unlike the 'Holy Sonnets', may properly be called hymns, since they unite the elements of prayer and praise; and, again unlike the 'Holy Sonnets', they are addressed to Christ. They are the only extant poems which fit the descriptions. But we cannot assume as certain that the poems which Donne sent to Mrs. Herbert have survived: indeed Walton says 'These *Hymns* are now lost to us'. Their identification with '*La Corona*' and the consequent dating of '*La Corona*' by the date of the letter, must therefore be regarded as not more than a highly probable conjecture.

The date of the letter was discussed by H. W. Garrod in 'Donne and Mrs. Herbert' (*R.E.S.* xxi, 1945). His suggested date is impossible, since he over-looked that Donne used Old Style. I. A. Shapiro informed me that he accepted the month and year; but David Novarr has argued convincingly that the letter cannot have been written in July 1607. See supplementary notes, p. 151. For a discussion of Donne's friendship with Mrs. Herbert, see Garrod's article and Appendix C, 'Lady Bedford and Mrs. Herbert' in Gardner, *Elegies etc.*, pp. 251-8.

Title: Walton's heading gives Mrs. Herbert a title she never bore. The error is repeated on the separate title-page to the *Letters* printed as an Appendix to the *Life of Herbert*, but the three letters from Donne are correctly headed '*To the worthiest Lady, Mrs. Magdalen Herbert*'. The error probably arose in shortening this longer title.

ll. 1-2. *Her of your name*, &c. Donne accepts here the tradition of the Western Church, enshrined in the Roman Breviary and in medieval legend, which identifies the woman who was a sinner (Luke vii) with Mary of Bethany and with Mary Magdalene, the demoniac (Mark xvi, Luke viii), who stood by the Cross and appears in the Resurrection narratives. This tradition appears not to have been questioned in the Church of England in the seventeenth century. Donne, Andrewes, and Taylor all take it for granted.

In late medieval legend Bethany is Martha's portion of the family estates (*Golden Legend*, iv. 74). In the earliest life of the Saint (written by Rabanus Maurus in the ninth century) Magdalo is the portion of Mary, but the shares of the others are not specified. I imagine Donne is thinking of Bethany as the family home of Mary Magdalene, as distinct from her dowry, Magdalo. I do not know of any authority for the form 'Bethina'.

l. 8. *think these* Magdalens *were two or three*. Donne may be writing loosely, and intending to say that some Fathers think *this* Magdalen to have been two or three women. But he may be referring to the further debate, occasioned by the discrepancy in the narratives of the Resurrection, as to whether there were not two Mary Magdalenes; see the Gloss on Mark xvi.

l. 11. *Take so much of th'example,' as of the name*. Mrs. Herbert is to add to the number of Mary Magdalenes, and since she bears the second name of the saint is to imitate the second half of her life. But unless we accept the identi-fication of the 'peccatrix' with Mary Magdalene the demoniac, the injunction has no force, and unless we accept the further identification of Mary of Bethany with Mary Magdalene, we cannot say that a Magdalene harboured 'Christ himself, a Guest'.

It is interesting to find Donne writing so forced and frigid a sonnet on the

Magdalene in an age when her cult was so intense. Neither here, nor in his sermons, is his imagination stirred by the favourite saint of the Counter-Reformation. She is to him primarily the herald of the Resurrection; cf. *Sermons*, ix. 195, where he even questions whether her sin was necessarily incontinence.

La Corona (*page 1*)

MSS.: Group I: *C 57*, *D*, *H 49*, *SP*; Group II: *A 18*, *N*, *TCC*, *TCD*, *DC*; Group III: *Dob*, *Lut*, *O'F*, *S 96*; *B*, *O1*, *S*; *W*; Miscellanies: *Hd*.

The text in *1633*, taken from its Group I MS., is good, and only six slight departures have been made from it. In 4. 4, only *C 57* supports it, and the reading of all the other MSS. has been adopted; in 1. 11 and 5. 8, only Group I supports it, and the reading of Groups I and II and *W* has been preferred; for the reading in 3. 8, 6. 12, and 7. 12, see notes.

The version preserved in Group III and *W* differs interestingly from that in Groups I and II and *1633*. *DC* has a poor Group II text. The texts in *O1* and *S* are extremely poor. *Hd* has a good Group III text.

In Group I 'La Corona' precedes the 'Holy Sonnets' under the general title of 'Holy Sonnets'. *H 49* has the heading 'Holy Sonnets written 20 yeares since'. This is probably a round figure, not a precise date, and it is impossible to say whether the statement is meant to refer to '*La Corona*' alone, or to include the 'Holy Sonnets'. Since the date 1629 occurs in the collection of poems immediately preceding the Donne collection in the MS., the heading supports us in putting '*La Corona*' (and possibly the 'Holy Sonnets') rather before 1610.

Title: Group III has 'The Crowne', except *O1* and *S* which have '*La Corona*'. The titles to the separate sonnets (2–7) are only found in Group II and *1633*. (They have been added in *O'F*.) The editor probably took them, with other titles, from his Group II MS. I retain them for convenience; but I do not think them authentic. The unity of the poem is obscured by the titles given to sonnets 2–7, which also make '*La Corona*' seem the title of the first sonnet instead of the title of the set. For supplementary note, see p. 152.

1. *Deigne at my hands this crown of prayer and praise* (*page 1*)

This sonnet might well be called 'Advent'. Its leading ideas and much of its phrasing are derived from the Advent Offices in the Roman Breviary. (Any Breviary Donne used would be a Roman one, since the Sarum Use fell into desuetude after the Reformation.) The contrast on which the sonnet is built is found in Isaiah xxviii: 'Vae coronae superbiae . . . et flori decidenti. . . . In die illa erit Dominus exercituum corona gloriae . . . residuo populi sui' (Lesson at Matins, Monday, third week of Advent, echoed in later versicles).

'Strong sober thirst' blends the admonition 'Sobrie, et juste, et pie vivamus
. . .' (Advent Sunday), with 'Omnes sitientes venite ad aquas' (Advent
Sunday) and 'Haurietis aquas in gaudio de fontibus Salvatoris' (Monday,
third week). 'My soul attends' recalls 'Ego autem ad Dominum aspiciam, et
exspectabo Deum Salvatorem meum' (Friday, third week). 'This first last
end' not only recalls the first chapter of Revelation, but also the first of the
Advent Antiphons: 'O Sapientia . . . attingens a fine usque ad finem (17 Dec.).
The final lines sum up the theme of the Advent Offices: 'Annuntiate populis
et dicite: Ecce Deus Salvator noster veniet.'

l. 2. *my low devout melancholie.* For the source of the reading 'lone' in *1635*,
see p. xc.

In general Donne regards melancholy as not conducive to true devotion,
but as its enemy; see *Letters*, p. 45, where he declares of sadness that for it
and wickedness 'the Italian allows but one word, *Triste*; And in full con-
demnation whereof it was prophesied of our blessed Saviour, *Non erit tristis'*.
'Low' may mean simply 'humble'; but Donne usually employs the word in
a derogatory sense.

l. 4. *All changing unchang'd Antient of dayes.* A name from Hebrew prophecy,
'the Ancient of Days' (Dan. vii), is combined with the philosophic conception
of the Unmoved Mover. Cf. the hymn 'Rerum Deus tenax vigor', ascribed
to St. Ambrose.

l. 9. *The ends crowne our workes, but thou crown'st our ends.* The fact that *S* (which
elsewhere, except in 3. 7, reads with Group III) agrees with Groups I and II
and *W* in reading 'our ends' suggests that 'our dayes' (Group III) may not
be a true early reading, and we need not ascribe to Donne's first version the
carelessness of rhyming the eighth and ninth lines and leaving the twelfth
unrhymed. It is difficult to account for 'dayes' as a scribal error for 'ends', and
'End crownes' (Group III) looks at first sight like the original reading, since
the proverbial saying is in the singular. But the currency of the proverb 'The
end crowns all' may have led a scribe to substitute the singular for the plural,
and 'dayes' might have been caught from l. 4.

The stress of the line falls on 'thou'. In the truism 'Finis coronat opus',
'crown' means 'completes worthily'; the other sense of the word is 'blesses
or rewards'. Christ 'crowns our ends' ('erit Dominus . . . corona') in being
himself our reward after death.

ll. 11–12.   *This first last end, now zealously possest,*
                    With a strong sober thirst, my soule attends.
1633 follows Group I in reading 'The first', which has been abandoned for the
more emphatic 'This' (Groups II, III, *W*). It refers back to the strongly
stressed 'thou' of line 9. 'Soberly possest' (Group III, *W*) may well have
stood in Donne's first version. The note of warning 'Be sober, be vigilant

is so characteristic of Advent that the repetition 'soberly/sober' may not have seemed excessive.

'Possest' qualifies the soul, which is 'wholly occupied' by its thirst. 'This first last end' is the expected Saviour. Cf. Rev. i. 8 and 11: 'I am Alpha and Omega, the beginning and the ending'; 'I am . . . the first and the last.'

l. 13. *heart and voice.* Group III (except *B*) and *W* read 'voice and heart'. If Donne had the Advent Offices in mind, it is natural that he should have thought of lifting up the voice and added 'heart' to fill his line. Cf. 'Clama in fortitudine . . . exalta in fortitudine vocem tuam (Wednesday in the third week). The order 'heart and voice' is more logical.

2. Annunciation (*page 2*)

In this and the next sonnet Donne recalls the *Horae B.V.M.*, which made part of the *Prymer*, the prayer book of the laity in the Middle Ages. References are from the most easily accessible version: *The Prymer*, ed. Littlehales, *E.E.T.S.*, O.S. cv (1895).

ll. 2–4. *That All, which alwayes is All every where*, &c. These lines are repeated, with only a change of tense, from 'The Progress of the Soul' (stanza VIII).

Cf. Aquinas, *S.T.* Iª Pars, Q. viii, Art. ii: 'Utrum Deus sit ubique?', which concludes 'Et ideo sicut anima est tota in qualibet parte corporis, ita Deus totus est in omnibus et singulis.'

l. 6. *In prison, in thy wombe.* The metaphor is natural—prison is normally interpreted allegorically as the world or the body; but medieval allegorists and poets celebrated the womb of Mary as 'palace', 'bower', and 'garden enclosed'.

ll. 9–10. *Ere by the spheares time was created* &c. Plato (*Timaeus*, 38ᵇ) says 'Time came into being with the heavens'; Aristotle (*Physics* iv. 223ᵇ) says 'Time is thought to be the movement of the sphere'. 'Begotten' (Group III, *W*) implies a world that 'comes into being' of itself; 'created' (Groups I, II, *1633*) is more suitable in a Christian context.

Cf. Ecclus. xxiv. 9, applied to the Blessed Virgin in her Office: 'Fro þe biginnyng & bifore worldis, y was maad; & y schal not ende vn-to world þat is to come; & in hooli wonyng y seruede bifore him' (*Prymer*, p. 21). On 'thy Sonne and Brother' Grierson cites Augustine: 'Maria ergo faciens voluntatem Dei, corporaliter Christi tantummodo mater est, spiritualiter autem et soror et mater' (Migne, *P.L.* xl. 399).

l. 12. *Thy Makers maker, and thy Fathers mother.* Cf. 'Þou brouȝtest forþ þe makere of þe world þat made þee' and 'Seynt marie . . . modir & douȝter of þe king of kingis' (*Prymer*, pp. 6 and 5). These paradoxes are familiar in medieval poetry.

l. 14. *Immensity cloysterd in thy deare wombe.* Cf.

> Quem terra, pontus, sidera
> Colunt, adorant, praedicant,
> Trinam regentem machinam
> Claustrum Mariae bajulat.

The English rendering of this Matins Hymn for feasts of the Blessed Virgin begins 'The cloistre of marie beriþ him whom þe erþe, watris & heuenes worschipen . . .' (*Prymer*, p. 2). Many medieval poets echo, as does Donne, the words of the *Prymer*; cf. 'Withinne the cloistre blisful of thy sydis' (Chaucer, *Prologue to the Second Nun's Tale*).

'Little roome' may echo Marlowe's adaptation of a Christian paradox: 'Infinite riches in a little room' (Marlowe, *Jew of Malta*, 1. i. 72).

3. Nativitie (*page 3*)

l. 8. *Th'effect of Herods jealous generall doome.* 'Effects' (*1633*) is supported by *D, H 49, SP* only and I have abandoned it on this ground. 'Zealous' (Group II) is plainly a mis-reading for 'jealous'; but 'dire and generall' (Group III, *W*) looks like an early reading which the poet has improved: for the merely dyslogistic 'dire', a motivating adjective has been substituted.

Grierson argued that 'effect' was the right reading since 'All the effects of Herod's doom were not prevented, but the one aimed at, the death of Christ, was'. But the infant Christ was saved by Joseph's warning dream, not by the journeys of the star and the Magi. 'Prevent' is used in its more common early sense of 'anticipate'. The 'effect' of Herod's doom is the Massacre of the Innocents, which the journey of the Wise Men just preceded. Cf. 'After he received the oblations of the kings . . . the next thing wherein he would be glorified, was that *Holocaust* and *Hecatombe* of the innocent children, martyrd for his name' (*Pseudo-Martyr*, p. 5).

l. 10. *Which fils all place, yet none holds him.* Cf. 'Holi modir of god, þat worþili disseruedist to conseyue him þat al þe world myȝte not holde!' and 'Blessid modir, . . . in whos wombe was closid, he þat is hiȝeste in alle craftis, & holdiþ þe world in his fist' (*Prymer*, pp. 6 and 2). Donne appears also, as in the preceding sonnet, to have in mind the discussion in Aquinas, *S. T.*, Iᵃ Pars, Q. viii. See Art. i. 2 and Art. ii. Conclusio: 'Deus non continetur a rebus, sed magis continet res. . . . Deus est in rebus, sicut continens res'; and 'Deus omnem locum replet, non sicut corpus . . . sed per hoc . . . quod dat esse omnibus locatis quae replent omnia loca.'

4. Temple (*page 3*)

l. 3. *Blowing, yea blowing out.* The Child Jesus by 'both hearing them and asking them questions' stimulated and baffled the sparks of reason in the Doctors. For 'asking them questions' earlier versions from Tindale to Geneva have 'posyng them'. *O.E.D.* cites Donne ('Satire IV', l. 20) as its earliest example of 'pose' in the sense of 'puzzle' or 'non-plus', which seems the meaning intended by 'blowing out' the 'sparks of wit'.

l. 5. *The Word but lately could not speake.* Donne refers this famous quibble 'Verbum Infans' to St. Bernard; see *Sermons*, vi. 184.

l. 9. *His Godhead was not soule to his manhood.* That Christ had no human soul was an early heresy which is explicitly rejected in the *Quicunque Vult*: 'Our Lord Jesus Christ . . . is Perfect God and perfect man: of a reasonable soul and human flesh subsisting.'

l. 11. *But as for one which hath a long taske, 'tis good.* I have retained the reading of *1633*, supported by Group I, although the line is clumsy, and it is contrary to Donne's normal practice to have an extra unelidable syllable. Group II supports Group I, except that *TCD, N* read 'hath long taskes'; *TCC, A 18* read 'hath long task'. The reading of *TCC, A 18* suggests that the agreement of *TCD, N* with Group III and *W* is only coincidence, 'long taskes' in *TCD, N* having arisen from a correction of an error in the archetype—the omission of the article—which *TCC, A 18* has reproduced.

'Long taskes' (Group III, *W*) may well have stood in Donne's first version, if he had in mind 'I must work the works of him that sent me' (John ix. 4); but it is so ugly followed by 'thinks', or even by ''tis' that he may well have preferred an uneven line to one so 'clogged and impeded by clusters of consonants'. There has obviously been revision in the line, but the earlier reading is in doubt. *B* reads 'But as one that hath long tasks thinks good', which is a syllable short. *S, S 96, W* insert 'to' before 'one', which gives no sense. *Dob* achieves a possible if limping line: 'but as one wch hath long taskes thinkes it good'. *Lut, O'F* read 'But as some one . . .', which gives good sense and metre. Although this may be only an ingenious improvement of *B*'s line, it may be the true early reading. The curious 'to' in *S, S 96, W* could have arisen from a misreading of 'sō', the suspension mark being taken as the crossbar of a 't'.

5. Crucifying (*page 4*)

l. 3. *weake spirits*: the 'poor in spirit', the 'weak things of the world' which God has chosen 'to confound the things which are mighty' (1 Cor. i. 27). Donne may have felt that 'meeke' was too obvious an antithesis to 'ambitious' and altered it to make the contrast between the Christian and worldly assessments of weakness and strength.

l. 8. *Measuring selfe-lifes infinity to'a span.* Cf. Ps. xxxix. 6: 'Behold, thou hast made my days as it were a span long' (*B.C.P.*). 'Measuring to' probably means 'reducing to': the infinity of life itself was reduced to the length of a human life—indeed to less, for Christ did not live out the allotted span. It may be used, however, as it is today, to express precision in measurement. The point is then the absurdity of measuring the hours, nay minutes, of life itself.

l. 12. *Now thou art lifted up, draw mee to thee.* Cf. John xii. 32: 'I, if I be lifted up . . . , will draw all men unto me.'

6. Resurrection (*page 4*)

l. 4. *starv'd*: withered, to balance 'dry' (l. 1); see *O.E.D.*, 'starve', 3.

l. 5. *abled*: endowed with power.

l. 6. *Death, whom thy death slue; nor shall to mee.* This line is a syllable short. Group II, *Lut, O'F* read 'nor shall nowe to me'. There are two similar lines in 'Holy Sonnets' (1633), 12:

> He keepes, and gives mee his deaths conquest

and

> None doth, but all-healing grace and Spirit.

In the first of these 1633, supported by *Lut, O'F* only, reads 'gives to me'; in the second 1633, supported by Group III only, reads 'but thy all-healing'. The three lines need to be considered together. I believe that we must ascribe their irregularity to the poet's intention; and that the agreement of Group II with *Lut, O'F* here, and of 1633 with *Lut, O'F*, and with Group III, on the other two occasions is due to independent patching of an unmetrical line. In each case Group I and *W* agree in a defective line; in each case it is the third foot which is defective; and in each case there is a marked pause within the line, which gives rhythmic compensation for metrical deficiency:

> Death, whom | thy death | slue; | nor shall | to mee
> He keepes | and gives | mee | his deaths | conquest
> None doth, | but all|-heal|ing grace | and Spirit.

There are some examples of similar lines in other poems:

> Know thy | foes: | The foule | Devill, | whom thou
> ('Satire III', l. 33)
> By cur|sed Cains | race | inven|ted be
> ('Progress of the Soul', l. 516).

The line recalls the Vulgate version of Hosea xiii. 14: 'Ero mors tua, o mors' and the Easter Preface in the Book of Common Prayer: 'Who by his death hath destroyed death.'

l. 7. *last death*. Cf. Rev. ii. 11: 'He that overcometh shall not be hurt of the second death.' This is glossed 'quae est gehenna'.

l. 8. *If in thy little booke my name thou'enroule.* Group III and *W* read 'life-booke', which gives a defective line of the type discussed above:

> If in | thy life|-booke | my name | thou'enroule.

It is difficult to see why Donne should have used the form 'life-booke', when 'Book of Life' was established by translators from Wyclif onwards.

It is even more difficult to suggest why he speaks of a 'little booke'. The 'little book' of Rev. x. 1–2 is interpreted as the Scriptures, which Christ, the Angel, opens to men's understandings and which the seer eats. It is plainly not the 'Book of Life' in which names are 'enrolled'. Grierson suggests that Donne had in mind the text 'Strait is the gate and narrow is the way, which leadeth unto life, and few there be that find it' (Matt. vii. 14); adding 'The grimmer aspects of the Christian creed were always in Donne's mind'. He quotes in support of this statement four lines from the Elegy on Mrs. Bulstrode. In Funeral Poems, as in Verse-Letters, Donne often takes up extravagant positions; but in his sermons he is very far from suggesting that only a few will be saved; see *Sermons*, vi. 76, viii. 370, and iv. 74. In this last, he declares that Christ used 'Metaphors of narrow wayes, and strait gates, not to make any man suspect an impossibility of entring, but to be the more industrious . . . in seeking it'. Even if he had held a grimmer view earlier in his life, it is most unlikely that he would have implied it in this joyful sonnet, where he has in mind the Book of Revelation, which insists on the multitude of the redeemed.

If 'little' is the right final reading, I can only suggest it is used vaguely with some such colour as 'thy own' or 'thy dear' book. But the spelling in Group II, 'litle', suggests the possibility that 'little' may be a misreading of 'title'. 'Title-book', a compound formed on the analogy of 'title-deed', would be the book containing our title, or claim to heaven, with a pun on the other sense of the word, 'name'. I do not feel sufficient confidence in this conjecture to emend a reading in which Groups I and II support *1633*, and put it forward only as a possible explanation of a difficulty I cannot otherwise explain.

l. 9. *Flesh in that long sleep is not putrified.* 'That long sleep' (*1633*) has the support of Group II. Group III and *W* read 'that last longe sleepe', which, with the obvious contraction 'sleep's', was probably the original version of the line. Group I reads 'that sleep' ('that steep'd', *H 49*), which may have arisen from the archetype of the group mistaking a deletion of 'last' for a deletion of 'last long'.

Donne means that putrefaction is not the ultimate state of the body. It is made that 'of which it was' by returning to dust; but it is also made 'that for which it was', since '*Adam* was made to enjoy an immortality in his body; He induced death upon himselfe: And then . . . man having induced and created death, by sin, God takes death, and makes it a means of the glorifying of his body, in heaven' (*Sermons*, vi. 72).

l. 11. *glorified.* 'Puryfy'd' (Group III, *W*) rather unpleasingly echoes the earlier 'putrified'; 'glorified' both avoids this assonance and is itself a much stronger word.

l. 12. *sinnes sleep, and deaths*. I have adopted 'deaths' from Group II and *W*. Groups I and III support *1633*; but the support of *W* turns the scale in favour of the Group II reading.

Ascention (*page 5*)

ll. 7–8. *Nor doth hee by ascending, show alone*, &c. Cf. Col. ii. 15: 'And having spoiled principalities and powers, he made a shew of them openly, triumphing over them in it' (Vulgate: 'palam triumphans illos in semetipso'). Christ does not triumph, or make display of himself, alone; he enters heaven at the head of his army. But he is not only first, as leader; he is also the first that ever passed this way.

ll. 9–10. *O strong Ramme*, &c. Cf. Mic. ii. 13: 'The breaker is come up before them: they have broken up, and have passed through the gate . . . and their king shall pass before them, and the Lord on the head of them.' Cf. also *Sermons*, iv. 357, where Donne applies this text to the Resurrection. Although the ram in the thicket (Gen. xxii. 13) is interpreted as Christ on the Cross, and the ram is the sacrificial victim elsewhere in the Pentateuch, in other places 'ram' is glossed as 'priest'; see Gloss on Prov. xxx. 31 and Ps. xxviii. 1. Rabanus Maurus (Migne, *P.L.* cxi. 202) explains that rams lead the flock and break down what bars the way. Christ enters Heaven as Victor and Victim, Priest and Offering: the 'strong Ramme,' and the 'mild lambe'.

l. 12. *thine . . . thine*. These readings have been adopted on the authority of Group II and *W*, supported by *Dob, Lut, O'F*. There are four occasions in the *Divine Poems* when Group III reads 'thy' before a vowel and *1633*, with all the other MSS., reads 'thine': 'Holy Sonnets' (1633), 1. 7, 5. 10, 'A Litany', ll. 13, 47. These four examples look like deliberate correction by the poet of what he had come to regard as an unpleasing hiatus. The position is different here; but the reading adopted agrees with what seems to be Donne's later practice.

To E. of D. with six Holy Sonnets (*page 5*)

MSS.: *DC*; *O'F*; *W*; *A 23*.

This sonnet, printed among the Verse-Letters in *1633*, is one of the few poems in the volume which are not extant in the Group I or Group II MSS. Grosart, followed by all subsequent editors, removed it from among the Verse-Letters, and placed it before '*La Corona*'. Grierson rejected Grosart's suggestion that 'E. of D.' was Doncaster, and proposed Richard, third Earl of Dorset. I accept this identification; but, as I believe Dorset was sent the first six of the 'Holy Sonnets' of *1633*, I have moved this sonnet to stand before them. See pp. xlviii–ix.

In 'Satire IV', l. 18, Donne employs the piece of 'natural history' on which this sonnet turns: that the sun generates creatures from the mud of the Nile.

See Pliny, *Nat. Hist.* ix. 84 and Ovid, *Met.* i. 422–9. That nature allows 'Seaven to be born at once' is also related by Pliny. He declares that more than three at a birth is portentous, except in Egypt, where drinking Nile water causes fecundity; and mentions that in Egypt there have been cases of seven infants at one birth (*Nat. Hist.* vii. 3).

Holy Sonnets (1633) (*page 6*)

MSS.: Group I: *C 57*, *D*, *H 49*, *SP*; Group II: *A 18*, *N*, *TCC*, *TCD*; *DC* (1–8 only); Group III: *B*, *Dob*, *S 96* (Sonnets 1–6, 11 and 12 only); *Lut*, *O'F*; *W*.

The twelve 'Holy Sonnets' of *1633* appear in the same order in the MSS. of Group I and Group II. For the order of the sonnets in Group III and *W* and in the second edition of *1635*, see p. xxxix. I give at the foot of each sonnet its number in Grierson's edition, which follows the order of *1635*, as do all editions subsequent to *1635*.

There is one important difference of reading between Groups I and II (3. 7), and here *1633* reads with Group II. Otherwise it follows Group I. The text in *1633* is good and the corrections made are only minor ones. Manuscript readings have been adopted on thirteen occasions: in 3. 6, 3. 14, 6. 10, 9. 14, 12. 14, *1633* has all the groups against it; in 1. 9, 7. 1, 9. 4, it has support from Group I only, and in 12. 9, it has support from *C 57* only; in 3. 4, 12. 4, and 12. 11, I believe the editor has patched what he thought to be a faulty line. In 4. 6, the reading of *W* has been adopted; see note.

As in '*La Corona*' there are interesting differences between the version in Groups I and II and that in Group III and *W*; there is also one striking one between Group III and *W* (11. 10).

For the demonstration that these twelve sonnets form a sequence, the reasons for dating them in the first part of 1609, and for a discussion of their dependence upon the meditation, see pp. xxxvii–lv.

Title: In Group II, where these sonnets follow '*La Corona*', they have no title: In Group I, where they also follow '*La Corona*', the heading 'Holy Sonnets' is put above '*La Corona*' and this set is untitled, except in *C 57* which heads them 'Sonnetts. Holy'. The editor of *1633*, following his Group I MS., kept the heading 'Holy Sonnets' before '*La Corona*', but repeated it before the second set. *W* has its nineteen sonnets before '*La Corona*'; its heading 'Holy Sonnets' may therefore refer to both groups. The Group III title 'Divine Meditations' is a much better description of the poems than the vague 'Holy Sonnets'; but the latter is well established and must remain. I have, however, added beneath it the Group III title, partly to distinguish these twelve sonnets and the four added to them in *1635* from the three which are found in *W* alone, which are not meditations.

1. As due by many titles I resigne (*page 6*)

l. 5. *thy sonne, made with thy selfe to shine.* Cf. Matt. xiii. 43: 'Then shall the righteous shine forth as the sun in the kingdom of their Father.'

l. 9. *usurpe in.* 'Usurpe on' (Group I, *1633*) is the more common phrase; but it is used normally with the person whose rights are 'usurped on'. It seems likely that Group I substituted the more familiar preposition after 'usurp', and *1633* followed its MS. in a minor uncorrected error.

ll. 13–14. *That thou lov'st mankind well, yet wilt not chuse me,*
  And Satan hates mee, yet is loth to lose mee.

The contraction 'wilt'not' (l. 13) in *1633* has no manuscript support. It gives a decasyllabic line with emphatic stress on 'mankind' and 'me':

That thou | lov'st man|kind well, | yet wilt'not | chuse me.

In l. 14 there are eleven syllables and the stress falls on 'hates' and 'lose':

And Sat|an hates | mee, yet | is loth | to lose mee.

This type of rhyme is discussed by Mr. Arnold Stein in 'Donne and the Couplet' (*P.M.L.A.* lvii, 1942), and by Dr. Percy Simpson in 'The Rhyming of Stressed with Unstressed Syllables in Elizabethan Verse' (*M.L.R.* xxxviii, 1943). Two types of licence must be distinguished. In rhyming two ten-syllabled lines, the stress may be inverted in the final foot of one, thus causing a stressed and an unstressed syllable to rhyme, e.g. 'Holy Sonnets' (1633), 12. 4–5 where 'conquest' rhymes with 'hath blest'. Or, as here, a masculine rhyme may be matched with the second syllable of a feminine rhyme, a tenth with an eleventh syllable. Cf. 'Holy Sonnets' (1633), 2. 6–7, where 'delivered from prison' rhymes with 'to execution' but not 'Holy Sonnets' (1633), 12. 9 and 11, where 'yet' rhymes with 'Spirit', pronounced as usual as a mono-syllable. Dr. Simpson collected examples of this second more unusual type of rhyme from Peele's *Arraignment of Paris*, Chapman's *Shadow of Night*, and from Jonson. But he stated that he found no examples in Shakespeare and Marlowe, and it is notable that he found only seven in the whole of Jonson. This suggests that the most sensitive metrists would either refuse this licence or use it sparingly—a suggestion confirmed by the fact, pointed out to me by Dr. Paul Maas, that there is an example in Shakespeare, but in Quince's play:

  Through which the lovers, Pyramus and Thisby
  Did whisper often very secretly.

Acceptance of the contraction 'wilt'not' gives a stress that gives better sense and Donne is fond of rhyming on the first personal pronouns. But the eye and ear are haunted by the true feminine rhyme 'chuse me' and 'lose mee'. On consideration I now reject the contraction; see supplementary notes, p. 152.

3. This is my playes last scene, here heavens appoint (*page 7*)

l. 4. *last point.* Although the reading I have adopted from Groups I and II and *W* gives a defective line, it is difficult to believe that these three good, independent witnesses are all in error. It is easier to believe that a defective line was patched in the obvious way in the archetype of Group III and in *1633*. There is a parallel in 'A Nocturnal' (l. 12):

$$\text{For I} \mid \text{am ev|ery dead} \mid \text{thing.}$$

(Donne, like other Elizabethan poets, treats 'every' as a dissyllable. It is hardly ever contracted in printing, which points to the contraction being an accepted one.) There is possibly another parallel in 'Holy Sonnets' (1633), 10. 9; see note. But even without parallels, the textual authority for 'last' is too strong to be rejected; and the crescendo of 'last . . . last . . . last . . . last . . . last point' is so powerful that it is impossible for the sake of metrical regularity to prefer the less authoritative and tamer 'latest'.

l. 7. *But my'ever-waking part shall see that face.* This is the only occasion in the *Divine Poems* on which Group II differs substantially from Group I. For a discussion of the two readings, see p. xlv.

l. 13. *Impute me righteous.* 'Righteous' could and still can be pronounced as a dissyllable or a trisyllable (*O.E.D.* and Fowler, *Modern English Usage*).

Although purged of its actual sins by penitence, the soul is not righteous—it bears the 'imputed guilt' of Adam; it can only be 'imputed righteous' by the merit of Christ. Cf. Article XI and *Paradise Lost*, iii. 290–4, where Milton sets out this distinctively Protestant doctrine.

l. 14. In *The Second Anniversary* (l. 214), Donne calls death the soul's 'third birth', adding 'Creation gave her one, a second, grace'. The final line of the sonnet recalls the renunciations which precede the administration of baptism in the Book of Common Prayer.

4. At the round earths imagin'd corners, blow (*page 8*)

l. 1. *the round earths imagin'd corners.* Cf. Rev. vii. 1: 'I saw four angels standing on the four corners of the earth.'

ll. 2–4. See pp. xliv–xlv for discussion of the implication of these lines.

l. 6. *dearth.* Grierson, followed by later editors, adopted this reading from *W*, saying: 'This reading . . . is surely right notwithstanding the consensus of editions and other MSS. in reading "death". The poet is enumerating various modes in which death comes; death itself cannot be one of these.' The choice of the right reading is not so simple. The argument from logic falls to the ground on reference to the Book of Revelation, where the Fourth Horseman

Death, has power 'to kill with sword, and with hunger, and with death, and with the beasts of the field' (Rev. vi. 8). The four plagues here are those of Ezek. xiv. 21: 'The sword, and the famine, and the noisome beast, and the pestilence'; and the Revised Version gives 'pestilence' as an alternative translation of θάνατος in Rev. vi. 8. In related passages (Jer. xv. 2 and Rev. xviii. 8) 'death' is also used for 'pestilence'. We cannot dismiss 'death' as obviously wrong in this Apocalyptic sonnet; and it is defensible on aesthetic grounds. Donne is, as often, cataloguing by the enumeration of opposites. First come those who have died suddenly, in multitudes—by war and pestilence; then those who have died one by one—by natural decay. After these contrasted pairs, come those destroyed by the will of others—'them that were slain for the word of God' (Rev. vi. 9); and those slain by their own will—the suicides. Then come those cut off by the deliberate processes of law, and those slain by chance. 'Dearth' comes more tamely as war's partner. Although multitudes die by Famine, it is a slow process. The 'vehemence, the violence, the impetuousnesse' of Pestilence (see *Sermons*, iv. 50) link it better with war.

In spite of these arguments, and its overwhelming textual authority, I have, though with misgivings, rejected 'death' on two grounds. First, the use of 'death' in a particular sense in l. 6, when it is used in its general sense in ll. 3 and 8, is very awkward. The second and more weighty argument is that I have found no parallel, outside the Bible, for the use of 'death', unqualified by an adjective, for 'pestilence'. The textual justification for reading 'dearth' is the ease with which it could be misread as 'death'. It is also possible to give a hypothetical explanation of how *W* might alone present the true reading. This poem appears not to have been revised. It is therefore possible that a slip of the pen or a badly written word in Donne's holograph remained uncorrected and was reproduced in the three independent manuscript groups; while, in the copy he wrote out for Woodward, he wrote the word he intended, 'dearth'.

l. 8. *deaths woe*: the return of the body to dust. See the discussion of the text 'We shall not all sleep . . .' (1 Cor. xvi. 51) in *Sermons*, iv. 74–76.

ll. 13–14. True repentance is a guarantee that the general pardon purchased by Christ's blood is sealed to a man individually.

5. If poysonous mineralls, and if that tree (*page 8*)

This sonnet has no *compositio loci*. The torments of the damned are usually handled at length in exercises of the kind which Donne is drawing upon.

ll. 9–10.   *But who am I, that dare dispute with thee?*
                   O God, Oh! of thine onely worthy blood . . .

I have retained the punctuation of *1633*, which has the support of Groups I and II, *Dob, S 96*. Although *B* has no stop at the end of l. 9, it agrees with

Dob, S 96 in having a comma only after 'God'. The punctuation of *Lut, O'F*, who put a point of interrogation after 'God', is possibly a correction of the error in *B*: the necessary question mark has been supplied, but in the wrong place. In view of the disagreement in pointing in Group III, the agreement of *Lut, O'F* with *W* has no significance. Grierson rejected *1633* for *W*; I have preferred *1633*, which follows Groups I and II. It gives, in my judgement, a finer rhythm. It throws the stress firmly on 'I' and 'thee', and makes a pause before the prayer which the question introduces.

ll. 13–14. *That thou remember them, some claime as debt*, &c. The reading of Group III is probably due to an error in the archetype, arising from the copyist carrying too many words in his head, and substituting the obvious 'remember them no more' for 'remember them, some claime'. Cf. 'As much as *David* stands in feare of this Judge, he must intreat this Judge, to remember his sinnes; Remember them, O Lord, for els they will not fall into my pardon' (*Sermons*, v. 320–1). That God will 'forget' sins has plenty of Scriptural warrant; cf. Jer. xxxi. 34: 'I will remember their sin no more.' Donne, in the same sermon says 'God himselfe, if I have repented to day, knowes not the sins that I did yesterday' (*Sermons*, v. 319); and Herbert says of repented sin that 'men's affections and words must turne, and forbear to speak of that, which even God himself hath forgotten' (*Works*, p. 288).

6. Death be not proud, though some have called thee (*page 9*)

In Dyce's copy of *1633* (Dyce Collection D 25 D 15), he has written by this sonnet: 'When I was preparing my *Specimens of English Sonnets*, Wordsworth wrote to me to request that I would not overlook this one, which he thought very fine.'

l. 1. *Death be not proud.* These words also open an Elegy on Mrs. Bulstrode, which is almost certainly not by Donne (Grierson, i. 422). For the bearing of this on the dating of the 'Holy Sonnets', see pp. xlvii–xlviii.

l. 7. *soonest our best men with thee doe goe.* The reference may be to the proverbial saying that the good die young, or to the death-bed of a righteous man; cf. 'Valediction: forbidding mourning':

> As virtuous men passe mildly 'away,
> And whisper to their soules, to goe.

l. 8. *soules deliverie.* Death is both the soul's birth, and its 'gaol-delivery'.

ll. 12–13. *better . . . wake.* 'Easyer' and 'live', the readings of Group III and *W*, stood, I believe, in Donne's first version. 'Easyer' merely means more pleasantly: 'better' gives us a hyperbole. The sleep of drugs is heavy and long; death's is short. 'Wake' gives a better antithesis to 'sleepe' than 'live' does.

l. 14. *And death shall be no more, Death thou shalt die.* I have restored the light pointing of this line in *1633*. It is supported by Group I, *TCC*, *A 18*, *W*. Grierson's 'no more; death, thou shalt die' has support from *TCD*, Group III. All the MSS. agree in giving the second 'death' a capital.

7. Spit in my face yee Jewes, and pierce my side (*page 9*)

Sonnets 7–11 are not found in the Group III MSS., except for *Lut* and its dependent *O'F*. Collation leaves no doubt that *Lut* took them from a Group II MS.; there is, therefore, no Group III text of these sonnets. There are, however, a few readings in *W* which may represent an earlier stage of the text than that represented in Groups I and II.

l. 5. *satisfied*: atoned for; see *O.E.D.*, 'satisfy', 2a.

l. 8. *Crucifie him daily.* Cf. Heb. vi. 6: 'They crucify to themselves the Son of God afresh, and put him to an open shame.'

l. 12. *supplant.* After Jacob had covered his neck and hands with the skin of goats to gain his father's blessing, Esau said 'Is he not rightly named Jacob? for he hath supplanted me these two times' ('supplantavit', Vulgate; 'hath deceived', Geneva); see Gen. xxvii. 36.

8. Why are wee by all creatures waited on (*page 10*)

l. 1. *Why are wee.* 'Why ame I' (*W*) is a more vivid opening, and is consistent with the use of the singular pronoun down to l. 10. The change to the plural may have been made, in order that the transition to the plural in l. 11 should seem less abrupt.

l. 4. *Simple, and further from corruption.* Group II, followed by *Lut*, *O'F*, reads 'Simpler', an error caused by the attraction of the comparative 'more pure' in the previous line.

Man, being compounded of the four elements, is mixed, not simple, and therefore more liable to corruption, which arises from inequality of mixture. But although the elements are 'simple', they have not absolute purity and incorruptibility, which are the properties of spirit alone.

l. 9. *Weaker I am, woe's mee, and worse then you.* With the contraction 'woe's mee', this is a decasyllabic line. The finer line in *W*, 'Alas I'ame weaker, wo'is me . . .' has an extra weak syllable in the third foot. As in the first line, one regrets the change to the final reading.

l. 11. *But wonder at a greater wonder.* The second 'wonder' is omitted in *1635*, perhaps in order to regularize the line, though the omission leaves it very lame. As it stands the line is clumsy:

$$\times \quad / \quad \overset{\times}{\frown} \quad \times \quad / \quad \times \quad / \quad \times \quad / \quad \times \quad /$$
But won|der at a great|er won|der, for | to us.

9. What if this present were the worlds last night (*page 10*)

l. 2. *Marke. W* reads 'Looke', which could at this period be used transitively; see *O.E.D.*, 'look', v. 6a.

l. 5. *amasing*: terrifying or dreadful. Donne speaks of Christ's tears on the cross in his sermon on the text 'Jesus wept' (*Sermons*, iv. 325).

l. 8. *fierce*. 'Ranck' (*W*) is more idiomatic. 'Fierce' accords with St. Luke's account of the trial of Jesus, where all English versions from Tindale (except Rheims, which depends on the Vulgate) have 'They were the more fierce' (Luke xxiii. 5).

l. 9. *my idolatrie*. 'Myne' (*W*) accords with what seems to have been Donne's later practice in avoiding *hiatus*; but Groups I and II support *1633*.

l. 14. *This beauteous forme assures a pitious mind*. Williamson (*M.P.* xxxviii, 1940) attempted a defence of 'assumes', the reading of *1633*. It is, I believe, not worth consideration, in face of the unanimity of the manuscripts.

Donne is addressing his soul, persuading it to be confident on the ground that the beauty of Christ is the guarantee of a compassionate mind. The question whether Christ was physically beautiful was much debated by the Fathers. Some took their stand on Isa. liii. 2: 'He hath no form nor comeliness; ... there is no beauty that we should desire him.' Others argued that Christ's humanity was perfect and must therefore have included physical perfection.

10. Batter my heart, three person'd God; for, you (*page 11*)

For a striking parallel in a sonnet by Ronsard, see supplementary notes, pp. 152–3.

l. 9. *1633* prints

> Yet dearely'I love you'and would be lov'd faine.

This gives a line defective in the final foot:

$$\overset{\times}{\text{Yet}}\ \overset{/}{\text{dear}}|\overset{\times}{\text{ely}}\overset{/}{'I}\ \text{love}\ |\ \overset{\times}{\text{you,}}\ \overset{/}{'\text{and would}}\ |\ \overset{\times}{\text{be}}\ \overset{/}{\text{lov'd}}\ |\ \overset{/}{\text{faine.}}$$

There is a parallel to this in 'Holy Sonnets' (1633), 3. 4; see note, p. 67. Grierson removed the contraction mark in 'lov'd' on the authority of the MSS., and their unanimity in writing 'loved' is impressive. But it seems extremely unlikely that in this forceful and colloquial sonnet Donne would use the poetical and archaic form 'lovèd' when elsewhere he almost invariably uses the contracted form. (The *Concordance* cites thirty-seven lines in which the word occurs; in only one other, in the doubtfully authentic 'Elegy XVII', is it uncontracted.) I have therefore preserved the contraction of *1633*, which accords with Donne's practice, and removed the elision mark before 'and'. This gives a powerful line, in which, characteristically, the metrical stress brings out the syntax: the contrast of the active and passive voice:

× / × ⌢ /   × ×   ×   /   /   /
Yet dear|ely'I love | you, and | would be | lov'd faine.

Cf. '*La Corona*', 3. 11:

× /   × /   × /   / ×   ×   /
That would | have need | to be | pittied | by thee.

11. Wilt thou love God, as he thee! then digest (*page 11*)

l. 4. *his Temple.* Cf. 1 Cor. vi. 19: 'Know ye not that your body is the temple of the Holy Ghost.'

l. 6. *still begetting, (for he ne'er begonne).* The Son is eternally, not temporally begotten.

l. 8. *Coheire to'his glory.* Cf. Rom. viii. 15–17: 'But ye have received the Spirit of adoption. . . . The Spirit itself beareth witness . . . that we are the children of God . . . heirs of God, and joint-heirs with Christ' ('coheredes', Vulgate; 'co-heires', Rheims; 'heyres anexed with', Geneva).

l. 10. *stolne stuffe.* The reading of Group III, 'stolen steede', though unsupported by *W*, is arguably not a copyist's error. 'Stuffe' and 'steede' are not easily read for each other; moreover, 'steede' gives a more apt analogy. Stolen goods, which had been sold, could be recovered by the owner by a writ of restitution, if he had procured the conviction of the thief. But Acts of 1555 and 1588–9 made special provisions in the case of sales of horses in markets; and even if these formalities had been complied with, the owner of a stolen horse (if the horse had been sold within six months of the theft, if claim had been made within the same period, and proof of ownership had been given within forty days of the claim) could buy back his horse by paying to the purchaser the price at which he had bought. See W. S. Holdsworth, *A History of English Law* (1922–45), iv. 522. By the rule of law merchant 'that a sale of goods in market overt passes the property to a purchaser, even though the vendor had no title to them', the owner of 'stolne stuffe' had to buy back his own stolen property; but in the case of the horse, the purchaser had to give it up, if the owner's claim was established and the proper price offered, whereas in the case of other goods he need not. 'Steede' then gives a better parallel with the old Ransom theory of the Atonement, by which Satan had no option but to release the souls for which Christ paid the just price. On the other hand, the word 'steede' is only used once elsewhere by Donne in his poetry—in a mythological context. This is the one example of a reading in Group III which cannot easily be taken as an error made in copying the text in *W*, but points to the text in Group III being independent.

12. Father, part of his double interest (*page 12*)

Donne expounds the theme of this sonnet at length in a sermon on John xiv. 20:

The two Volumes of the Scriptures are justly, and properly called two Testaments, for they are *Testatio Mentis*, The attestation ... of the will and pleasure of God, how it pleased him to be served under the Law, and how in the state of the Gospell. But ... the Testament, that is, The last Will of Christ Jesus, is this speech ... to his Apostles, of which this text is a part. . . . By this Wil then, ... having given them so great a Legacy, as *a place in the kingdome of heaven*, yet he adds a codicill, he gives more, he gives them the evidence by which they should maintain their right to that kingdome, that is, the testimony of the Spirit, *The Comforter, the Holy Ghost*, whom he promises to send to them (*Sermons*, ix. 232).

l. 1. *his double interest*: his two-fold claim.

l. 3. *joynture*: 'the holding of an estate by two or more persons in joint-tenancy' (*O.E.D.*, now obsolete).
    knottie: entangled, or inextricably tied together; and 'full of intellectual difficulties, hard to explain' (*O.E.D.*).

l. 4. See note to '*La Corona*' 6. 6, where this type of line is discussed, and note to ll. 9–14 of this sonnet.

l. 6. *from the worlds beginning slaine*. Cf. Rev. xiii. 8: 'the Lamb slain from the foundation of the world'. All English versions before A.V. have 'from the beginning'.

ll. 7–8. *two Wills, which ... doe*. Only *1633* reads 'doe'. Groups I and II and *W* read 'doth'. It is possible that 'doth' is the old Southern plural; but it seems more likely that it is an uncorrected singular left over from the original reading in Group III:

> and he
> Hath made two Wills; he with the Legacy
> Of his and thy kingdome doth thy Sonnes invest.

I accept here what looks like an editorial correction in *1633*.
    The two Wills are the two Testaments. Both are of force by the death of the Testator; cf. Heb. ix. 15–17.

ll. 9–14. In the last six lines there are three differences of reading which need to be considered together.

l. 9. thy laws	Group III, *W*
those laws	D, H 49, SP, Group II
these laws	C 57, 1633

This is an example of *1633* agreeing with *C 57* against the other Group I MSS.; see pp. lxxiv–lxxv. We may take it that the true Group I reading is the same as Group II's.

l. 11. thy all-healing grace	Group III, *1633*
all-healing grace	Group I, Group II, *W*

It is probable that *1633*'s agreement with Group III is accidental: the editor has patched a defective line in the obvious way. The weight of authority points to the irregularity of the line being due to the poet's intention; see note to 'La Corona', 6. 6.

l. 14. thy last Will	Group III
that last Will	Group I, Group II, *W*
this last Will	*1633*

1633 has here no manuscript support, although there is a possibility that it has taken 'thy' (Group III) as 'thys'.

These three differences of reading would seem to have arisen from the poet's deliberate correction. We can suggest reasons why Donne should have been dissatisfied with the Group III version. First, the word 'thy' occurs far too often in the sestet. Secondly, in the octave the Father is carefully distinguished from the Son, 'thy' being used for the Father and 'his' for the Son. Since in l. 8 Donne speaks of 'his and thy kingdome', it is awkward in the very next line to use 'thy' for the laws which the Son, the maker of both Testaments, has laid down. The omission of 'thy' in l. 11, though it gives a defective line, throws special emphasis on 'all-healing' and makes distinct the reference to the work of the Third Person of the Trinity. The reading 'that', in l. 14, specifying the Testament referred to—Christ's last speech before his death—is stronger than the repetition of 'thy', already used twice in the previous line. In each case, I have adopted the reading of Groups I and II, which in the two last cases is supported by *W*, as the reading most likely to be the poet's final one.

ll. 11–12. *grace and Spirit . . . law and letter*. Cf. John i. 17: 'The law was given by Moses, but grace and truth came by Jesus Christ'; and 2 Cor. iii. 6: 'The letter killeth, but the spirit giveth life.' I do not doubt that the capital of 'Spirit' is right, and that Donne intends a reference to the Holy Spirit, the bequest of Christ in his 'last Will'. 'Spirit' and 'Holy Spirit' are used frequently without an article in the Greek New Testament, a fact which Donne discusses; see *Sermons*, v. 60–61.

l. 13. *Thy lawes abridgement*. Cf. 'Where the Jews had all abridged in *decem verba* . . . the Christian hath all abridged in *duo verba*, into two words, *love God, love thy neighbour*' (*Sermons*, ix. 150).

thy last command. Cf. John xiii. 34: 'A new commandment I give unto you, That ye love one another.'

Holy Sonnets (added in 1635) (*page 12*)

MSS.: Group III: *B, Dob, Lut, O'F, S 96; W*

The resemblances in text and accidents of punctuation between *1635* and *O'F* make it virtually certain that the editor of *1635* took these sonnets from *O'F*; see p. lxxxviii. As elsewhere, *Lut, O'F* differ at times from the other

Group III MSS. On these occasions, the support which *W* gives to *B*, *Dob*, *S 96* points to *Lut*, *O'F*, and consequently *1635*, being in error. I have emended *1635* on this assumption in the following places: 1. 12, 2. 6, 3. 5, 3. 7, 3. 8, 4. 8. I have also corrected *1635* to the reading of the MSS. in 1. 7, 2. 11, 4. 10, and to the reading of *W* in 4. 14.

The order in which the second and third sonnets occur in the MSS. and in *1635* has been reversed. The sonnet which I place second is a general meditation on sinfulness. This should precede the one I have placed third, which considers a particular sin and leads on to the fourth.

I date these sonnets, tentatively, after the preceding set, but before *The First Anniversary*: that is, between the latter half of 1609 and the first half of 1611; see p. l, and note to ll. 5–6 of the second sonnet.

1. Thou hast made me, And shall thy worke decay (*page 12*)

ll. 13–14.   *Thy Grace may wing me to prevent his art*
              And thou like Adamant draw mine iron heart.

'Prevent': frustrate. Satan's art is to make men fall into despair. 'And', used as a conditional conjunction, takes the subjunctive. 'Adamant' implies both steadfastness and an attractive force which is irresistible. Donne comments on the dangers of the doctrine of the 'irresistibility of grace' in a sermon; see *Sermons*, vii. 156.

2. I am a little world made cunningly (*page 13*)

ll. 5–6.   *Tou which beyond that heaven which was most high*
            Have found new sphears, and of new lands can write.

It has been suggested (C. M. Coffin, *John Donne and the New Philosophy*, 1937, p. 186) that the reference is to the 'new lands' of the moon, as seen through Galileo's telescope. If this is so, the sonnet cannot have been written earlier than 1610, the year in which Galileo's *Sidereus Nuncius* was published at Venice. It came into Donne's hands in the same year, since he refers in *Ignatius His Conclave* (entered in the Stationers' Register, January 1610–11) to Galileo's having 'instructed himselfe of all the hills, woods, and Cities in the new world, the *Moone*' (Healy, *Ignatius*, p. 81). The finding of 'new sphears' 'beyond that heaven which was most high' may be a reference to the newly revealed immensity, and possibly to the infinity, of the universe.

But a precise meaning can be given to these words. The original outermost heaven was the eighth sphere, the sphere of the fixed stars. Ptolemy had added a ninth, the Primum Mobile, to account for the two motions of the eighth sphere, and Alphonsus of Castile had added a tenth, to account for a third motion. Copernicus observed a 'fourth motion'; and those who rejected his hypothesis of a heliocentric universe explained this fourth motion by postulating an eleventh sphere. This theory can be found set out at length by the Jesuit mathematician Clavius, in his revision of his Commentary on

Sacrobosco's *De Sphaera* published in 1607. It is referred to as common knowledge by Purchas; see *Purchas his Pilgrimage* (2nd edn., 1614), p. 10.

This interpretation makes it a little doubtful whether by 'new lands' Donne can be referring to Galileo's discoveries, which powerfully supported the Copernican hypothesis and made such attempts to 'save appearances' unnecessary. He may be referring to astronomers of the old and new schools— those who find 'new sphears' and those who find 'new lands'; but I think it is more likely that he is calling on discoverers generally: astronomers who find new spheres and explorers who find new lands.

ll. 9–10. *Or wash it*, &c. Cf. the promise to Noah (Gen. ix. 9–17), and the belief derived from 2 Pet. iii (for which the Fathers found much support in classical writers) that the world would end by fire.

l. 11. *have burnt*. *Lut*, *O'F* read 'hath burnt'. *1635*'s omission of the auxiliary was perhaps to correct what seemed a false concord in *O'F*.

l. 13. *a fiery zeale*. Cf. Ps. lxix. 9: 'The zeal of thine house hath eaten me up.' As often, Donne abandons an extended parallel for a contrast. The fires of lust and envy, unlike earthly fires, have not purged, but made him 'fouler'. The fire he prays for, unlike the fire which will destroy the world, will 'in eating heale'.

3. O might those sighes and teares returne againe (*page 13*)

l. 6. *rent*: obsolete infinitive, derived from past participle, of 'rend'.

l. 7. *That sufferance was my sinne, now I repent*; *1635*, agreeing with *O'F*, reads 'sinne I now repent,'. *Lut*, *S 96* have the same reading, except that they omit the comma. *B* reads 'syn now I repent': *Dob* has 'synne, nowe I repent': and *W* 'sin, now I repent;'. I have adopted the order of the words in *B*. *Dob*, *W*, because *B*, in spite of its errors, seems often near the root of the Group III tradition, and it here agrees with *W*. I have adopted the punctuation of *W* because I believe it gives the sense intended and that Grierson's interpretation of the line is right against Williamson's defence of *1635*. Williamson argued that the line in *1635* should be interpreted as 'That suffering was the sin which I am now repenting of' (*M.P.* xxxviii, 1940). But it would have been more natural for Donne to have used the present tense if this had been his meaning: 'That old suffering *is* the sin which I now, at this moment, bewail.' The contrast in the line is between past and present, his 'unholy' and his 'holy' discontent. '*That* suffering in the past was sin: *now* I am engaged in a good work, repentance—but I still suffer.'

l. 8. *Because*. *1635*, again following *Lut*, *O'F*, reads 'Cause'. There is no other example in the *Concordance* of Donne's using this abbreviation. I have no doubt that 'Because' is right, and that this is an example of *Lut*'s being edited for publication. Since the final syllable of 'suffer', as pronounced, can be elided, there is no irregularity in the line, which should be read with the stress on the contrasted auxiliaries:

$$\times \quad / \quad \times \quad / \quad / \quad / \quad / \quad / \quad \times \quad /$$
Because | I did | suffer'I | must suff|er paine.

l. 9. *hydroptique*. The more the dropsical man drinks the more he thirsts.
night-scouting: skulking by night.

l. 10. *itchy*: having an uneasy desire or hankering: the 'lecher' is forever unsatisfied.
selfe-tickling proud. The proud man will owe his pleasure to nobody but himself.

4. If faithfull soules be alike glorifi'd (*page 14*)

This sonnet rests on the distinctions drawn by the Schoolmen between the mode of knowing of angels and the modes by which men know; see Aquinas, *S. T.*, Iᵃ Pars, Qq. liv–lviii. Angels do not apprehend by means of images, nor do they need to reason from inferences; they know by immediate intuition. Donne begins by wondering whether souls out of the body will know as angels do; but, at the close, by a characteristic twist he remembers 'Solus Deus cogitationes cordium cognoscere potest.'

l. 10. *vile blasphemous Conjurers*. *1635* misprints 'stile'. Donne used both 'vile' and 'vild'; but 'vile' is better here, since 'vild' gives an awkward collocation of consonants.
Like Milton, Donne accents 'blasphemous' on the second syllable. 'Conjurers' conjure spirits by employing words of power, such as the Sacred Name.

l. 14. *Thy true griefe, for he put it in my breast*. I follow Grierson in adopting the reading of *W*. Group III and *1635* read 'Thy griefe for he put it into my (thy *B, S 96*) breast'. It seems likely that the archetype of Group III omitted 'true' in error, and that this was patched by the alteration of 'in' to 'into'.

Holy Sonnets (from the Westmoreland MS.) (*page 14*)

These sonnets are printed from the MS. Contractions are expanded, and the writer's usage with *i* and *j*, *u* and *v* has been modernized. Woodward uses the capital forms of initial *L* and *S* far more often than he can have intended a capital. Since it would be absurd to print 'feare Least' and 'or Like', but inconsistent not to do so if one printed 'my Love' or 'make Love', in the following lines, I have reproduced his capital *L* and *S* only at the beginning of a line.

I would suggest that the reason why these sonnets did not circulate, and so did not come to the notice of the seventeenth-century editors of Donne, was that they were written after his ordination, when he was anxious not to be thought of as a versifier. The verses which he wrote on the Marquis of Hamilton in 1625 provoked the comment from John Chamberlain: 'though they be reasonable wittie and well don yet I could wish a man of his yeares and place to geve over versifieng.' Chamberlain's earlier comment on hearing that Donne had been made Dean of St. Paul's suggests that Donne's decision to 'inter his Muse' on his ordination would be approved by serious persons: 'yf Ben Johnson might be made deane of Westminster, that place, Paules, and Christchurch, shold be furnished with three very pleasant poetical deanes' (*Letters of John Chamberlain*, ed. N. E. McClure, Philadelphia, 1939, ii. 613 and 407). Of the poems we can date with certainty after Donne's ordination (except for the Hamilton Elegy, written at the direct request of Sir Robert Carr) only the 'Hymn to Christ' and the 'Hymn to God the Father' appear to have circulated freely. Donne may well have felt that there was a difference between the hymns, inspired by solemn occasions—his journey overseas and his grave illness—and these sonnets inspired by what appear to have been casual moods.

1. Since she whome I lovd, hath payd her last debt (*page 14*)

Donne's wife died 15 August 1617, in her thirty-third year, on the seventh day after the birth of her twelfth child. She was buried in the church of St. Clement Danes. The epitaph Donne wrote for her monument (which disappeared when the church was rebuilt) was printed in the 1633 edition of Stow's *Survey* (p. 889); see Milgate, *Anniversaries etc.*, p. 78. The writer of *Lut* included it at the close of his 'Epicedes and Obsequies'.

It seems likely, from its tone of resignation, that the sonnet was not written immediately after Donne's bereavement. He tries to find in the infelicities of his life a proof of God's love, by seeing them as a lover's stratagems. The same idea is handled in 'A Hymn to Christ'. Since the sonnet reads like a first working-out of an idea more powerfully expressed in the hymn, I am inclined to date it just before Donne's journey of May 1619.

The sonnet also recalls a letter which Donne wrote to his mother in 1616, 'comforting her after the death of her Daughter:

God hath seemed to repent, that he allowed any part of your life any earthly happinesse, that he might keep your Soul in continuall exercise, and longing, and assurance, of comming immediately to him. . . . His purpose is, to remove out of your heart, all such love of this world's happinesse, as might put Him out of possession of it. He will have you entirelie (*Tobie Mathew Collection*, pp. 325 and 326).

ll. 1–2.   *Since she whome I lovd, hath payd her last debt*
               To Nature, and to hers, and my good is dead,
The first line is of a type which Donne often employs: speech stress and metrical stress pull against each other. The beauty of the line depends on our giving the metrical stress some weight:

Since she | whome I | lovd, hath | payd her | last debt.

Cf. 'A Valediction: of Weeping':

$$\acute{} \quad \acute{} \quad \times \quad \acute{} \quad \times \quad \acute{} \quad \acute{} \quad \times \quad \times \quad \acute{}$$

Weepe me | not dead, | in thine | armes, but | forbeare.

For possible interpretations of l. 2, see supplementary notes, p. 153.

ll. 4 and 6. Gosse, followed by Grierson and Hayward, misread 'in' as 'on' and 'yᵉ' as 'yʳ'. Both errors were corrected by Bennett.

l. 6. *so streames do shew the head.* Cf. Thomas Twyne, *Phisicke against Fortune*, translation of Petrarch *De Remediis* (1579), f. 57ᵛ: 'All earthly delyghtes, if they were gouerned by discretion, would styre men vp to the heauenly loue, and put them in minde of their first original. For, I pray thee, who euer loued a riuer, and hated the head thereof.'

l. 10. *Dost wooe my soule, for hers offring all thine.* The punctuation in *W* is 'Dost wooe my soule for hers; . . .'. The line apparently presented no difficulty to Grierson and Hayward, but Bennett punctuated as I do. As the line stands in *W*, I can give no sense to 'for'. Repunctuation gives not the meaningless antithesis between 'my soule' and 'hers', but a proper antithesis between 'hers' and 'thine': 'How can I ask for more love, when Thou art my wooer, who in place of *her* love offers me all *thine*.' Throughout the sonnet the stress falls constantly on the personal pronouns. See supplementary notes (p. 154) for another interpretation.

ll. 13–14. I imagine Donne is thinking of the general misfortunes of his life. God has not only removed his 'saint and Angel', fearing that he might love her too much; but has also guarded him against temptation by continual disappointments and mortifications.

2. Show me deare Christ, thy spouse, so bright and cleare (*page 15*)

The interpretation of this sonnet, and its date, are discussed in Appendix C, pp. 121–7.

l. 1. *thy spouse, so bright and cleare.* Cf. Rev. xix. 7–8: 'The marriage of the Lamb is come, and his wife hath made herself ready. And to her was granted that she should be arrayed in fine linen, clean and white ('splendenti et candido', Vulgate; 'pure fyne lynen cloth and shining', Geneva).

l. 2. *What, is it she.* The MS. has no stop after 'What'. I have inserted a comma for Grierson's exclamation mark, since it seems unlikely a scribe would miss an exclamation mark. There is no justification for singling out this 'she' from the other 'she's' of the sonnet by giving it a capital, as Gosse, followed by Grierson and Hayward, did.

'What' is an exclamation of astonishment, introducing a series of rhetorical questions, expecting a negative answer.

l. 8. *On one, on seaven, or on no hill*. The 'one hill' is Mount Moriah, where Solomon built the Temple. There was dispute between the Jews who worshipped there, and the Samaritans, who worshipped on Mount Gerizim; cf. Christ's words to the woman of Samaria: 'The hour cometh, when ye shall neither in this mountain, nor yet at Jerusalem, worship the Father' (John, iv. 21). The Church on seven hills is the Roman Church, and the Church on no hill' is the Genevan; cf. '*The Word of God is not above thee*, says Moses, *nor beyond the Sea*. We need not clime up seven hills, nor wash our selves seven times in a Lake for it' (*Sermons*, iv. 107); and 'Trouble not thy selfe to know the formes and fashions of forraine particular Churches; neither of a Church in the lake, nor a Church upon seven hils' (*Sermons*, v. 251).

ll. 9–10. *Dwells she with us* &c. Two conceptions of the Church are given here in terms of two conceptions of love—the domestic and the romantic. Donne had not much sympathy with the latter; and allusions to medieval romance are very rare in his poetry.

l. 12. *thy mild Dove*. Cf. Song of Sol. v. 2: 'Open to me, my sister, my love, my dove, my undefiled.'

A Litanie (*page 16*)

MSS.: Group I: *C 57, D, H 49, Lec, SP*; Group II: *A 18, N, TCC, TCD; DC*; Group III: *Dob, Lut, O'F, S 96*; *B, O1, (S), (D 17, JC), O2*; Miscellanies: *Hd, HK 2, S 962*.

The text in *1633*, taken from its Group I MS., is extremely good, and its punctuation is careful and expressive. Two obvious misprints (ll. 153 and 163) escaped the proof corrector; both occur in the same forme, which exists in a corrected and uncorrected state. Otherwise, I have abandoned *1633* five times only: ll. 61, 100, 109, 122, and 191.

Groups I and II preserve fundamentally the same text. *DC* has a good Group II text, avoiding some errors common to *TCC* and *TCD. S* and *JC* (with its copy *D 17*) have the text of Group I in this poem. (*S*, contrary to its usual practice, reproduces it with few errors: *JC* reproduces it very badly, with some ludicrous readings.) I have bracketed these *MSS*. to indicate that they do not read with their usual group. *B* and *O2* have fair Group III texts, but the text in *O1* is very poor. The three miscellanies have the characteristic Group III readings with a great deal of individual error. *Hd* and *HK 2* would seem to have been copied from a manuscript that was defective or illegible.

The number of plausible readings common to the Group III manuscripts suggests they may preserve an earlier version. But, if Donne did revise this poem, his revisions were trivial.

In a long undated letter to Goodyer Donne writes:

Since my imprisonment in my bed, I have made a meditation in verse, which I call a Litany. . . . Amongst ancient annals, I mean some 800 years, I have met two Letanies in Latin verse, which gave me not the reason of my meditations, for in good faith I thought not upon them then, but they give me a defence, if any man; to a Lay man, and a private, impute it as a fault, to take such divine and publique names, to his own little thoughts. The first of these was made by *Ratpertus* a Monk of *Suevia*; and the other by *S. Notker* . . . ; they were both but Monks, and the Letanies poor and barbarous enough; yet Pope *Nicolas* the 5, valued their devotion so much, that he canonized both their Poems, and commanded them for publike service in their Churches: mine is for lesser Chappels, which are my friends. . . . That by which it will deserve best acceptation, is, That neither the Roman Church need call it defective, because it abhors not the particular mention of the blessed Triumphers in heaven; nor the Reformed can discreetly accuse it, of attributing more then a rectified devotion ought to doe (*Letters*, pp. 32–34).

Later in the same letter, Donne refers to 'my Book, of which it is impossible to give you a copy so soon, for it is not much less then 300 pages'. As he goes on 'I have not appointed it upon any person, nor ever purposed to print it', he must be referring to *Biathanatos*, and not to *Pseudo-Martyr*. (*Biathanatos* can be dated after 1607 and before the early part of 1609.) Some phrases from another letter to Goodyer, dated September 1608 (see p. 88), are echoed in 'A Litany'. This suggests that the autumn of 1608 is a possible date for the poem. See supplementary notes, pp. 154–5, for the dating of *Biathanatos* and for the source of Donne's knowledge of the ancient litanies.

Title: Only the Group I MSS. support *1633* in using the definite article. I have adopted the indefinite article from Groups I and III. It is obviously more appropriate and Donne uses it in his letter. I retain the spelling of the edition.

ll. 5–6. *My heart is by dejection, clay*, &c. Melancholy, the cold and dry humour, corresponds to earth. The clay of his heart is red because by sin we 'wound our soule away'. Cf. 'We are made but men . . . and man . . . is but *Adam*: and *Adam* is but earth, but red earth, earth dyed red in bloud, . . . the bloud of our own soules'(*Sermons*, ix. 49). Donne often refers to the notion that 'Adam' means 'red earth', the Hebrew for 'red' being *adom*. This interpretation goes back to Jerome.

l. 8. *vicious tinctures*: 'the adhering but not essential impurities' in metals, which must be purged before the true 'tincture' which will transmute them is projected. See E. H. Duncan, 'Donne's Alchemical Figures' (*E.L.H.* ix, 1942), and note to 'Resurrection', ll. 9–16, p. 95.

l. 15. *crucified againe*. 'Be nailed to my heart, and though by my sins thou art crucified there, leave me not.' Cf. Heb. vi. 6: 'They crucify to themselves the Son of God afresh.'

l. 25. *intend*: intensify. Paradoxically, the tears of repentance do not quench but increase the 'flame'.

l. 26. *this glasse lanthorne, flesh*. B, Dob, S 96 read 'darke lanterne'; but *Lut*, O'F read with Groups I and II and *1633*. The stanza contrasts the impermanence of the body with the eternal sameness of the Spirit. It is only of 'mudde walls', a phrase Donne used in his *Devotions* (Sparrow, p. 109); it has been profaned by the fires of lust and must suffer the storms of sickness in age. Its fragility, not its darkness, needs emphasis. It seems likely that 'darke' is an error and not an early reading, as *Lut* and *O'F* have 'glasse'. I do not believe Donne wrote 'darke' but, as a possible reading, it is recorded.

Cf. 'Epitaph on Himselfe':

> Parents make us earth, and soules dignifie
> Us to be glasse. . . .

The comparison of the body of man to a glass is not unusual in Elizabethan literature; cf. Spenser, *Ruins of Time*, l. 50, and Chapman, *Byron's Tragedy*, v. iv. 37.

'Glasse lanthorne' unites two commonplaces: the body is both a glass vessel, containing the breath of life, and a lantern containing the candle of the soul.

l. 27. *be the same*: be unchanged. The Fire is the flame of the Spirit, which burns on the Altar of his heart; the Priest is his soul, which offers the Sacrifice of a troubled spirit. The prayer is for perseverance.

l. 29. *Bones to Philosophy, but milke to faith*. Donne speaks of the resurrection of the body as 'one of the hardest bones in the body, one of the darkest corners in the mysteries of our Religion' (*Sermons*, vii. 211). What is a hard bone to Philosophy is food to faith. Cf. 'These notions . . . of God, as a Father, as a Son, as a Holy Ghost . . . are . . . so many breasts, by which we may suck such a knowledge of God, as that by it wee may grow up into him' (*Sermons*, iii. 263).

ll. 30–31. *Which, as wise serpents, diversely* &c. Christ praised the wisdom of serpents, and the serpent lifted up is a type of Christ; but the qualities Donne gives his 'wise serpents' are those which belong to the serpent as a type of evil: his 'volubility and lubricity' (Bacon, *Advancement of Learning*, II. xxi. 9), and '*tortuositas serpentis*, The wryness, the knottiness, the entangling of the Serpent' (*Sermons*, i. 178). Tertullian described the serpent as 'tenax ad occupandum, tortuosa ad obligandum, liquida ad elabendum' (Migne, *P.L.*, i. 651; quoted in the Gloss on Gen. iii. 1). Donne's comparison seems, therefore, more ingenious than suitable. The meaning is either that the doctrine contradictorily eludes our grasp and yet involves us in endless complications; or, that the Persons of the Trinity, in our notions, are either too 'distinct'—they slip apart—or too 'undistinguished'—they are 'entangled' together.

l. 33. *power, love, knowledge*. The attribution of Power, Wisdom, and Love (or Goodness) to the Persons of the Trinity goes back to Augustine's *De Trinitate*, where it is based on an analogy with the powers of the mind. Donne's order here, which attributes love to the Son and wisdom to the Holy Ghost, has no theological authority that I can discover, although it is current in the seventeenth century; see Cowley, note to *Davideis* II. But 'distinguish'd undistinct' makes clear that no attribute is confined to a single Person; and 'You'unnumbred three' declares that the Persons are not to be placed in a series. Cf. *Sermons*, iii. 327–8 and i. 199.

ll. 34–35.   *Give mee a such selfe different instinct,*
                  Of these let all mee elemented bee,
I have retained the idiomatic 'a such selfe' (Group III, *1633*). Grierson cites a similar use in 'The Dream': 'after a such fruition'.

The punctuation is questionable. Grierson reads

> Give mee a such selfe different instinct
> Of these; let . . .

He claimed the support of Group I; but only *D*, *SP* support him. *C 57*, *Lec* punctuate as I do. *H 49*, although it has a comma after 'these', has a semi-colon after 'instinct', thus agreeing with *C 57*, *Lec* in separating the lines. (The Group II punctuation is not helpful; it is the only pointing which makes sense of its erroneous reading 'Of thee'.) The fine emphatic line in Group III 'Of all these let all me elemented be', which may be the original version of the line, demands to be read without a pause, and is so punctuated, except in *S 96*. I have corrected *1633* by supplying a comma at the end of l. 34, since it is prone to omit final commas. This punctuation accords best with the MSS.

'As You are distinguished as Power, Love, Knowledge, yet are One God, All-Powerful, All-Loving, All Wise, bestow on me an animating power which likewise differs within itself while remaining one: let my whole soul be composed only of power, knowledge and love, directed towards You.' Cf. *Sermons*, ix. 83.

Stanzas V–XIV. In Cranmer's Litany of 1544, based on the Sarum Litany, the long bead roll of saints was removed and only the headings were kept: 'Saint Mary, mother of God . . . pray for us. All holy angels and archangels . . . pray for us. All holy patriarchs and prophets, apostles, martyrs, confessors and virgins and all the blessed company of heaven, pray for us.' These clauses, retained in 1545, were omitted in the Litany of Edward VI and never restored. Donne adds one category, the Doctors. In the Roman Litany, the clause 'Omnes sancti Pontifices et Confessores' had been followed by 'Omnes sancti Doctores' since at least the thirteenth century. Although Donne follows the Roman use in distinguishing the Doctors from the Confessors, he has not put them in the right place. Wit, which sees a link between Confessors and Virgins, has triumphed over liturgical propriety. Donne has also given his own interpretation to the last invocation, 'Omnes Sancti', which he interprets as meaning the whole Church, triumphant and militant. Cf. a sermon preached on All Saints' Day: 'It is truly a festivall, grounded upon that Article of the Creed, *The Communion of Saints*, and unites in our devout contemplation, the Head of the Church, God himselfe, and those two noble constitutive parts thereof, The Triumphant, and the Militant' (*Sermons*, x. 42). This Scriptural and Protestant use of the word 'saint' is familiar from Charles Wesley's hymn: 'Let saints on earth in concert sing'.

V. *The Virgin Mary. Dob, S 96*, and *HK 2* give this stanza the characteristically Catholic title 'Our Ladie'. Since the other Group III manuscripts read with *1633*, the variant is probably merely scribal.

ll. 38–39. *Whose flesh redeem'd us; That she-Cherubin,* &c. The Virgin opens the gate of Paradise, shut against man by the Cherubim (Gen. iii. 24):

> Evae crimen nobis limen
> Paradisi clauserat,
> Haec, dum credit et obedit,
> Caeli claustra reserat.
>   (Dreves, *Analecta Hymnica*, l. 428.)

Cf. 'Good Friday', l. 31, where the Virgin is called 'Gods partner'. In later life Donne deprecated such language: 'God forbid any should say, That the Virgin *Mary* concurred to our good, so, as *Eve* did to our ruine. . . . The Virgin *Mary* had not the same interest in our salvation, as *Eve* had in our destruction; nothing that she did entred into that treasure, that ransom that redeemed us' (*Sermons*, i. 200).

l. 40. *disseiz'd sinne.* The Virgin can make 'one claime for innocence': she committed no actual sin. This had been generally held since Augustine. She cannot make the further claim of being innocent of original sin. To 'disseize' is 'to put out of actual seizin; to dispossess (a person) of his estates, etc., usually wrongfully, or by force; to oust' (*O.E.D.*). By committing no actual sin the Virgin puts sin out of possession of her, though sin still has the right to her that it has to all Adam's posterity. Donne, agreeing with Aquinas (*S.T.*, Pars 3ᵃ, Q. xxvii, Art. i. 3), wittily denies the Immaculate Conception. The doctrine was not declared to be an Article of Faith until 1854.

l. 45. *titles unto you*: just claims upon you. *O.E.D.* gives no parallel to the use of 'title to' with the person from whom something is claimed.

l. 49. *denizen'd*: admitted, though an alien, to residence and rights of citizenship.

l. 55. *thy Patriarches Desire*: the desire which the Patriarchs felt for the Kingdom of Heaven; cf. Heb. xi. 16: 'They desire a better country, that is an heavenly.'

l. 56. *great Grandfathers, of thy Church.* The Patriarchs are fathers of the Apostles, who are fathers of the Fathers.

l. 57. *More in the cloud, then wee in fire.* The pillar of cloud by day and the pillar of fire by night (Ex. xiii. 21) are glossed as 'Obscuritas veteris testamenti' and 'Lux evangelii'; cf. *Sermons*, ix. 233–4.

l. 58. *clear'd*: enlightened (*O.E.D.* 'clear', *v.* 4) or 'freed from the imputation of guilt' (*O.E.D.* 9). Cf. Heb. xi, with its catalogue of those who 'obtained a good report by faith'. The Patriarchs saw more, and obeyed God better, by the light of Nature than we do by the lights of Law and Grace.

l. 61. *satisfied.* This is the most striking example in the *Divine Poems* of *1633* reading with *C* 57, *Lec* against all other MSS.; see pp. lxxxiv–lxxxv. Their reading, 'sanctified', is explicable as a misreading if the spelling was 'sattisfied'. The first 't' might be read as a 'c', and its cross-bar taken as a suspension over the 'a'. The 'sf' would then be read as 'ff'.

l. 63. *Nor Faith by Reason added, lose her sight.* The Patriarchs are the great types of Faith. Donne may mean that we may dim or extinguish the light of faith by the activity of reason; cf. *Sermons*, iii. 357. It seems more in keeping with the rest of the stanza to take it that he fears that we who have reasonable grounds for faith may, on that account, have a faith less strong. Cf. Sir Thomas Browne, *Religio Medici*, i. 9: 'As we have reason, we owe this faith unto History: they only had the advantage of a bold and noble Faith, who lived before his comming, who upon obscure prophecies and mystical types could raise a belief.'

l. 65. *thy Churches Organs.* Taylor has the same idea: 'God spake by the prophets, transmitting the sound as through an organ pipe, things which themselves often understood not' (*Works*, iv. 336).

l. 66. *That harmony.* Cf. 'On the Translation of the Psalms', ll. 15–16. Christ is the harmony which the Prophets sounded. They foretold his Office as Mediator of both Covenants, reconciling the old law of works and the new law of faith (Rom. iii. 27–31); and they foretold his Person, which united, but did not confound the Natures of God and Man. Cf. *Quicunque Vult*: 'One altogether; not by confusion of substance; but by unity of person.'

l. 70. *In rythmique feet.* Cf. 'The style of the Scriptures is a diligent, and an artificial style; and a great part thereof in a musical, in a metrical, in a measured composition, in verse. The greatest mystery of our Religion . . . is conveyed in a Song, in the third chapter of *Habakkuk*' (*Sermons*, ii. 171).

l. 72. *Poëtiquenesse.* There is no other example of the word in *O.E.D.* Donne is speaking of two kinds of 'curiosity': striving to know too much, and being too much delighted in the 'curious' or artful. Cf.

In the way to knowledge there is curiosity too; In seeking such things as man hath no faculty to compass, unrevealed mysteries. . . . In seeking things which . . . appertain not to our profession. . . . It is so, in us, in Church-men, *si Iambos servemus, & metrorum silvam congerimus*, If we be over-vehemently affected or transported with Poetry, or other secular Learning (*Sermons*, iv. 142–3).

l. 74. *ingirt*: the shortened form of the preterite 'ingirded'. The Zodiac, with its twelve signs, encircles the Universe; the apostolic band, in their legendary journeys, encompassed the whole world.

l. 76. *throw downe, and fall*. The Group III readings give an instructive picture of progressive corruption. *B* reads with *1633*; *S 96* has 'throwne downe and fall'; *Dob, Lut, O'F* have 'throwne down do (doth, *Lut, O'F*) fall'. It is clear that *Dob, Lut, O'F* are only making sense of the error which *S 96* has been content to reproduce. The editor of *1635* adopted the *O'F* reading, which is plausible enough, until one sees all the Group III readings.

'Whoever do not derive their light from the Apostles cast down their followers into pits of darkness, even as they fall into them themselves.' Cf. Matt. xv. 14: 'And if the blind lead the blind, both shall fall into the ditch.'

l. 78. *bookes*. 'Workes' (Group III) may be an earlier reading, altered by Donne to avoid ambiguity.

l. 80. *Th'old broad way in applying*. Jeremy Taylor quotes St. Gregory Nazianzen against subtle interpretations of Scripture: 'Thou goest a hard and untrodden path: I go the king's highway, and that in which many have been saved' (*Works*, ix. 656).

decline: bring low, or humble (*O.E.D.*, 'decline', 17).

l. 86. *In Abel dye*. In 'The Progresse of the Soul' (l. 405), Abel and his sheep are 'the first type' of 'Church and kingdomes'. The mystic body of Christ, the Church, is from the beginning of the world; see Peter Lombard on the text 'Initio cognovi de testimoniis tuis' (Migne, *P.L.* cxci. 1121). Donne may have had in mind a passage from Paulinus of Nola, quoted by Taylor in his sermon on 'The Faith and Patience of the Saints' (*Works*, iv. 435–6): 'Ab initio seculorum Christus in omnibus suis patitur . . . in Abel occisus a fratre . . . et multis ac variis martyrum crucibus frequenter occisus' (Migne, *P.L.* lxi. 359). Cf. 'But though all were finished in his Person, he hath a daily passion in his Saints still' (*Sermons*, vi. 220).

l. 92. *A Virgin Squadron of white Confessors*. 'Confessors' is accented on the first syllable. 'Squadron' is appropriate for those who, with the martyrs, were called by Cyprian 'Milites Christi'. Virgins and Confessors share the liturgical colour white, in contrast to the red of martyrs; this gives Donne his conceit.

ll. 98–99. *Tentations martyr us alive*; &c. The comparison of temptations with persecutors is a commonplace; see Rabanus Maurus (Migne, *P.L.* cxi. 89). By adding 'A man is to himselfe a Dioclesian', Donne twists it to mean that we tempt ourselves and are our own worst enemies. Cf. Henry King's phrase 'this homebred tyrranie' ('A Labyrinth').

l. 100. *snowie Nunnery*. The extreme High Anglican Anthony Stafford addresses those 'who have vowed Virginity mentall, and corporall' in words that seem to be taken from this stanza: 'Approach with Comfort, and kneele downe before the Grand White Immaculate *Abbesse* of your snowy *Nunneries*' (*The Femall Glory*, 1635).

ll. 105–6.   *That or thy Church, or I,*
                   Should keep, as they, our first integrity;
Donne has in mind a famous saying of Eusebius, quoted by Hooker in the Preface to *The Laws of Ecclesiastical Polity*, that the Church only remained a pure Virgin as long as the Apostles lived; see Migne, *P.G.* xx. 283. It is awkward to use 'virginity' metaphorically in a stanza in honour of 'virgins' in the literal sense.

l. 109. *Academe*. 'Academie' and 'Academe' had the same accentuation at this period; see Cooper, *Grammatica Linguae Anglicanae* (1685), iii. 9. Since most readers are unaware of this, I have adopted the form which makes the accentuation obvious.

l. 111. *Both bookes of life*. Cf. 'God hath two Books of life; that in the *Revelation* . . . which is an eternall Register of his Elect; and this *Bible*. . . . Our orderly love to the understanding this Book of life, testifies to us that our names are in the other' (Simpson, *Essays*, pp. 6–7). See also *Sermons*, vii. 353–4.

l. 112. *wrought*. This spelling appears in the MSS. as well as in the editions. To alter to 'wrote' suppresses a possible pun: if our names are written in the Book of Life, we are 'made new'.

ll. 116–17.   *Lord let us runne*
                 Meane waies, and call them stars, but not the Sunne.
Donne says briefly here what he says at length in a sermon, in which he refutes the Roman accusation that the Church of England, and Protestants generally, undervalued the Fathers; see *Sermons*, ix. 158–9. 'Let us take the middle course: steering by them, as a mariner steers by the stars, but not taking them as our chief light.'

l. 122. *Pray ceaslesly*. *1633* reads 'Prayes ceaslesly' and Group III 'Ceasleslie prayes'. 'Pray' is cognate with 'hearken'; both verbs should be in the same mood. The readings of *1633* and Group III suggest that while the Church certainly prays, God only possibly listens. 'Whilst' used concessively, as almost equivalent to 'although', takes the subjunctive.

l. 124. *treble*. With a flash of wit, Donne makes us bear the 'treble part'. 'Though the whole Church in heaven and earth pray, and though thou hear their prayers, yet because we on earth, in order to be acceptable, need to suffer and do good as well as to pray, hear this special prayer . . .'.

Stanzas XV–XXII. The tenor of these stanzas resembles that of a letter to
Goodyer of September 1608 (*Letters*, pp. 48–52), and there are some resem-
blances in phrasing. Donne, complaining of his inactivity, says of the 'primi-
tive Monkes' that they 'were excusable in their retirings', for 'they ought
the world no more since they consumed none of her sweetnesse'; cf. 'this
worlds sweet' (stanza XV). He goes on

if I were able to husband all my time so thriftily, as not onely not to wound my
soul [cf. stanza XVI] in any minute by actuall sinne, but not to rob and cousen her
by giving any part to pleasure or businesse, but bestow it all upon her in meditation,
yet even in that I should wound her more, and contract another guiltinesse: As the
Eagle were very unnaturall if because she is able to do it, she should pearch a whole
day upon a tree, staring in contemplation of . . . the Sun, and let her young Eglets
starve in the nest.

Cf. the close of stanza XVI:

> From thinking us all soule, neglecting thus
> Our mutuall duties, Lord deliver us.

See also note to 'measuring ill by vitious' (l. 147). The number of parallels
suggests that the letter and poem may belong to the same period.

l. 127. *secure*: careless.

l. 128. *clods*. Group III reads 'clouds', which is plainly an error: it destroys the
contrast with 'squibs' and the implied play on the humours.

   A 'clod' is both a lump of earth, the element corresponding to the humour
of melancholy, and a boorish or dull person. A 'squib' is both a flash of fire
and 'a mean, insignificant or paltry fellow' (*O.E.D.*).

l. 133. *maim'd*: incapacitated. The use of 'maimed' with 'from' has no parallel
in *O.E.D.* The word brings with it the suggestion of the extremer forms of
mortification. Donne appears to be denying that to 'seek first the kingdom of
God' involves asceticism.

l. 142. *light affecting, in religion, newes:* frivolously taking up new beliefs and
habits in religion. Donne is perhaps glancing at the attraction of 'Roman
innovations'. Cf. a long passage on the 'snares' of Rome which ends: 'If it
be levity, and affectation of new things, there may be a snare of things so
new in that Religion, as that this Kingdom never saw them yet, not then
when this Kingdom was of that Religion. For we had received the Reforma-
tion before the Council of *Trent*, and before the growth of the Jesuits'
(*Sermons*, iv. 139).

l. 143. *From thinking us all soule*. Cf. 'Man hath many offices, that appertaine to
this world, and . . . must not withdraw himselfe, from those offices of mutuall
society, upon a pretence of zeale, or better serving God in a retired life'
(*Sermons*, ix. 63). This is a favourite theme with Donne later; see *Sermons*, iv.
226 and vii. 104, Simpson, *Essays*, p. 37.

l. 147. *measuring ill by vitious*: excusing faults by comparing them with vices, instead of measuring them by the standard of virtue. In his letter to Goodyer, September 1608, Donne says 'God doth thus occasion, and positively concurre to evill, that when a man is purposed to do a great sin, God infuses some good thoughts which make him choose a lesse sin' (*Letters*, p. 49). The petition in the poem seems to follow on from this rather paradoxical remark: that we may not be led into thinking these lesser sins are not sins at all, by comparing them with the greater sins we have avoided.

l. 149. *indiscreet humilitie*: Donne rates discretion highly; cf. *The First Anniversary* (ll. 337-8):

> For good, and well, must in our actions meete:
> Wicked is not much worse then indiscreet.

An excessive neglect of reputation and an excessive self-depreciation casts 'reproach on Christianitie' by suggesting that Christianity unfits men for positions of dignity and responsibility. Donne, with Hooker, holds that 'Religion unfainedly loved, perfecteth mens abilities unto all kinds of vertuous services in the Common-wealth' (*Laws of Ecc. Pol.* v. 1). Cf. 'God can suffer even thy humility to stray, and degenerate into an uncomly dejection and stupidity, and senselesness of the true dignity and true liberty of a Christian' (*Sermons*, ii. 243).

l. 152. *to spies pervious*: 'accessible to the influence of' spies (*O.E.D.*, but not before the nineteenth century). Curiosity—repeating or listening to gossip —is a prime example of 'sins spawne, Vanitie'.

l. 153. *thirst, or scorne of fame*. Cf. 'They that rest in the testimony of their owne consciences, and contemne the opinion of other men, *Imprudenter agunt*, & *crudeliter*' (*Sermons*, vii. 250); also, '*For fame*, . . . *I so esteem opinion, that I despise not others thoughts of me*, . . . *nor so reverence it, that I make it alwayes the rule of my Actions*' (Simpson, *Essays*, p. 38).

l. 164. *th'agonie of pious wits*: both 'the grief' and 'the occasion of contest' of theologians. Cf. 'To this day, thy Church, thy School cannot see, what kinde of arrow thou tookest into thy soul, what kinde of affliction . . . made thy soul heavy unto death, . . . in thine agony' (*Sermons*, ii. 70).

ll. 167-71: *And through thy free confession* &c. The reference is to the narrative of the betrayal in John xviii: 'Jesus saith unto them, I am he. . . . As soon then as he had said unto them, I am he, they went backward, and fell to the ground.' The traditional interpretation is that Christ's question, 'Whom seek ye', shows that those who came to take him were blinded, since in spite of their lanterns they did not recognize him until his 'free confession'. The commentators contrast this occasion with two others (John viii. 59 and x. 39) when Christ hid himself from his enemies. Donne takes the falling to the ground as a 'blinding', and is struck by the paradox that Christ's 'free confession' prostrated his enemies, and, revealing the truth, blinded them, so that he might have escaped. But in his petition he ignores his parenthesis and uses 'blind' in its figurative sense. He prays that we may learn when we may not and when we may 'blinde unjust men', by hiding the truth.

This is a clear reference to the bitter contemporary debate on 'equivocation'. The incident chosen presents an obvious parallel to a suspected priest being challenged. Examples of equivocation by Christ were freely cited by Parsons. Morton, in replying to him, accepted that many of the sayings of Christ had a double sense, but denied that they constituted a parallel to a priest who, when challenged, replied 'I am no priest', with the mental reservation 'I mean, of Apollo'.

ll. 172-5. *Through thy submitting* &c. The syntax is difficult; there is a kind of double zeugma. 'Through thy surrendering all—surrendering thy face to blows, thy clothes to be the soldiers' spoil, thy good name to obloquy—through thy submission to all the ways known to the enmity of man and the processes of law, by which thou couldest show that thou wast truly born of woman.'

l. 173. *clothes*. The reading of B, 'Robe' ('Robes' in *Dob, Lut, O'F, S 96*), was possibly in Donne's first version, and referred to the seamless coat for which the soldiers diced (John xix. 24). He might have altered it because the homelier 'clothes' is more suitable in a stanza on Christ's humility.

l. 178. *expresse*: press out, expel. Cf. 'He did dye, before the torments could have extorted his soule from him; . . . Christ did not die naturally, nor violently, as all others doe, but only voluntarily' (*Sermons*, ii. 208).

l. 194. *thine Angell*. Cf. 2 Sam. xxiv. 15-16, where the angel of the Lord is his agent in bringing pestilence.

l. 196. *Heresie, thy second deluge.* This is a commonplace, which Donne, in a sermon, refers to Augustine; see *Sermons*, ix. 329.

l. 198. *sinister.* The word has the accent on the second syllable up to the time of Pope. It has primarily its original Latin meaning: cf.

> Inter oves locum praesta
> Et ab haedis me sequestra
> Statuens in parte dextra.
> ('Dies Irae')

In reference back to the whole stanza, it can be given its general meaning of 'worse'.

Stanzas XXIII–XXVIII. The Supplications are rather too like the Deprecations; and the response has led to a disproportionate emphasis on the sense of hearing.

l. 206. *Jobs sicke day*: the day when sickness fell on Job; cf. Job. ii. 4–7.

l. 207. *Heare thy selfe now*, &c. Cf. 'It is the Holy Ghost himselfe that prayes in us' (*Sermons*, iii. 153).

l. 218. *Labyrinths*. Cf. 'Labyrinths of eares' in *The Second Anniversary* (l. 297). The first use of the word anatomically, for the passages of the inner ear, which *O.E.D.* records is in 1696.

ll. 219–20. *That wee by harkning*, &c. 'That by lending a ready ear, we do not procure flattery from others, nor invite them to speak against others.'

l. 221. *slipperinesse*: carelessness; but the word leads to the idea of sliding down a slope in the next line.

l. 223. *excesse*: excellence or superiority. Cf. 'Certainly those men prepare a way of speaking negligently, or irreverently of *thee*, that give themselves that liberty, in speaking of thy *Vice-gerents, Kings*' (Sparrow, *Devotions*, p. 44). Bacon puts 'great persons' after religion and matters of state, as things which 'ought to be privileged' from jest ('Of Discourse').

Stanza XXVI. 'When the Magistrate, the Law in Person, who, for our own good, and that of others who may profit by the example, makes our sins appear worse than they are; when Satan, the Accuser, and envious men, who rejoice at our failings, charge us with sin; may they see us listen and amend our lives: but may they see thee Lord decline to listen.'

l. 231. *Which well, if we starve, dine*. Group III (except *S 96* which omits the stanza) and *C 57*, *Lec* read 'will', although *Lec* corrects to 'well'. 'Will' was corrected to 'well' by the proof-corrector of *1633*.

l. 239. *wit, borne apt, high good to doe*. The understanding or reason is given man that by it he may know God. If, born for that, it contents itself with the study of the creation, worthless without its Creator, it will become worthless itself.

l. 242. *That our affections kill us not, nor dye*. Cf. 'To every sick soule, whose cure he undertakes, he sayes so too, '*Surge, Tolle, Ambula*. Our beds are our naturall affections; These he does not bid us cast away, nor burne, nor destroy. . . . Arise from this bed . . . walke sincerely in thy Calling, and thou shalt heare thy Saviour say . . . These affections . . . shall not destroy thee' (*Sermons*, v. 351–2). See also iv. 329–30, where Donne declares that Christ came nearer an 'excesse of passion' than 'a privation of naturall affections'.

l. 243. *Heare us, weake ecchoes, O thou eare, and cry*. B, *Dob*, *S 96* read 'weake wretches'; the fact that *Lut* and *O'F* read with *1633* points to this being an error. 'Wretches' is an obvious substitution in a litany for a word a scribe could not read or thought unintelligible. Group III reads 'eare and eye': again a scribe might read the difficult phrase 'eare and cry', according to expectation, as 'eare and eye', or correct it to this. *TCC* originally read 'eye', but corrected to 'cry'.

Grierson explains: 'God is both the source of our prayers and their answerer', and refers back to l. 207.

l. 246. *Gaine to thy self, or us allow.* Grierson paraphrases: 'If we perish, neither Christ nor we have gained anything by his death.' Cf. Simpson, *Essays*, pp. 99–100 and

> Recordare, Jesu pie,
> Quod sum causa tuae viae,
> Ne me perdas illa die.
>
> Quaerens me sedisti lassus
> Redemisti crucem passus;
> Tantus labor non sit cassus.
> ('Dies Irae')

l. 252. *As sinne is nothing, let it nowhere be.* Cf. 'You know, . . . in what sense we say in the Schoole, *Malum nihil*, and *Peccatum nihil*, that evill is nothing, sin is nothing; that is, it hath no reality, it is no created substance, it is but a privation, as a shadow is, as sicknesse is' (*Sermons*, vi. 238); cf. also 'That sin is nothing. . . . This is true; but that will not ease my soul, no more then it will ease my body, that *sicknesse* is nothing, and *death* is nothing' (*Sermons*, ii. 99). Donne's paradoxical petition includes the philosophic and the moral view.

OCCASIONAL POEMS

The Crosse (*page 26*)

MSS.: Group I: *C 57, D, H 49, Lec, SP*; Group II: *A 18, N, TCC, TCD; DC*; Group III: *Dob, Lut, O'F; B, S; A 25, D 17, JC, O, P*; Miscellanies: *CCC, Grey, Hd, HK 2, La, RP 117 (2), S 962, Wed*.

The text of *1633* has been abandoned on six occasions: in l. 26 for the reading of Groups I and II; in ll. 50, 61, and 63 for the reading of all MSS. collated; in l. 55 where it follows *C 57, Lec* against the other manuscripts. For the reading in l. 52, see note.

Both its style and its wide circulation suggest that the poem is an early one. It is more a Verse-Letter than a Divine Poem. At this period a cross on an altar would be very rare, except in royal chapels: King James observed to the Puritans: 'the materiall *Crosses*, which in the time of Popery were made, for men to fall down before them . . . are demolished as you desire' (Barlow, *The Sum of the Conference*, 1604, p. 74). Donne is defending the cross as a pious and proper personal possession.

The poem may be compared with Herbert's 'The Crosse' and his *De*

Signaculo Crucis (*Works*, pp. 164 and 389).

l. 14. *No Crosse is so extreme, as to have none.* Cf. 'There cannot be so great a crosse as to have none. I lack one loaf of that dayly bread that I pray for, if I have no crosse; for afflictions are our spirituall nourishment' (*Sermons*, iii. 166).

ll. 17–24. All these likenesses to a cross were noted by early Christian writers and collected by Lipsius, *De Cruce* (Antwerp, 1595), Book I, chap. ix. See supplementary notes, p. 155.

l. 27. *extracted chimique medicine.* Galenists held disease arose from dispropor-tion of the humours, and was cured by drugs which had the qualities opposite to the humour which was in excess. Paracelsians held that each disease had an essence or 'spiritual seed', which could be purged by an antagonistic remedy. They tried to find this remedy, in its purest form, by chemical extraction. They also believed in the use of these 'extracted virtues' to pre-serve or restore 'our naturall inborn preservative'; see *Letters*, pp. 97–98.

l. 37. *Alchimists doe coyners prove.* 'Authority for such a charge against alchemists is not hard to find, even among their own brethren', writes E. H. Duncan in 'Donne's Alchemical Figures' (*E.L.H.* ix, 1942). He quotes from Paracelsus, and from Lodge's *A Fig for Momus*.

l. 48. *Make them indifferent; call nothing best.* Grierson departed from *1633*, which has the support of Groups I and II, and conflated the reading of *1633* with that of *1635*, taken from *O'F.* 'Make them indifferent all, nothing best' (*Lut, O'F*) plainly arose from a mis-reading of 'call' as 'all'.

'Make your senses indifferent to pleasure or displeasure; have no pre-ferences.'

l. 50. *To th'others th'objects must come home.* The great majority of the MSS. read 'others'. The sense demands the plural; the contrast is between the eye and the four other senses.

'The eye most needs "crossing", for it can perceive at a distance and by moving choose its objects: the other senses are in fixed organs and must have their objects presented directly to them.'

l. 52. *Points downewards, and hath palpitation. 1633*, supported by Group I, and a majority of the Group III manuscripts, reads 'Pants'. Group II reads 'Points'. *O'F* has been corrected to 'Pants', so this reading stood in *1635*. I follow Grierson in adopting 'Points'. He argued that 'Pants' anticipates 'hath palpitation' and cited a parallel: 'O man . . . only thy heart of all others, points downwards, and onely trembles' (Simpson, *Essays*, p. 30).

Aristotle (*De Partibus Animalium* iii. 6, 669[a]) declares that 'man is practically the only animal whose heart presents this phenomenon of jumping, inasmuch as he alone is influenced by hope and anticipation of the future'. The earliest use of the word 'palpitation' which *O.E.D.* records is by King James in 1604.

l. 53. *dejections.* *Dob, P* read 'defections', probably the word misread as 'dissections' by *A 25*, as 'desertions' by *S* and as 'dissentions', corrected from 'disthentions', by *S 962*. *Lut, O'F* read 'detortions', which looks like an attempt by *Lut* to make sense of one of the poor Group III readings. 'Detortions' was, if so, an intelligent emendation as it can be taken with both the following clauses.

ll. 55–56.   *And as thy braine through bony walls doth vent*
              By sutures, which a Crosses forme present.

Aristotle ascribes the size of the human brain to the excessive heat in the region of the heart and lungs in man, who has, as a counterpoise, superabundant fluidity and coldness in his brain. Owing to this superabundance 'the cranial bone, which some call the Bregma, is the last to become solidified; so long does evaporation continue to occur through it under the influence of heat. . . . Man, again, has more sutures in his skull than any other animal. . . . The reason is again to be found in the greater size of the brain, which demands free ventilation, proportionate to its bulk' (*De Partibus Animalium* ii. 7, 653^b). The frontal, or metopic suture continues the line of the sagittal, across the coronal, making the front of the skull present 'a Crosses forme'. This suture is present in all human skulls in infancy; it closes normally at about two years of age, but it persists in about nine per cent. of adults. See J. E. Frazer, *The Anatomy of the Human Skeleton*, 4th edn. (1940), p. 202. Since the brain 'vents' thus through a cross, let us cross or correct the child of the brain, wit.

l. 61. *fruitfully.* I follow Grierson in adopting the reading of all the MSS. Grierson objected: 'A preacher may deal "faithfully" with his people. The adverb refers to his action, not its result in them. The Cross of Christ, in Donne's view, must always deal faithfully; whether its action produces fruit depends on our hearts.'

Resurrection, imperfect (*page 28*)

MSS.: Group II: *A 18, N, TCC, TCD; DC*; Group III: *Lut, O'F*; Miscellanies: *Grey.*

E. H. Duncan in 'Donne's Alchemical Figures' (*E.L.H.* ix, 1942) points out that the alchemical conceit in this poem occurs in a modified form in the Elegy on Lady Markham (Milgate, *Anniversaries etc.*, p. 57). He comments that it is impossible to say which poem was written first. I owe to this article the interpretation of the figure and the alchemical quotation illustrating it.

l. 1. *repast*: recovered from. This is the only example of the word in *O.E.D.*; it is derived from an obsolete French verb *repasser* 'to cure'.

ll. 9–16. *Whose body, having walk'd on earth* &c. Cf. Eph. iv. 9–10: 'Now that he ascended, what is it but that he also descended first into the lower parts of the earth? . . . that he might fill all things.' Christ would 'allow Himselfe', or grant his presence, to all parts of the universe; his body, having been above the earth, like the animal and vegetable creation, became by burial a mineral. The alchemical sense of the word—used to express the 'remote matter' whence common minerals and metals spring—leads to the conceit. All things strive towards the perfection of gold, and in earth base metals change gradually to gold; cf. 'here to grow gold we lie' ('Epitaph: on Himself'). Christ's body was all gold when he was buried; but gold itself, through mortification and regeneration, can be refined into a 'tincture', which then has power to transmute other metals to itself. Cf. Michael Sendivogus, *The New Chemical Light* (*Hermetic Museum*, ed. Waite, 1893, ii. 99): 'The Stone or Tincture is nothing other than gold digested to the highest degree. *Common* gold resembles a plant without seed; when such a plant is matured, it produces seed . . . so, when gold is ripened, it produces its seed, or the Tincture.' Christ's body has become this Tincture of Gold, which 'disposes to good' wills of lead and iron, the base metals, and transmutes sinful flesh to its own perfection. Cf. Phil. iii. 21: 'Who shall change our vile body that it may be fashioned like unto his glorious body.'

l. 22. *of the whole.* The risen body of Christ is 'anima mundi', the principle of life.

Upon the Annunciation and Passion falling upon one day. 1608
(*page 29*)

MSS.: Group I: *C 57, D, H 49, Lec, SP*; Group II: *N, TCD; DC*; Group III: *Dob, Lut, O'F, S 96; B, O1, S; O, P*; Miscellanies: *La, HK 2*.

The text of *1633* has been abandoned three times: in l. 33, it misprints 'those' for 'these'; for the readings in ll. 10 and 37, see notes. It is an excellent example of illogical but expressive poetic punctuation; the full stop being used sparingly to mark the end of a train of thought.

There are some Group III readings which seem likely to have stood in Donne's first version; see the inversions in ll. 13 and 15 and the readings in ll. 1 and 33.

The date, 1608, is confirmed by reference to a perpetual calendar. Whether we begin the year on Lady Day, 25 March, or on 1 January, the year remains 1608. The poem has obvious affinities with '*La Corona*', which was probably written in the same year.

Forty-eight lines on the life of Christ, in couplets, follow Donne's poem in *Lut, O'F*; see Grierson, Appendix C, i. 443. The poem is certainly not by Donne, and it is not a continuation of Donne's poem. It is separated from it by a line in *Lut*, and by a space in *O'F*. Grierson refers to Sir John Beaumont's poem on the coincidence of the Annunciation and Easter in 1627 (*Bosworth*

Field, 1629); and to Herbert's poem '*In Natalia et Pascha Concurrentes*'. Beaumont's poem was possibly inspired by Donne's; but Herbert's is naturally much more personal, since his subject is the concurrence of his own birthday with Good Friday. It is a little surprising that Donne made no use of the tradition that the first Good Friday fell on March 25 (*Golden Legend*, iii. 100).

Title: Group I has the inadequate title 'The Annuntiation', which *1633* expanded to 'The Annuntiation and Passion'. *TCD*, *N* have 'Vppon the Annunciation, when Good-Friday fell upon the same daye'. All the Group III MSS. (except *P*, which has no title) have, with minor variations, the title I have adopted from *Dob*. (*Lut* and *La* wrongly give 1618 for 1608.)

l. 1. *Tamely*: submissively. The soul has so much to feed on that the body should not feel rebellious at abstaining.

l. 4. *of them both a circle embleme is*. Christ's human life, coming to an end on the day it had begun, makes up a circle and 'One of the most convenient Hieroglyphicks of God, is a Circle' (*Sermons*, vi. 173).

l. 7. *She sees him nothing*. As a preacher Donne is careful to insist that man does not become 'nothing' at death, though by the separation of body and soul, whose union makes man, he becomes 'no man'; see *Sermons*, viii. 283 and x. 236.

l. 8. *a Cedar*. The Cedar typifies the Godhead; see Rabanus Maurus, Migne, *P.L.* cxii. 891. Cf. the sequence 'Laetabundus' (*English Hymnal*, no. 22).

l. 9. *put to making*: subjected to being made. 'Making' is a verbal noun used instead of the passive form of the gerund.

l. 10. *and dead*. Only poor witnesses, *B* (which altered 'but' to 'yet'), *S*, *O*, *P*, *HK 2*, *La*, support *1633* in reading 'yet'. 'And' avoids the use of 'yet' twice, and in two different senses, in the same line.

l. 12. *Reclus'd*. The Angel 'found her alone, enclosed in her chamber', according to *The Golden Legend* (iii. 97). 'Reclus'd', like 'enclosed', relates the Virgin at her prayers to the nun or anchoress, a connexion made in *Ancren Riwle* (ed. Morton, 1835, p. 161). Donne would possibly have avoided this suggestion later.

l. 14. *At almost fiftie, and at scarce fifteene*. 'When our Lady had conceived Jesu Christ she was of age of fourteen years, and she was delivered in her fifteenth year, and lived and abode with him three and thirty years' (*Golden Legend*, iv. 234).

l. 17. *Orbitie*: 'bereavement, especially of children' (*O.E.D.*).

l. 21. *plaine*: flat; cf. 'Take a flat Map, a Globe *in plano* . . .' (*Sermons*, ii. 199)· Cf. note to 'A Hymn to God my God', p. 108.

· ll. 25–28. *As by the selfe-fix'd Pole* &c. Cf. 'Neither is that starre which we call the North-pole, or by which we know the North-pole, the very Pole it selfe; but we call it so, and we make our uses of it, and our conclusions by it, as if it were so, because it is the neerest starre to that Pole' (*Sermons*, vii. 245)

l. 32. *his Church, as cloud.* The standard interpretation of the pillar of cloud is 'Obscuritas veteris testamenti'. Donne's interpretation here is, as far as I can tell, original. In many places 'cloud' is glossed generally as 'flesh' and particularly as 'the humanity of Christ'. Donne may be extending this to the Church, which is Christ's body.

l. 33. *daies.* ' Feasts', the reading of Group III, although it seems at first sight improbable, may have been used by Donne metaphorically, with reference back to 'my soule eates twice'. He perhaps altered it because it is too paradoxical to speak of Good Friday as a 'feast'.

l. 37. *had made.* Only Group I supports *1633* in reading 'hath'. Although to God there is no distinction of tenses, to Christ, as man, living in time, creation was in the past. This is brought out by the use of the pluperfect.

l. 38. *one period*: the same point of time. Cf. 'The first *Fiat* in the Creation of *Adam*, and the last note of the blowing of the Trumpets to judgement . . . are not a minute asunder in respect of eternity, which hath no minutes' (*Sermons*, vi. 331). Cf. *Religio Medici*, i. 11.

l. 42. *Accepted.* Cf. 'Though then one drop of his bloud had beene enough to have redeemed infinite worlds, if it had beene so contracted . . .' (*Sermons*, iv. 296). In Protestant doctrine no works, not even Christ's, are of themselves pleasing to God: 'If wee could consider the passion of Christ, without the eternall *Decree*, and *Covenant*, and *Contract* with his father, his worke (saving the dignity which it had by Acceptation, by which the least step of his humiliation might worthily have redeemed tenne thousand worlds) had not naturally merited our salvation' (*Pseudo-Martyr*, p. 98).

l. 44. *busie'a life.* The agreement of the Group III manuscripts in reading 'buy a life' is striking. I am convinced it is an error, although Bennett adopted it. The Church is being compared to Christ in generosity. Although one drop of his blood would have saved us, Christ shed all; so, although the least of his sufferings, miracles, or words could give us matter for a life-time's meditation, the Church gives us all on this one day.

l. 46. *my life.* Group III reads 'thy', also adopted by Bennett. But Donne has a habit of speaking of his soul as distinct from himself; cf. 'Holy Sonnets' (1633), 9. 2 and 'Holy Sonnets' (1635), 4. 14.

Goodfriday, 1613. Riding Westward (*page 30*)

MSS.: Group I: *C 57, D, H 49, Lec, SP*; Group II: *A 18, N, TCC, TCD; DC*; Group III: *Dob, Lut, O'F, S 96; B, S; A 25, Cy*; Miscellanies: *A 23, Grey, Hd*. For discussion of two copies in the hand of Sir Nathaniel Rich, see supplementary notes, pp. 155–6.

The text of *1633* has been abandoned on three occasions: in l. 4 all the MSS. are against it and in l. 27 all but one; for the reading in l. 24, and that in l. 22, where I retain the reading of *1633*, see notes.

The copyists of Group I were prone to eye-slips in this poem; only *H 49* has a complete text. Group III shows no substantial variation from Groups I and II. The absence of 'Group III readings' here strengthens the case for regarding them when they do occur as deriving from a different version of the poem.

The date, 1613, established by the general agreement of the MSS., puts the poem just under two years before Donne's ordination.

Title: The title of *1633* is sufficiently descriptive. Group I has 'Goodfryday. 1613. Ridinge towards Wales', except for *H 49*, which has 'Riding to Sᵣ Edward Herbert in wales'. Group II has 'Goodfriday / Made as I was Rideing westward, that daye'. This sounds like a title Donne had himself written above his poem, and supports the view that the compiler of the Group II collection had access to his papers. It also allows us to believe that in some of Donne's poems spontaneity is not merely an artistic illusion. The title varies in Group III; that in *A 25* is of interest: 'Mᵣ J. Dun*ne* goeinge from Sᵣ H G: on good fryday sent him back this Meditacion on the waye.' Good Friday fell on 2 April in 1613. After the royal wedding in February of that year, Donne visited Goodyer in Warwickshire; but on 7 April he wrote a letter dated from Montgomery Castle (Hayward, p. 464). The castle was at this time in the possession of Edward Herbert's cousin, Philip, but there is no reason why he should not have been staying with his kinsman. See Bald, pp. 269–71.

ll. 1–10. *Let mans Soule be a Spheare*, &c. The soul is the moving principle, or 'forme' to the body; the Intelligence, or Angel, which moves a sphere, is then its 'naturall forme'. Devotion is the Intelligence or 'form' of the soul; cf.

> in good men this
> Vertue, our formes forme and our soules soule is.

But the spheres had more than one motion. Their natural motion, guided by their Intelligences, was from west to east; but the movement of the Primum Mobile hurried them against this from east to west every day. There were also other motions: that of the ninth sphere, postulated to account for irregularities which could not be accounted for by the orbital and diurnal motions, and the 'fourth motion' observed by Copernicus. The spheres 'seldom, in the course of the year, are not deflected from their own path'.

Cf. a letter to Goodyer, in which Donne uses this conceit to contrast true and indiscreet friendship, and ends by saying that friendship 'which is not moved primarily by the proper intelligence, discretion, and about the naturall center, vertue, . . . returns to the true first station and place of friendship planetarily, which is uncertainly and seldome' (*Letters*, pp. 26–27).

Donne's moralization of the heavenly system is directly opposed to the standard one. In Sacrobosco's *De Sphaera*, the diurnal motion of the 'first mover' is 'motus rationalis', and the contrary motion of each sphere is 'motus irrationalis sive sensualis'; for the Primum Mobile is a type of the First Mover, God. See supplementary notes, pp. 156–7.

l. 17. *Who sees Gods face, that is selfe life, must dye.* Cf. Exod. xxxiii. 20: 'Thou canst not see my face: for there shall no man see me, and live.'

l. 20. *his footstoole.* Cf. Isa. lxvi. 1: 'The earth is my footstool.'

l. 22. *tune all spheares.* The line is missing in *C 57, Lec. H 49, D, SP* support *1633* in reading 'tune'. Group II reads 'turne'. The majority of the remaining manuscripts read 'tune'.

Grierson, who adopted 'turne', wrote: 'Donne was more of a Schoolman and Aristotelian than a Platonist, and I think there can be little doubt that he is describing Christ as "first mover". On the other hand "tune" may include "turne".' Hayward restored 'tune', commenting that Donne was an eclectic and could not be tied to any school. Grierson replied, defending 'turne' in a letter to *T.L.S.* (5 Dec. 1929). The authority is evenly divided; but 'tune', being the more difficult reading, is less likely to be a scribal substitution. Its defence is Grierson's statement that 'tune' includes 'turne', since the music arises from the rate of turning. In his poem on the Sidneian Psalms Donne speaks of Christ as 'tuning heaven and earth'. He is not only the First Mover, but the Wisdom which 'sweetly ordereth all things'.

l. 24. *and to'our Antipodes. 1633* reads 'and our'. It is supported by *TCC, A 18* in Group II, *Lut, O'F* in Group III, and *A 25. H 49,* the only Group I MS. in which the line is not omitted, agrees with the other MSS. in the reading I have adopted. It makes the sense clearer and it seems more likely that 'to' or 't' dropped out, than that it was inserted. Wherever we are on the earth's surface, God is our Zenith.

l. 26. *The seat of all our Soules, if not of his.* In a sermon Donne speaks of blood as '*sedes animae*, the seat and residence of the soule' and of Christ's blood as 'the seat of his soule' (*Sermons*, iv. 294). The Fathers, discussing the text 'Anima enim omnis carnis sanguis est' (Lev. xvii. 11), and refuting Tertullian's ascription of corporeality to the soul, deny that the soul can be said to reside in any part of the body. The Gloss on this text cites Augustine on the double sense of 'anima'. Whether or not we think of Christ's blood as the seat of his soul, mystically it is the seat of the souls of all of us, who have new life by it.

l. 27. *Make durt of dust.* Only *Dob* supports *1633* in reading 'Made'. Both were probably influenced independently by the past participles before and after. 'Made durt of dust' can only mean 'made vilest of the vile'. The reading of the MSS. is far more vivid: the blood mingles with the 'dust' of the ground to make unregarded 'durt', that is mud or filth.

l. 30. *miserable.* *1635* reads 'On his distressed mother', one of the very few of its readings not derived from *O'F*, or from any other MS. Presumably the editor thought the contractions in 'mis'r'ble' excessive. Cf.

> Quis est homo qui non fleret
> Matrem Christi si videret
> In tanto supplicio?

To Mr. Tilman after he had taken orders (*page 32*)

MSS.: Group III: *Dob, O'F*; Miscellanies: *Wel.*

The text in *1635*, where this poem was first printed, is too different from that in *O'F* for us to believe that *1635* took it from there. Bennett printed from *Dob*; but its independent readings, here as elsewhere, are suspicious. *O'F* presents the best text, but no single text is good enough to rely on. I print, therefore, from *1635*; but wherever all three MSS., or *Dob* and *O'F* agree against it, their reading has been adopted. It is in almost all cases manifestly superior. The independent readings of *Dob* are considered in the notes, but not recorded in the apparatus, since I do not believe they have any authority.

The MS. which I call Welbeck was formerly in the possession of Mr. Glass of Tavernham Hall, near Norwich. He allowed Mr. Harvey Wood to describe it and to print from it Mr. Tilman's verses; see *Essays and Studies*, xvi (1931). It was sold at Maggs' in October 1935, and bought by the Duke of Portland. It is beautifully written in a small Italian hand, and the poems are arranged under headings, with spaces left for additions under the different categories. A number of Donne's secular poems are included; but the texts are not good. The MS. contains a good many Oxford poems, and was probably bound at Oxford. The binding is contemporary calf and portions of John Reinold's *Epigrammata* (Oxford, 1612) are bound in at the end. A good many of the topical poems belong to 1621-2, but the MS. also contains verses on the death of James I in 1625. It was probably written around 1630.

For the facts of Tilman's life, and a consideration of the light his and Donne's poems throw on Donne's own reluctance to take orders, see Appendix D, pp. 127–32. Tilman took deacon's orders in December 1618; Donne's poem must, therefore, be after that date. Walton made good use of phrases from this poem in his *Life of Donne*.

l. 6. *in the vintage.* 'Since' (*Wel* and *1635*) destroys the parallel with 'bringst thou home': the ripe grapes 'in the vintage' correspond to the sheaves brought home at harvest. 'In the voyage' (*Dob*), a clumsy anticipation of the later metaphor of the trading ship, destroys this natural and Biblical metaphor for a matured purpose; cf. Ecclus. xxiv. 26–7.

ll. 13–18. *Art thou* &c. All three MSS. agree in making these lines questions. By making them statements *1635* destroys the sequence of rhetorical questions, ending with a direct appeal: 'Deare, tell me . . .'. Also, if they are statements, the point of contrast with ll. 19–22 is lost: 'Is the change only outward—a mere change of stamp, which does not affect the value of the coin—or is there an inward change, by which you are "new feather'd", that is given new powers and functions?'

Dob reads 'new birth' for 'new stampe' (l. 18).

l. 18. *thy Coronation*. Cf. 'What a Coronation is our taking of Orders, by which God makes us a Royall Priesthood' (*Sermons*, vii. 134).

l. 25. *gayning*. The singular, the reading of *Dob*, *O'F*, makes 'doe' subjunctive, which agrees with Donne's usual practice in conditional clauses.

l. 29. *As if their day were onely to be spent*. The reading of *1635* has no manuscript support; but that of *Dob*, *O'F*, which I formerly adopted, I now reject as hopelessly unmetrical, although supported by a similar line in *Wel*. Since ll. 29–30 in *1635* depend on the main interrogative clause in ll. 27–28, I have reversed the query (l. 28) and semi-colon (l. 30).

l. 30. *In dressing, Mistressing and complement*. This is plainly the right reading, confirmed by the reference to 'cloathes and beauties' three lines later and by Herbert's borrowing of the line in 'The Church-Porch' (l. 80), and his adaptation of it in *A Priest to the Temple* (*Works*, pp. 9 and 277). Herbert died before the poem was in print. 'Mis-dressing' (*O'F*) is an obvious mis-reading; and 'undressing' (*Dob*) looks like an ingenious attempt to make sense of it. *O'F*'s mistake makes it seem certain that *1635* did not take the poem from there; it is highly unlikely that anyone faced with 'mis-dressing' would hit on the true reading, which is an unusual use of the noun 'Mistress' as a verb.

l. 32. *refined*. 'Sublimed' (*1635*) is an anticipation of 'sublimed clay' in l. 34.

l. 33. *beauties*. This reading (*Dob*, *O'F*) is superior to 'beauty' (*Wel* and *1635*), since it refers back to 'Mistressing', and the concrete 'beautiful women' are more fitly described as 'sublimed clay' than the abstract 'beauty'.

l. 38. *Embassadour to God*. Cf. 2 Cor. v. 20: 'Now then we are ambassadors for Christ' ('legatione fungimur', Vulgate; 'messengers', Geneva).

l. 43. *As Angels out of clouds*. Walton's adaptation of these words to Donne as a preacher 'alwayes preaching to himself, like an Angel from a cloud, but in none' suggests that he took them to mean simply 'from on high'. Reference to the sermons suggests a rather fuller meaning. 'Clouds' are traditionally interpreted as preachers: 'ut in Isaia "Nubes pluant justum", praedicatores nuntient Christum' (Rabanus Maurus, Migne, *P.L.* cxii. 1008). 'Cloud' is also frequently glossed as 'flesh'. Angels are messengers of God and when appearing to men were held to make themselves bodies out of clouds. Donne has fused these commonplaces. As angels appear to men in clouds, so preachers through and in spite of the weakness of the flesh convey the messages of God. Cf.

Clouds are but the beds, and wombs of distempered and malignant impressions ... yet by the presence of Christ, and his employment, these clouds are made glorious Chariots to bring him and his Saints together. Those ... *Clouds* which *David* speaks of, *S. Augustin* interprets of the Ministers of the Church (*Sermons*, iv. 83).

Donne goes on to define these clouds as various human defects. Cf. also *Sermons*, vii. 134 and x. 60.

l. 46. *Opticks*: telescopes, which are compared to the 'engines' or instruments of the minister: preaching and the sacraments.

l. 54. *Hermaphrodite*. The word is used figuratively at this period for any striking conjunction of opposites; cf. 'Of study'and play made strange Hermaphrodits' ('Epithalamium at Lincoln's Inn'). The wit of this climax lies in the demonstration that the opposites here conjoined are masculine and feminine.

Upon the translation of the Psalmes &c. (*page 33*)

MS.: Group III: *O'F*.

There can be no doubt that *1635* took this poem from *O'F*; see p. lxxxviii.

Although *O'F* includes as Donne's some poems which are not his and others which are doubtfully so, there is no reason to question its attribution here. The opening lines are much in Donne's manner and there are parallels to other Divine Poems throughout. The poem must have been written after 1621, when the Countess of Pembroke died, since her death is referred to at the close.

The version of the Psalter made by Sidney and his sister (not published until 1823) is extant in a good many manuscripts. From a note in one (Rawlinson Poetical MS. 25), it appears that Sidney's share stopped with Psalm xliii, and that the remainder were paraphrased by his sister after his death. The Sidneys, unlike the majority of paraphrasers of the Psalms, employed a wide variety of metres. Comparisons between their stanza-forms and Herbert's in *The Temple* have been made by Joseph Summers, *George Herbert: His Religion and Art* (1954) and Louis L. Martz, *The Poetry of Meditation* (1954).

ll. 1–4. *Eternall God* &c. Donne adds to the description of God as a circle, a favourite commonplace of his, the jesting reference to squaring the circle—a problem much debated in his century—and the play on the two meanings of 'corners': 'hidden nooks' and 'angles of a square'. Cf. 'God is a circle himselfe, and he will make thee one; Goe not thou about to square eyther circle, to bring that which is equall in it selfe, to Angles, and Corners . . .' (*Sermons*, vi. 175).

ll. 17–19. *Two that make one* John Baptists *holy voyce*, &c. These two make a single 'voice . . . crying in the wilderness' and, being islanders, carry out the precept of Ps. xcvii. 1. Donne is plainly not aware that Sidney's share ended with Ps. xliii.

l. 38. *So well attyr'd abroad*, &c. 'Abroad', that is in 'chambers', the Psalms can be found in this admirable version: 'at home', that is in Churches, they are sung in a bad version. There are constant complaints of the badness of the Old Version at this period. Puritans attacked it for not being sufficiently literal, while men of letters complained of its feeble style.

l. 44. *More hoarse, more harsh than any other.* This is probably a reference to the excellence of the French versions of the Psalms, by Clement Marot, and possibly also to the richness in hymnody of the Lutheran Churches.

l. 46. *this* Moses *and this* Miriam. Cf. Exod. xv. 20, where Miriam, the sister of Moses, takes up her brother's song.

The Lamentations of Jeremy (*page 35*)

MSS.: Group II: *N*, *TCD*; *DC*; Group III: *O'F*; *B*; *O2*.

The text in *1633*, which was here following its Group II MS., is poor. In addition to having inferior readings, it notably lacks necessary contractions and elision marks. No single manuscript is satisfactory. *B* is above its usual level and can be used to support *O'F*. *DC* has a fair text, avoiding some of the errors of *TCD* but having more of its own. The text in *O2* is poor.

Grierson put forward as an objective test of the merits of variants closeness to the Latin of Tremellius, since Donne was attempting a close paraphrase. But he also thought that Donne consulted the Vulgate, a view I formerly accepted. J. J. Pollock (*English Studies*, December 1974) has shown conclusively that reference to the Vulgate is not necessary to explain Donne's departures from Tremellius, since in each case where Donne appears to follow it his deviation can be explained by reference to the Genevan and Authorized Versions. In particular the wording of the Genevan version pervades Donne's choice of English words to render Tremellius's Latin. The most striking example is 'bread and drinke' (l. 134) where Tremellius has 'frumentum et vinum', the Vulgate has 'triticum et vinum', *A.V.* has 'corn and wine', but Geneva has 'bread and drink'. This might justify, in disputed readings when Tremellius and Geneva disagree, the adoption of the reading that agrees with Geneva; but I have thought it better to follow Tremellius: see notes to ll. 157, 355, 374.

Although the poem cannot be dated exactly, it seems safe to put it after Donne's ordination. We may connect it with the poem on the Sidneys' paraphrases (after 1621) and possibly with the events of the years 1620–2, when the distress of the German Protestants turned men's minds to the captivity of Zion. Donne discusses the interpretation of Lamentations in a sermon preached 5 November 1622 (*Sermons*, iv. 237–63).

Donne's motives may not have been primarily artistic. His lines on the Sidneian Psalms show that he shared the current discontent with the Old Version. He may have wished to enrich the worship of his Church with matter suitable for singing in penitential seasons. The first two stanzas were set by Thomas Ford in three parts (Christ Church MSS. 736–8). Donne's superiority to most paraphrasers is partly due to his metre, which is capable of supporting Biblical rhythms. This can be seen by comparing his version with Drayton's rendering of the last chapter of Lamentations into fourteeners in his *Harmonie of the Church* (1591).

Tremellius (1510–80) was by birth an Italian Jew. He became a Christian at the age of twenty, was a Calvinist and a famous Hebrew scholar. His translation of the Old Testament, which he made with Francis Junius, was published at Frankfurt in 1575–9. It was printed in London in 1580, along with a translation of the New Testament, made by Tremellius alone, from the Syriac. In the following year, Tremellius's Old Testament with Beza's New Testament, translated from the Greek, were published together in one volume. This was the Latin Bible of Protestants.

As the heading suggests, Donne did not follow Tremellius slavishly. At times he follows the Vulgate, and sometimes he blends the two versions. In some places his choice of version seems affected by the Authorized Version.

ll. 33–34. *Her foulnesse* &c. 'Inmunditiae suae in fimbriis suis mercedem esse nondum recordata' *Tr*: 'Her filthiness is in her skirts: she remembered not he last end' *Gen*: 'remembereth' *A.V.*

l. 50. *hath spred*. 'hath spred' *Gen* and *A.V.* 'Spred' (*1633*) would make 'heaven' a dissyllable, which is contrary to Donne's practice.

l. 58. *invite*. 'Accite' (*B, O'F*) renders 'convocat' rather better than 'invite' does. But, although the word occurs more than once in *Essays in Divinity*, there is no example of Donne's using it in poetry.

l. 76. *and none could get*. This reading from *O'F* gives the best sense, and is probably the reading which lies behind *B*'s 'they none could gett', which is in turn probably the source of the impossibly abrupt reading of *TCD* and *1633*.

l. 81. *Of all which heare I mourne*. Grierson explains as 'hear that I mourne', quoting Tremellius: 'Audientium me in gemitu esse . . .' and adding ' "me in gemitu esse" is not quite the same thing as "me gementem".'

l. 95. *and prophan'd*. 'Ut prophanum abjicit regnum cum principibus ipsius' *Tr*: 'Polluit regnum, et principes ejus' *V*: 'He hath polluted the kingdom and the princes thereof' *Gen* and *A.V.*

l. 114. *hand.* Geneva agrees with Tremellius in the singular here and in ll. 158, 246, 354. It agrees with Tremellius in the plural in ll. 122, 298, 304.

l. 157. *against.* I retain 'against' ('contra' *Tr*), although both Geneva and *A.V.* have 'unto'. It seems most unlikely that the unusual preposition 'against' would have been substituted for the familiar 'unto'.

l. 174. *his.* The change from second to third person reflects a similar change in the originals: 'in die furoris Domini' *V*: '. . . the Lord's wrath' *Gen*: '. . . the Lord's anger' *A.V.* Grierson changed 'his' to 'thy' in 1929.

l. 183. *With hemlocke, and with labour.* 'Cicuta et molestia' *Tr*: 'Felle et labore' *V*: 'gall and labour' *Gen*: 'gall and travail' *A.V.*

l. 220. *yet there.* TCD omits 'there'; *1633* reads 'yet then'. I suspect this was a patch of a defective line.

l. 233. *Both good and evill from his mouth proceeds.* This is a question in *Tr*, *V*, *Gen*, and *A.V.*

l. 234. *for his misdeeds.* 'Propter poenas peccatorum suorum' *Tr*: 'Pro peccatis suis' *V*: 'for his sin' *Gen*: 'for the punishment of his sins' *A.V.*

l. 245. *water rivers.* Donne appears to be trying to render 'rivis aquarum' by using the noun 'water' attributively.

l. 249. *my city daughters sake.* As in l. 245, B, O'F have a less idiomatic reading 'city's'. There is a good analogy in 'city fathers' for the use of the uninflected genitive.

l. 252. *cast on mee a stone.* 'Projiciunt lapides in me' *Tr*: 'Posuerunt lapidem super me' *V*: 'Cast a stone upon me' *Gen* and *A.V.* The application of the Vulgate text prophetically to the burial of Christ probably made Donne reject the prosaic rendering of Tremellius.

l. 274. *as.* Both Geneva and *A.V.* read 'as'.

l. 289. *have sinn'd more.* 'Et major est poena . . . supplicio Sodomi' (*margin* 'Heb. *iniquitas filiae*') *Tr*: 'Et major effecta est iniquitas . . . peccato Sodomorum' *V*: 'For the iniquity . . . is become greater than the sin . . .' *Gen*: 'The punishment of the iniquity . . . the punishment of the sin . . .' *A.V.*

l. 296. *Saphirine.* The spelling 'Sapherine' (*B*, *TCD*), which disguises the derivation from 'Sapphire', may have led to the absurd 'Seraphine' (*1633*).

l. 299. *their bone.* Grierson adopted 'the bone' (*B*, *O'F*), but in his note said 'The reading of the editions is probably right', citing Tremellius: 'Concreta est cutis eorum cum osse ipsorum'. Geneva and *A.V.* have 'their bones'.

l. 302. *by penury.* Grierson adopted 'through penury' (*B*, *O'F*), saying that Donne was echoing the parallelism of 'confossi gladio, quam confossi fame' in the line before. Reference to Geneva and *A.V.* does not help.

l. 337. *Th'anointed Lord.* In his Gunpowder Plot sermon of 1622, preached on this text (*Sermons*, iv. 237–63) Donne takes the reference here to be historical, to a King of Israel, and not, as the Vulgate rendering makes it, prophetic of Christ. Here, and in another sermon (x. 192–212) he interprets Lamentations literally and historically as does Tremellius throughout his rendering and commentary.

l. 342 *Uz.* Since both Geneva and *A.V.* have this form I now adopt it, although 'her' (*1633*) suggests 'Huz' or 'Hus' may be Donne's form.

l. 355. *drinke.* Both Tremellius and the Vulgate have 'bibimus'; but Tremellius continues with the present tense, whereas the Vulgate has the past. It seems likely, as Donne has preserved the present tense of Tremellius in the second verb, that he took the first verb, 'bibimus', to be in the present.

l. 374. *fall . . . beare.* Here again, Tremellius uses the present tense, where the Vulgate has the past: but the Vulgate renders the first half of the text quite differently. In Tremellius this clause is a parallel to the preceding one: 'Juvenes ad molendum portant, et pueri ad ligna corruunt.' It seems likely that Donne would preserve Tremellius's tense in the second clause, as he has followed him in the first.

A Hymne to Christ, at the Authors last going into Germany
(*page 48*)

MSS.: Group II: *A 18, N, TCC, TCD*; Group III: *Dob, Lut, O'F, S 96; B; O2, P.*

1633 took this poem from its Group II MS. I have emended it once (l. 12) where all the MSS. (except *P*) agree against it.

In *1635*, the editor, as well as adopting a bad Group III reading, 'Face' for 'Fame' (l. 28), printed 'this flood' for 'our seas' and 'thy blood' for 'thy sea' (ll. 11 and 12). I do not believe he had manuscript authority for this, and think he took his corrections from the 'flood' and 'blood' of the first stanza.

All the MSS. agree in setting the poem in a seven-line stanza ending with a fourteener. *1633* divides the final line into two lines of eight and six syllables. For reasons for adopting the setting of the manuscripts, see supplementary notes, p. 157.

Donne left England, as chaplain to Doncaster on his mission of mediation to the German Princes, on 12 May 1619. They returned in January 1620, having travelled as far as Vienna. On 18 April 1619, Donne preached a farewell sermon at Lincoln's Inn. The close of the sermon strikingly anticipates the words of the Hymn: 'Christ Jesus remember us all in his Kingdome, to which, though we must sail through a sea, it is the sea of his blood, where no soul suffers shipwrack' (*Sermons*, ii. 249).

l. 9. *I lov'd there, . . . lov'd.* *1635* adopted present tenses from *O'F*, but made the further alteration of 'there' to 'here'. The word 'there' points to the past tenses of Group II, *1633* being right. In sacrificing 'this Island', Donne puts all he offers into the past, as if it were no longer 'here'.

ll. 12–14. See supplementary notes, p. 157.

l. 15. *controule*. In a soul that is well-ordered, neither Christ nor the Christian religion censures or checks love. See *O.E.D.* 'control', *v.* 3b and 4b.

ll. 19–21. *Thou lov'st not* &c. The prayer to be freed from 'loving more' than Christ echoes Augustine: 'Minus te amat qui tecum aliquid amat, quod non propter te amat' (*Confessions*, x. 29). But the conceit of Christ as a lover who should be jealous, since all true lovers are so, is Donne's own. Cf. the close of the sonnet on his wife's death. There is in both poems something uncharacteristic of Donne's thought, which we may perhaps ascribe to his deep unhappiness after his wife's death.

l. 28. *An Everlasting night*. The close of the poem is a prayer for death, by which our divorce from the world is sealed or ratified. In his first sermon at Court after his return Donne took for his text Amos v. 18: 'Woe unto you that desire the day of the Lord! . . . the day of the Lord is darkness, and not light.' In his third part he applied his text to the dejected 'them in whom a wearinesse of this life, when Gods corrections are upon them . . . works an over-hasty and impatient desire of death' (*Sermons*, ii. 359, preached 3 March 1620). Donne had returned from his journey, according to Walton, 'with his sorrows moderated and his health improved'. In this sermon he takes his usual view that the afflictions of this life are 'corrections'.

Hymne to God my God, in my sicknesse (*page 50*)

MSS.: Group III: *S 96*; *A 34* (Sir Julius Caesar's papers).

This Hymn was first printed in 1635. Spelling and punctuation do not suggest any direct contact between the two manuscript versions, or between either of them and *1635*. I have corrected *1635* twice: ll. 5 and 12.

The date of this poem is discussed in Appendix E, pp. 132–5.

l. 5. *now*. I have adopted the reading of both MSS. for 'here' of *1635*, which would seem to have been caught from the line above.

l. 6. *love*. Grierson was misled in stating that in Caesar's copy the reading is 'loer', sc. 'lore'.

By their loving attention to him Donne's doctors have turned into geographers and he a map which they pore over. It is a map of the whole world, for man is a little world. They chart his symptoms and find that the course which they have charted shows a 'South-west discoverie'. The South is the hot quarter; the West the quarter of the Sun's declension. He is to die by the 'raging heat' (*fretum*) of fever, or to travel by the 'strait' (*fretum*) of fever.

l. 12. *theire*. I follow Grierson in adopting 'theire' from *S 96*. 'Theis' (*A 34*) may well be a misreading of 'their', which has given rise to 'these' read as 'those' in *1635*.

ll. 13–15. *As West and East* &c. Cf. 'Upon the Annunciation and Passion', l. 21; cf. also *Sermons*, ii. 199. These three lines condense a passage in a sermon:

In a flat Map, there goes no more, to make West East, though they be distant in an extremity, but to paste that flat Map upon a round body, and then West and East are all one. In a flat soule, in a dejected conscience, in a troubled spirit, there goes no more to the making of that trouble, peace, then to apply that trouble to the body of the Merits, to the body of the Gospel of Christ Jesus, and conforme thee to him, and thy West is East, thy Trouble of spirit is Tranquillity of spirit. The name of Christ is *Oriens, The East*; And yet Lucifer himselfe is called *Filius Orientis, The Son of the East*. If thou beest fallen by *Lucifer* . . . and not fallen as *Lucifer*, to a senslesnesse of thy fall . . . but to a troubled spirit, still thy Prospect is the East, still thy Climate is heaven, still thy Haven is Jerusalem (*Sermons*, vi. 59).

Both text and conceit occur in a letter to Sir Robert Carr, where Donne says his imagination is full of a sermon he is about to preach (*Tobie Mathew Collection*, pp. 305–7). The text is the Vulgate version of Zech. vi. 12: 'Ecce vir, Oriens nomen ejus', used by Donne in his own epitaph.

ll. 16–17.   *Is the Pacifique Sea my home? Or are*
                     The Eastern riches? Is Jerusalem?

Cf. 'A narrower way, but to a better Land; thorow Straights; 'tis true; but to the *Pacifique* Sea' (*Sermons*, ix. 185). 'The Easterne riches' refers to the fabled land of Cathay. The name 'Jerusalem' means 'Vision of Peace'.

Behind the questions lie the speculations of medieval geographers as to the location of the Terrestrial Paradise. In most medieval maps Jerusalem is at the centre, the East is at the top and Paradise is placed at the farthest East, beyond Cathay; see the Hereford *Mappa Mundi*. But since it was believed that Paradise was hedged about by a wall of flame, some thinkers identified this with the torrid zone and placed Paradise in the Southern Ocean, as Dante does. In Donne's day, however, all authorities, Catholic and Protestant, were agreed that the Terrestrial Paradise was in Mesopotamia, in the same part of the world as Jerusalem. The earthly Paradise is a type of the heavenly, as the earthly city of Jerusalem is a type of 'the Jerusalem which is above'.

ll. 18–20. Anyan, *and* Magellan, *and* Gibraltare &c. The 'Streto de Anian' appeared first on a map of 1566, as a narrow strait separating America from Eastern Asia. 'Anian' placed on the west coast of America, was Marco Polo's Anica or Anin, modern Annam.

The world as known to the early Fathers was divided between the sons of Noah: Japhet's inheritance was Europe, Ham's was Africa, and Shem's, Asia. On old sketch-maps their names can be seen for the names of the continents.

Donne cannot mean that the Pacific or Cathay can only be reached by straits in the geographical sense; cf. 'Men go to *China*, both by the Straights, and by the *Cape*' (*Tobie Mathew Collection*, p. 68); see also *Sermons*, viii. 371. He is punning: 'Anian, Magellan and Gibraltar, ways to the East, the Pacific and to Jerusalem, are all straits, and however we travel to them—

ll. 21–22. Paradise *and* Calvarie &c. See Appendix F, pp. 135–7, for an extended discussion of these lines.

l. 30. *Therfore that he may raise the Lord throws down.* The text of Donne's sermon to his own soul is not apparently Scriptural. Cf. 'But thine *Apostles* feare takes hold of mee, *that when I have preached to others, I myselfe should be a cast-away*; and therefore I am *cast downe*, that I might not. be *cast away*' (Sparrow, *Devotions*, p. 13, cited by Grierson). Cf. also: 'Death who destroys me, re-edifies me: . . . man was fallen, and God took that way to raise him, to throw him lower, into the grave' (*Sermons*, iv. 126). The nearest text I can find is Job xxii. 29: 'When men are cast down, then shalt thou say, There is lifting up' ('Qui enim humiliatus fuerit erit in gloria', Vulgate).

A Hymne to God the Father (*page 51*)

MSS.: Group II: *A 18, N, TCC, TCD*; Group III: *Dob, Lut, O'F, S 96*; Miscellanies: *Ash, E 20, S 962*.

The differences between this Hymn, as it appears in *1633* and Walton's *Life of Donne* (1640), and as it appears under a different title in the MSS., led Grierson to print two texts. But the variants in *1633*, with one possible exception, are weaker readings, in most cases obscuring the sense. I do not believe there was more than one version of this poem, and therefore print a single text, based on *1633*, but emended from the MSS.

The texts in the miscellanies are poor. In *Ash*, whose text shares some readings with *S 962*, the line-division in the last verse is wrong, and has been put right by another hand. This suggests that the writer was not copying from another manuscript, and that his variants may be the result of oral transmission. *E 20* has the hymn with a setting by John Hilton (d. 1657); see Grierson, ii. 252 and *English Hymnal*, no. 515.

Walton gave the Hymn in full, with only insignificant variations from *1633*, in the first edition of his *Life*. There is no reason to doubt his accompanying statement that Donne wrote the poem during his grave illness of 1623, or the additional information he gave in 1658, that Donne had it set to music.

Title: The title of *1633* is not found in the MSS. Group II, *Dob, Ash* have 'To Christ'; *Lut, O'F, S 96* have 'Christo Salvatori'. There is no title in *E 20, S 962*.

The titles of Donne's poems do not generally have much authority. (See my article 'The titles of Donne's poems', *Friendship's Garland: Essays presented to Mario Praz*, ed. V. Gabrieli (Rome, 1966), i. 189–207.) The manuscript

titles may have arisen here because the other Hymn which appears with this
one is addressed to Christ. Although the first two verses might properly
be addressed to either the Father or the Son, in the third verse the memory
of the promise to Abraham seems more natural in a prayer to the Father,
and, if the prayer is addressed to Christ, the pun on Sun and Son is lost.
For these reasons I reject the manuscript titles. The title of *1633* is probably
only editorial in origin, but titles are a convenience and this one is estab-
lished. The best title would be no title at all. The poem has no sense of distinc-
tion of Persons; it ends with an appeal to the Godhead. 'Sweare by thy selfe'
is the cry of the man who, as Walton reports, 'would often say in a kind of
sacred extasie—Blessed be God that he is God only, and divinely like himself'.

l. 2. *is.* The present tense is plainly right against 'was' (*1633*). Cf. Ps. li. 5:
'Behold I was shapen in iniquity: and in sin did my mother conceive me.'
This sin, though committed before he was born, is still his; he inherits from
his parents, as they from theirs, the taint of original sin.

l. 3. *those sinnes.* The singular of *1633*, 'that sinne', looks like a correction made
to bring this petition into line with the others, which has led to the further
correction in the next line of 'doe them still' to 'do run still'. It is impossible
that Donne, in speaking of his daily sins, should limit them to one.

l. 5. *When thou hast done, thou hast not done.* Donne's pun on his own name, on
which the poem turns, is brought out by the spelling in some of the MSS.
Group III spoils the point by reading 'I have not done'.

l. 7. *by which I'have wonne.* I have adopted the reading of *TCD*, supplying an
elision mark. Without this the line is irregular. *Dob* and *O'F* have regularized
by omitting 'by' and *1633* by omitting 'have'.

The sin here is possibly the writing of licentious poetry.

ll. 15–16.   *Sweare by thy selfe, that at my death thy Sunne*
                        Shall shine as it shines now,

1633 is without support, except from *E 20*, in reading 'thy sonne' and 'as
he shines'. At first sight these readings are tempting; but this is the only
occasion in the poem on which *1633* is not manifestly inferior to the MSS.

Donne constantly uses the Sun as a type of God's mercy. That mercy is
manifested in his Son, and a pun is intended here, as elsewhere. By using
the neuter pronoun Donne compresses what may be extended as: 'Swear that
thy Sun of mercy—shown to us in Son—shall shine . . .'. There is a kind of
parallel in a sermon: 'I shall see the Sonne of God, the Sunne of glory, and
shine my self, as that sunne shines' (*Sermons*, iv. 162). This mercy he feels
now, in his assurance of forgiveness; his fear is that in the pangs of death
'an horror of great darkness' may fall upon him as it fell upon Abraham
(Gen. xv. 12), and that his faith may fail and he himself be cast away. Cf. the

promise to Abraham, 'By myself have I sworn, saith the Lord' (Gen. xxii. 16) and the comment on it in Hebrews vi. 13–19.

l. 18. *I have no more.* The reading of Groups II and III makes the full close to the poem. *1633* reads 'I feare'; *Ash* reads 'I aske' (*S 962*, 'I'le aske'); *E 20* reads 'I need'. The variants in this line may have arisen because 'have' is an unsatisfactory word for a singer to rest on.

LATIN POEMS

To Mr. George Herbert, with my Seal, of the Anchor and Christ (*page 52*)

This Latin poem, with its translation, was first printed in the 1650 edition of Donne's poems. Its date and the nature of the verses by Herbert which were printed with it are discussed in Appendix G, pp. 136–47. I give reasons there for my emendation of the title.

l. 3. *Adscitus domui Domini.* This should mean 'having been baptized' and the translator appears to have understood the phrase so, for he rendered 'Adopted in Gods Family'. Cf. a sermon in which Donne speaks of those 'who are of the houshold of the faithfull . . . matriculated, engraffed, enrolled in the Church, by that initiatory Sacrament of Baptisme' (*Sermons*, ix. 319). On the other hand, in the dedication to his *Devotions*, Donne speaks of his ordination as his second birth, a phrase which normally refers to baptism. If we take the words the first way, we may render: 'I, who used formerly to seal my letters with my family crest, have, by my baptism, a right to new arms.' The poem then begins with a conceit: our renunciation of our natural inheritance at baptism is marked by our taking the Arms of the family into which we are adopted. But, unlike other Arms, the Cross, borne for a long time, changes; so his new seal is not Christ upon the Cross, but Christ upon an Anchor. If we take the words the other way—'I . . . on my ordination take new arms'—the conceit is lost; but the parallel with the *Devotions* inclines me to the second interpretation.

l. 5. *lavacro.* Cf. Tit. iii. 5: 'through the washing of regeneration' ('per lavacrum', Vulgate).

l. 7. *desinit.* There may be an echo here of Horace, *Ars Poetica*, 3–4:

ut turpiter atrum
Desinat in piscem mulier formosa superne.

l. 10. *Jesu.* The scansion with a short 'e' is most extraordinary. Although there is a licence allowed in the scansion of proper names, it can hardly be extended to the sacred name.

ll. 11–16. 'Nor am I wholly deprived of the serpents I had by birth; God does not give in such a way that he takes away what was given before. In as much as he is wise, the serpent is a gift from God; in as much as he licks the dust and goes on his belly, he is death; but on our Cross he is our cure, if nature is nailed to the Cross, and if all grace flows out upon us from him who is nailed there.'

The serpent is a type of wisdom, a type of evil or death, and a type of Christ upon the Cross; cf. Matt. x. 16; Gen. iii. 14–15; and John iii. 14: 'And as Moses lifted up the serpent in the wilderness, even so shall the Son of man be lifted up.' Cf.

The creeping Serpent . . . is Craft; the exalted Serpent, the crucified Serpent, is Wisdome. All your worldly cares, all your crafty bargaines . . . savour of the earth. . . : But crucifie this craft of yours, . . . and then you have changed the Serpent, from the Serpent of perdition creeping upon the earth, to the Serpent of salvation exalted in the wildernesse. Creeping wisedome, that still looks downward, is but craft; Crucified wisedome, that looks upward, is truly wisedome.

Later in the same paragraph, Donne passes from the moral to the mystical sense:

But in the other Serpent, the crucified Serpent, God hath reconciled to himself, all things. . . . That creeping Serpent, Satan, is war. . . . The crucified Serpent Christ Jesus is peace. . . . The creeping Serpent eats our dust, the strength of our bodies, in sicknesses, and our glory in the dust of the grave (*Sermons*, x. 189–90).

l. 18. *Catechismus*. Donne's scansion, with a short 'e', may be due to his having mistaken the word's derivation. More probably he is influenced by its currency in English with a short 'e'. A catechism is an epitome of the faith; this seal will be the faith in miniature.

l. 21. *sanctus cognominis*. The reference is to the George that hangs from the Garter on the seated figure of the King on the reverse of the Great Seal.

Epigraph to the Portrait of Donne in his Shroud, &c. (*page 53*)

Corporis haec Animae sit Syndon, Syndon Jesu. Amen. Both the scansion and the translation of this line of hexameter verse present some difficulty. The line either ends with two spondees: 'Syndon Jesu', or there is a false quantity in the second 'Syndon' and the 'J' of 'Jesu' is vocalized: 'Syndon Jesu'. The first scansion is highly improbable; it gives a line ending with four successive spondees. A false quantity in 'Syndon' would be a parallel to that in 'Catechismus' in the last poem. In both cases we have a Greek word, borrowed into Latin and then into English. Reference to *O.E.D.* shows that 'sindon', from Matt. xxvii. 59, was in current use. Donne uses it in *Pseudo-Martyr* (p. 86), though with italicization. I therefore scan the line

Corporis haec Animae sit Syndon, Syndon Jesu.

In construing, 'Jesu' might be taken as in the vocative, and the meaning would then be: 'May this shroud of the body be (i.e. typify) the shroud of the soul, O Jesu.' The other way to construe gives preferable sense, since it makes use of the typological meaning of the shroud of Christ, and brings out the theological implications of the prayer. By this method, the predicate, being the same as the subject, is taken as suppressed, the second 'Syndon' as in apposition to the first, and 'Jesu' as in the genitive. The literal meaning is: 'May this shroud of the body be (i.e. typify) the shroud of the soul: the shroud of Jesus.' Paraphrased this means: 'As the body is shrouded in white linen, may the soul be shrouded in a white garment also, which is not its own but is the white garment of Jesus.' The line is a rather tortured rendering of the sense of a couplet in *The Second Anniversary* (ll. 113–14):

> Thinke that they shroud thee up, and think from thence
> They reinvest thee in white innocence.

There is a parallel in 'A Hymn To God my God': 'So in his purple wrapp'd receive me Lord', where we find the same idea of being wrapped in the garment of another. In the hymn the garment is the purple robe set on Christ in mockery, which typifies his blood; in the hexameter it is the shroud in which Joseph of Arimathæa wrapped his body for burial, which typifies the righteousness of Christ. John Sparrow has suggested that the words have been transposed by a puzzled copyist and that Donne actually wrote

    Corporis haec Syndon, Syndon animae sit Jesu,

that is,

This the shroud of my body, may the shroud of my soul be the shroud of Jesu. (*T.L.S.*, 13 March 1953.)

I cannot believe that anyone but Donne wrote this line of verse, and it was plainly written for one purpose only: to stand beneath this picture of himself in his shroud. It has no point without the picture. I wish to suggest that Donne's last sermon, with this striking frontispiece prefixed, was published in accordance with instructions which he himself gave; and that we should add to his activities in his last illness, the arrangements for the publication of his last sermon and the composition of this epigraph. He wished that, being dead, he might yet speak.

APPENDIX A

Donne's Views on the State of the Soul after Death

THE two points on which Donne as a preacher insists are that the soul is immortal, not in its essence, but by the will of its Creator, who will not let it perish;[1] and that at death the virtuous soul goes at once to heaven, and does not wait for its reward until its reunion with the body at the Last Day. The first point was not disputed. Donne's insistence on it is probably because of its bearing on the second point, and because the 'heresy of the Arabians'—that the soul died with the body, to be raised with it at the Last Day—had been revived in his time by the sect of Mortalists. On the second point, which was disputed, Donne differs from the majority of Protestants in taking up a definite position. What is more, he takes up the Roman position, although he appears to have arrived at it late in life and as a result of his polemical writings against the Roman Church.

Both points are made in a passage cited by Grierson in his long note on the line 'Soules but preserv'd, not naturally free':[2]

We have a full cleernesse of the state of the soule after this life, not onely above those of the old Law, but above those of the Primitive Christian Church, which, in some hundreds of yeares, came not to a cleere understanding in that point, whether the soule were immortall by nature, or but by preservation, whether the soule could not die, or onely should not die. Or (because that perchance may be without any constant cleernesse yet) that was not cleere to them, (which concernes our case neerer) whether the soule came to a present fruition of the sight of God after death or no. But God having afforded us cleernesse in that....[3]

Here Donne suggests that there is still some possibility of dispute on the first point, though the second is certain. Usually he is equally certain on both. At times he refers to the state of the soul after death casually, without indicating that any different view had ever been held or was possible.[4] At other times he refers to the testimony of the

---

[1] This is not to be defined, as Grierson defined it, as 'a form of the doctrine of conditional immortality'. Donne does not suggest that some souls only are preserved, and others are allowed to perish. He is asserting that the soul, as a created thing, is dependent upon its Creator; see *Sermons*, ix. 82 and Simpson, *Essays*, p. 76.

[2] Grierson, ii. 160–2.

[3] *Sermons*, v. 385.

[4] But as my soule, as soone as it is out of my body, is in Heaven, and does not

Fathers on this point, either stating that their witness was conflicting, or that the majority were in error here;[1] or he specifies the various heresies which have been held on the subject;[2] but, again and again, in speaking of the Resurrection he is careful to make clear the distinction between the fate of the soul and the fate of the body at death. Often the theme is handled with a poet's imagination:

Saint Augustine hath seen Christ in the flesh one thousand two hundred yeares; in Christs glorifyed flesh; but, it is with the eyes of his understanding, and in his soul. Our flesh, even in the Resurrection, cannot be a spectacle, a perspective glasse to our soul. We shall see the Humanity of Christ with our bodily eyes, then glorifyed; but, that flesh, though glorifyed, cannot make us see God better, nor clearer, then the soul alone hath done, all the time, from our death, to our resurrection. But as an indulgent Father, or as a tender mother, when they go to see the King in any Solemnity, or any other thing of observation, and curiosity, delights to carry their child, which is flesh of their flesh, and bone of their bone, with them, and though the child cannot comprehend it as well as they, they are as glad that the child sees it, as that they see it themselves; such a gladnesse shall my soul have, that this flesh, (which she will no longer call her prison, nor her tempter, but her friend, her companion, her wife) that this flesh, that is, I, in the re-union, and redintegration of both parts, shall see God.[3]

Donne is perfectly correct in saying that the majority of the early Fathers held that the souls of the righteous were not admitted to the Beatific Vision before the Last Day. But by the fifth century, when the

stay for the possession of Heaven, nor for the fruition of the sight of God, till it be ascended through ayre, and fire, and Moone, and Sun, and Planets, and Firmament, to that place which we conceive to be Heaven, but without the thousandth part of a minutes stop, as soone as it issues, is in a glorious light, which is Heaven. . . .' (*Sermons*, vii. 70–71).

¹ 'The Fathers, in a great partie denied, that the soules of good men departed were to enjoy the sight of God, till the Resurrection' (*Sermons*, vii. 202).

² 'The Gnosticks . . . acknowledged a Resurrection, but they said it was of the *soul* onely, and not of the body, for they thought that the soul lay dead (at least, in a dead sleep) till the Resurrection. Those Heretickes that are called the *Arabians*, did (as the Gnosticks did) affirm a temporary death of the soul, as well as of the body, but then they allowed a Resurrection to both soul, and body . . .' (*Sermons*, iii. 115).

³ *Sermons*, iii. 112. Other passages where Donne speaks of this immediate possession of heaven at death are: *Sermons*, ii. 267, v. 212, vi. 74–75, 266, and 359, vii. 122, 182, and 257–8, ix. 160, x. 227. See also *Devotions*, Meditation xviii (Sparrow, pp. 103–5). This list is not exhaustive; references are to places where the subject is handled explicitly; there are many others where the doctrine is implied. I have found only three passages in which Donne speaks of 'rising from the grave' or 'sleeping in the grave', without distinguishing between the fates of the soul and the body: *Sermons*, iv. 126 and 162, vi. 213.

original Christian belief in the imminence of the Last Day had faded,
it came to be believed that the righteous did not have to wait for the
consummation of all things, but that their souls, either at death, or
after a time of purification in purgatory, were admitted to the full bliss
of heaven. Although this was the general belief in the West after
Gregory the Great, it did not, however, receive formal definition until
1336. The occasion was the revival of the older view by Pope John XXII
(1316–34). He was condemned by the Faculty of Theology at Paris, and
is said to have recanted on his death-bed. His successor, Benedict XII,
treated the subject fully in *De statu animarum ante generale judicium*, and
put forward a lengthy definition on 29 January 1336, which was ac-
cepted throughout the West, but not in the East. The Greek repre-
sentatives at the Council of Florence in 1438 accepted both this
definition and the allied doctrine of purgatory; but all their decisions
were repudiated on their return home. Jeremy Taylor is well aware
that the Greek Church did not accept the Roman view, but Donne
either does not know this, or ignores it.

At the Reformation this doctrine was not specifically attacked, as
was the doctrine of purgatory. The doctrine of purgatory was rejected
on the ground that it could not be proved out of Scripture; but on this
point, texts could be cited to support either view. Protestants held that
where Scripture gave doubtful testimony the matter could not be one
of faith, but could only be a matter of opinion. Thus Calvin, although
he himself thought, like Luther, that both full reward and full punish-
ment were not experienced by the soul until the Last Day, judged the
whole debate on what befell the soul at death to be 'bien frivole et
sotte', adding 'C'est folie et témerité de nous enquérir de choses in-
cognues, plus haut que Dieu ne nous permet d'en savoir'.[1] I have not
found an expression of opinion by a contemporary of Donne's in the
Church of England; but, in the next generation, Taylor is as emphatic
as Donne on the other side.[2] He declared that the belief that the
righteous receive their full reward at death was a 'recession from
antiquity'; and that the doctrine was designed by the Roman Church
to support its doctrines of purgatory and the intercession of saints.

I believe that the question first presented itself to Donne when he

---

[1] *Institution de la religion chrétienne*, III. xxv. 6. See also IV. i. 12, where Calvin
uses this question as an example of an indifferent matter on which Churches should
not divide.

[2] Taylor refers to the question many times, handling it at length in *The Great
Exemplar*, and in his Funeral Sermon on Sir George Dalston (*Works*, ii. 715–17
and viii. 543 et seq.).

was writing *Pseudo-Martyr*, which is the earliest of his works in which he gives definite expression to his later view. There is some irony in the fact that he seems to have accepted this Roman doctrine, in order to overturn another—purgatory. The Roman controversialists produced, in support of purgatory, many passages from the Fathers which spoke of a purging fire. These were bandied to and fro—one side claiming that they referred to purgatory; the other, that they referred to the general conflagration at the Last Day. Anyone who has attempted to follow the controversy between Morton and Parsons, as to whether Bellarmine had or had not twisted the testimony of the Fathers, must appreciate Donne's good sense and controversial skill in cutting the whole question short, by asserting that the testimony of the Fathers on the state of the soul after death was too confused to be used to prove anything at all.[1] Donne takes the shortest way to put the Fathers out of court, by accepting the definition of Pope Benedict XII as the voice of the Church, having arrived at 'cleernesse' on a point on which the testimony of the Fathers was 'obscure and various'. Since they showed such 'irresolution' here, and there was such 'perplexity in collating their opinions', it was useless to call them as witnesses for or against the allied doctrine of purgatory. The acceptance of the definition was not impossible for a Protestant, since it had not been explicitly attacked by the Reformers, and was not, as the Reformers held purgatory to be, unsupported by Scripture.

But, as I have said in the Introduction, although Donne may have been led to accept this view for purposes of controversy, it plainly seized his imagination and became of great importance to him personally. We cannot otherwise explain why he should insist on it so often, when Protestants either rejected it, or regarded the whole matter as indifferent. He usually accepts whole-heartedly the Protestant distinction between beliefs and pious opinions.

[1] See *Pseudo-Martyr*, p. 111, and cf. Morton, *Encounter against M. Parsons* (1610), pp. 116–57.

APPENDIX B

Verbal Alterations in the Divine Poems *in the edition of 1635*

THE alterations which the editor of *1635* made in the poems he reprinted from *1633* are of no textual value; but since the majority appeared in later editions, until the Grolier Club editor and Grierson returned to the text of *1633*, they are of interest to students of Donne. They are given here together in tabular form. When they are presented in this way, their origin is clear. With the exception of 'Good Friday', l. 30, and 'A Hymn to Christ', ll. 11 and 12, all those which cannot be regarded as obvious corrections, slips, misprints, or minor alterations are to be found in *O'F*. The majority are readings which *O'F* shares with the other Group III manuscripts; but some are peculiar to *Lut*, *O'F*, and two are found in *O'F* alone.

The editor of *1635* worked from a copy of *1633* which had the outer forme of Aa in its uncorrected state. He corrected its obvious errors, but printed 'still is' for 'is still' and 'will' for 'well' in 'A Litany', ll. 164 and 231; see p. xcvi.

In the following table the manuscripts are listed alphabetically in their groups.

	1633	1635	MSS. agreeing with 1635
'La Corona'			
1. 2	low	lone	*O'F*
1. 10	end	ends	*Dob, S, S 96*
3. 9	eyes	eye	Group II
6. 8	little	life	Group III; *W*
7. 3	just	true	Group III; *W*
'Holy Sonnets'			
(1633)			
1. 12	doe	shall	Group III
3. 6	my	*omitted*	Group I; Group II; *Lut, O'F; W*
6. 5	pictures	picture	
6. 10	doth	dost	All *MSS.*
8. 4	Simple	Simpler	Group II; *Lut, O'F*
8. 11	greater wonder	greater	

	1633	1635	MSS. agreeing with 1635
11. 11	Sonne	Sunne	
11. 12	stolne	stole	B, Lut, O'F, S 96; W
12. 8	doe	*omitted*	

'A Litany'

34	a such	such	
52	which	what	Lut, O'F, S
58	then	that	
61	sanctified	satisfy'd	All MSS. but C 57, Lec
76	throw . . . and	thrown . . . do	Dob, Lut (doth), O'F (doth)
109	Thy	The	Group II; JC
	Academie	Academ	Group II; Dob, Lut, O'F, S 96
112	wrought	wrote	Lut, O'F
128	clods	clouds	B, Dob, Lut, O'F (corrected to clods in margin), S 96; S 962
134	sweet	sweets	Group II; Lut, O'F, S
153	flame	fame	All MSS.
154	for	through	B, Dob, Lut, O'F, S 96; JC; S 962
163	though	through	All MSS.
164	is still/still is	still is	C 57, Lec
173	clothes	robes	B (Robe), Dob, Lut, O'F, S 96; JC; S 962
217	wee	me	
231	well/will	will	B, Dob, Lut, O'F; S 962
246	or	and	B, Dob, Lut, O'F, S 96; S 962

'The Cross'

48	call	all,	Lut, O'F, S; P
50	th'other	th'others	All MSS.
	th'objects	objects	B, Dob, Lut, O'F, S; JC; S 962
53	dejections	detorsions	Lut, O'F

'Annunciation and Passion'

1	body	flesh	B, Dob, Lut, O'F, S 96
10	yet	and	Group I; Group II; Dob, Lut, O'F, S 96

	1633	*1635*	MSS. agreeing with *1635*
31	as	and	
33	daies	feasts	B, Dob, Lut, O'F, S (feast), S 96; P
34	is	are	B, Lut, O'F, S, S 96; P

'Good Friday'

	1633	*1635*	
10	toward	to	Lut, O'F
13	this	his	N, TCD; B; Cy
30	Upon . . . miserable	On . . . distressed	
40	rusts	rust	A 18, TCC

'Lamentations'   (Only in N, TCD; B, O'F)

	1633	*1635*	
56	whence	whom	All MSS.
58	invite	accite	B, O'F
76	they could not	and none could	O'F
78	return'd	o'rturned	B, O'F
95	strengths	strength	B, O'F
121	Their	The	
141	For, the	For thee	B, O'F
157	against	unto	B, O'F
161	poure, for	powre out	
174	his	thy	B, O'F
229	wrong	wrung	All MSS.
245	water	watry	B, O'F
296	Seraphine	Saphirine	All MSS.
302	by	through	B, O'F
318	garments	garment	
342	which	that	
	her	Uz	B (Huz), N, TCD (Hus), O'F (Uz)
355	drunke	drinke	B, O'F
368	Ocean	Oven	All MSS.

'A Hymn to Christ'

	1633	*1635*	
10	lov'd there . . . lov'd	love here . . . love	B, Dob, Lut, O'F, S 96 (love there . . . love)
11	our seas	this flood	
12	thy seas	thy blood	
28	Fame	Face	B, Dob, Lut, O'F, S 96

APPENDIX C

The Interpretation of Donne's Sonnet on the Church

THE interpretation of the sonnet 'Show me deare Christ, thy spouse, so bright and cleare' is a matter of dispute, and since the manner in which we understand it has a bearing on our judgement of Donne's later life,[1] it calls for a rather fuller discussion and more lengthy illustrative quotation than is desirable in a commentary.

Two authoritative voices give quite different interpretations. On the one hand Grierson, agreeing with Gosse who discovered the sonnet, writes:

It is clear enough why this sonnet was not published. It would have revealed Donne, already three years in orders, as still conscious of all the difficulties involved in a choice between the three divisions of Christianity—Rome, Geneva (made to include Germany), and England. This is the theme of his earliest serious poem, the *Satyre III*, and the subject recurs in the letters and sermons.

Evelyn Simpson, on the other hand, writes:

The sonnet may best be interpreted as a poetical expression of the thought found in the *Essays in Divinity*, and set forth earlier in Donne's life in the third *Satire*—that so long as the Church of Christ is rent into so many portions, men will have difficulty in recognizing her, and will be bewildered by the claims of different factions. Donne longed passionately for the reunion of Christendom. He readily admitted that Rome and Geneva, as well as Canterbury, were branches of the One Church, and he was troubled all through his life by the thought of 'our unhappy divisions', but this was perfectly compatible with loyalty to the Church of England.[2]

I agree with this latter view, but I would put it more strongly. The subject of the sonnet is not 'Which is the best of existing Churches?'; but the contrast between the Church promised in Scripture and the Church as it appears in the world and throughout history. In the first four lines, Donne sets two figures beside the image of the Bride of the

---

[1] Cf. the implications of such a statement as the following: 'If the philosophic doctrine of the relativity of truth helped to open the doors of the Church, it also left them ajar. "Show me deare Christ, thy spouse, so bright and cleare", Donne could write, two or three years after his ordination, in a sonnet discreetly omitted from his collected *Poems*' (Douglas Bush, *English Literature in the Earlier Seventeenth Century*, 1945, p. 133).

[2] See Grierson, ii. 235 and Simpson, *Prose Works*, p. 101.

Apocalypse. Contrasted as they are, they are alike in one thing: they are both totally unbridelike. Grierson speaks of 'a choice between the three divisions of Christianity—Rome, Geneva (made to include Germany), and England'. But, apart from the fact that to say 'Germany' is an odd way of saying 'Geneva (including Germany)', there is no third figure. There is the proud harlot, who is plainly not the Bride, and there is the ravished virgin, mourning and dishevelled, found in Germany and here in England, who is also certainly not the promised 'spouse, so bright and cleare'. Donne does not place over against them a third figure, modest yet comely, such as Herbert praised in his poem 'The British Church'. Instead, in his last lines, he opposes to these two figures a third, who represents the Church Universal, at present hidden from our sight by the divisions which obscure her unity in her Lord. He prays that we may see the Spouse of Christ appear to men, as a wife who delights to welcome all her husband's friends, and whose husband, unlike earthly husbands, delights in her approachability.

The sonnet is not merely 'compatible with loyalty to the Church of England'; it could hardly have been written by anyone but an Anglican.[1] The Anglican, at this period, differed from the Roman Catholic and the Calvinist in not holding a doctrine of the Church which compelled him to 'unchurch' other Christians. The Anglican Fathers, while defending episcopacy against the Puritans, did not, as Keble had to own in his edition of Hooker, defend it as a necessity for the valid administration of the Sacraments. They distinguished between matters of faith and matters of order, and regarded the Roman additions to the *credenda* as a far more serious obstacle to unity than the Calvinist defects in the *agenda*. They thought of themselves as Protestants, who had made a wise and godly reformation, preserving the true Catholic Faith, and a manner of Church government that was primitive and apostolic; but they did not assert exclusive validity for an episcopal ministry, and so did not feel themselves to be more truly members of the Church than their Protestant brothers abroad.[2] Similarly, they did not hold that what they regarded as Roman deviations from 'primitive purity' made the Church of Rome no Church. Donne's sarcastic wit in lines 5–8 of his sonnet is turned against those, either Calvinist or Roman, who would confine the meaning of the word Church.

[1] I use this term for those who accepted and carried further Hooker's defence of the Elizabethan settlement.
[2] See Leonard Hodgson, *The Doctrine of the Church as Held and Taught in the Church of England* (Oxford, 1948), and Norman Sykes, *The Church of England and Non-Episcopal Churches in the Sixteenth and Seventeenth Centuries* (S.P.C.K., 1948).

There are many parallels to the thought of this sonnet in Donne's letters and sermons; but we should not, I think, cite 'Satire III'. The subject of the satire is the problem of authority: 'Where is "true Religion" to be found?' The subject of the sonnet is 'What is the mark of the Church of Christ?' Having mocked at other answers, Donne gives his own at the close: 'unity and godly love'. His views can be found set out systematically in the *Essays in Divinity*, where he declares that the unity of the Church lies in its profession of faith in its Founder, and not in 'one precise forme of exterior worship, and Ecclesiastick policie'. The 'spacious and specious super-edifications' of Rome, and the refusal of Order and Hierarchy by Geneva do not destroy the fact that both are built upon 'the same foundation and corner-stone Christ Jesus'; but he concludes by declaring his longing for greater outward unity:

And though to all my thanksgivings to God, I ever humbly acknowledg, as one of his greatest Mercies to me, that he gave me my Pasture in this Park, and my milk from the brests of this Church, yet out of a fervent, and (I hope) not inordinate affection, even to such an Unity, I do zealously wish, that the whole catholick Church, were reduced to such Unity and agreement, in the form and profession Established, in any one of these Churches (though ours were principally to be wished) which have not by any additions destroyed the foundation and possibility of salvation in Christ Jesus; That then the Church, discharged of disputations, and misapprehensions, and this defensive warr, might contemplate Christ clearly and uniformely.[1]

The difference between such a passage and the sonnet lies not in the ideas expressed, but in the tone: in the wit of the contrasted images of the opening, in the mockery of the central lines, where Donne speaks as a man impatient of 'disputations and misapprehensions', and in the daring conceit of the close. If Donne deliberately withheld it from publication, it might well be because he thought it was too witty a poem for a man of his profession to write.

The sonnet opens with a prayer to Christ to reveal his Bride to men's sight. This is followed by an expression of incredulity as Donne looks out upon the world of his day and sees how unbridelike are those who claim to be the Spouse of Christ. The first figure he speaks of is obviously the Church of Rome; but the figure which

> rob'd and tore
> Laments and mournes in Germany and here

is not so easy to identify. Donne plainly means more than a mere

[1] Simpson, *Essays*, pp. 51–52.

unbridelike sluttishness, which is his complaint in 'Satire III' (ll. 50–52), where he speaks of her

> who'at Geneva's call'd
> Religion, plaine, simple, sullen, yong,
> Contemptuous, yet unhansome.

The contrast between the Church of Rome with its ceremonies and the Church of Geneva 'unfurnished of such Ceremonies as should make it comly and reverend' he makes more than once in his sermons, where he speaks of 'a *painted Church*' and 'a *naked Church*'.[1] But the image in the sonnet is not merely of lack of comeliness, but of spoliation, even of loss of virginity, and Donne does not speak of Geneva, but of Germany. It might be argued that he has been led away by his desire to find two contrasting images, both contrasting with the Bride, but it is unlike Donne not to be precise, and there is a Scriptural figure, a type of the Church, which fits well his image of a woman who 'laments and mournes' and is 'rob'd and tore': Jerusalem, the once proud city, now desolate, of Lamentations.[2] I would suggest that Donne has seen a parallel between the captivity of Israel and the total collapse of the Protestants after the defeat of the Elector in the battle of the White Mountain, outside Prague, on 29 October 1620.

The news of the Elector's defeat reached London on 24 November and caused consternation.[3] In an undated sermon (dated 1620–2 by Evelyn Simpson), Donne, among references to the Elector's loss of his patrimony, and to the rumour which had reached England earlier in 1620 that the Elector was calling in the help of the Turks, speaks of seeing 'God abandon greater persons, and desert some whole Churches, and States, upon whom his glory and Gospel depends'.[4] But the cause which seemed thus to be deserted by God was felt by many in England to be their cause. On 26 March 1620, when the attack on the Palatinate was pending, the Bishop of London preached at Paul's

---

[1] See *Sermons*, i. 246, vi. 284.

[2] Cf. Lam. ii. 5: 'The Lord was as an enemy: he hath swallowed up Israel, he hath swallowed up all her palaces: he hath destroyed his strong holds, and hath increased in the daughter of Judah mourning and lamentation'; and Lam. ii. 13: 'What thing shall I liken to thee, O daughter of Jerusalem? what shall I equal to thee, that I may comfort thee, O virgin daughter of Zion? for thy breach is great like the sea: who can heal thee?'

[3] See S. R. Gardiner, *History of England 1603–42* (1893), iii. 383–5; also Simpson, *Prose Works*, 349–54, where Evelyn Simpson discusses the dates of five undated sermons, which she places in 1620–2 on account of their obvious references to the calamities which had befallen the Protestant cause.

[4] *Sermons*, v. 273.

Cross, ostensibly to raise money for the repair of St. Paul's. He had been forbidden to touch on politics, but

as he spoke of the necessity of prayer and action on behalf of the spiritual Zion, and exhorted his hearers to nourish the truth of the Gospel in every place, there were probably many present who would have responded to the words with which one of the bystanders recorded his impressions. 'The Bishop', he wrote, 'said that there was not the poorest hewer of wood who would not give one penny out of twopence to build up the walls of Zion. He did not, he durst not apply it; but gave every man liberty to make the application; but I believe his heart was then in Bohemia.'[1]

If men so naturally thought of the Protestant Church in Germany as Zion, what would be more natural than for Donne to identify it in its disasters with the afflicted Zion of Lamentations. And since the feeling of unity with their Protestant brethren abroad was so strong in England, where there was a widespread demand for war on behalf of the German Protestants, he would see only one figure, lamenting and mourning, 'in Germany and here'.

The opening lines are an expression of distress at the spectacle Christendom presented at the beginning of the Thirty Years War. Where is the promised bride? On the one hand there is a figure more like the Babylonish woman of the Apocalypse;[2] on the other, one like the desolate Virgin of Zion, once beloved, now, for her sins, abandoned by her Lord and left to be the prey of her enemies.

Contemplating a world in which the Church as promised is not to be seen, Donne passes to the arguments on the nature of the Church which vexed his age and vexed history. He ironically echoes in his questions the charges each side brings against the other's claims. If the true mark of the Church is Primitive Discipline, as the Calvinists insist, then the Church 'slept' between primitive times and the Reformation, to 'peepe up' with Calvin.[3] If the true mark of the Church is infallibility,

[1] Gardiner, op. cit. iii. 342.
[2] See Rev. xvii. 4.
[3] Cf. Bancroft's famous sermon against the Puritans, preached at Paul's Cross, 9 February 1588: 'A very strange Matter, if it were true, that Christ should erect a Form of Government for the ruling of his Church, to continue from his Departure out of the World until his coming again; and that the same should never be once thought of or put in Practice for the Space of 1500 Years, or at the least ... that the Government and Kingdom of Christ should then be overthrown, when . . . the Divinity of his Person . . . was so godly, so learnedly, and so mightily established against the *Arrians*, in the Council of *Nice*'; see Hickes, *Bibliotheca Scriptorum Ecclesiae Anglicanae* (1709), pp. 247–315, for a reprint of Bancroft's sermon. Donne's thousand years would be roughly from the Council of Nicaea to the Reformation.

where is there an infallible Church? The errors of Popes, the alterations
and additions of the Roman Church, make her claim untenable.[1] Donne
recalls how, throughout history, there have been rival claims that here
and here only can the true Church be found, and wonders whether it
will always be so. From this he passes to one of the great points at
issue between Rome and Geneva: the debate as to whether the true
Church of Christ is the Visible or the Invisible Church.[2] Donne's state-
ment of the two opposite views, in the form of questions—as if neither
were tenable—is a sign of his sympathy with the Anglican refusal to
choose one of two mutually exclusive positions. Taylor, in his chapter
'Of the Church' in *The Second Part of the Dissuasive from Popery*,[3] after
defining the word 'Church' in both senses, goes on:

> Not that there are two churches, or two societies, in separation from each
> other; or that one can be seen by men, and the other cannot; for then either
> we must run after the church, whom we ought not to imitate; or be blind in
> pursuit of the other that can never be found; and our eyes serve for nothing
> but to run after false fires. No, these two churches are but one society; the
> one is within the other.

This would seem to be what Donne intends by setting the two doc-
trines against each other. If we think of the Church as dwelling 'with
us', where is there any body worthy to be called the Bride of Christ?
If we think of her as only revealed to us after this life, what guidance
have we on our travels?

Donne's concluding prayer, that Christ will 'betray' his Bride to
men's sight, rests on the assumption that, for all her apparent disunity,

---

[1] Donne recurs to this theme often in his sermons; cf. 'Pope *Stephen* abrogates all
the Decrees of Pope *Formosus*, and so gives that ly to him: Next yeere Pope *Romanus*
abrogates all his, and so gives that ly to him; and within seven yeers, *Servius* all
his; and where was *fidelis sermo*, the faithfull word all this while ? . . . If for the
space of a 1500 years, the twelve Articles of the Apostles Creed might have sav'd
any man, but since as many more, *Trent* Articles must be as necessary; still
where is that *fidelis sermo*, that faithfull word which we may rely upon ?' (*Sermons*,
i. 297).

[2] 'In sixteenth-century Reformation theology the distinction between the visible
and the invisible Church has a cardinal place. . . . Catholics and Protestants were all
agreed that the sins and corruptions of the actual Church on earth could not be
predicated of Christ, and also that to God alone is known which human beings are
men of faith whose lives are hid with God in Christ. Protestants alone formulated
the definite doctrine by which this hidden company of men of faith were held to
form the invisible Church which could be identified *simpliciter* with the body of
Christ' (Hodgson, op. cit., pp. 17 and 24). Article XIX 'Of the Church', like so
many Anglican formularies, can, as Hodgson points out, bear two interpreta-
tions.

[3] *Works*, vi. 340.

the Church is still one. He makes this point in a letter to Goodyer to whom he speaks as 'one who cannot be scandalized, and that neither measure Religion (as it is now called) by Unitie, nor suspect Unity, for these interruptions':

They whose active function it is, must endevour this unity in Religion: and we at our lay Altars (which are our tables, or bedside, or stools, wheresoever we dare prostrate our selves to God in prayer) must beg it of him: but we must take heed of making misconclusions upon the want of it: for, whether the Maior and Aldermen fall out, (as with us and the Puritans; Bishops against Priests) or the Commoners voyces differ who is Maior, and who Aldermen, or what their Jurisdiction, (as with the Bishop of *Rome*, or whosoever) yet it is still one Corporation.[1]

To sum up, I offer a paraphrase of the sense of the sonnet as I understand it, in the hope that any who challenge this interpretation will produce a paraphrase to support the challenge:

Make visible, dear Lord, the Church as she is described in Scripture. Can she be either the insolent, proud Church of Rome, or the mourning and desolate Protestant Church in Germany and here? Am I to believe that for a thousand years or more there was no true Church on earth? Or, that a Church claiming to be truth itself, yet constantly erring—both innovating and deserting what she formerly held—can be she? Am I to believe that now, as of old, and in future, as long as the world lasts, she is to be found in one place only—here, or there, or elsewhere? Am I to believe that she is to be found here on earth, or am I to hold that only in heaven, after our pilgrimage, can we see her as she is? Lord, do not thus hide thy Bride from our sight, but let me woo the gentle spouse of thy marriage song, who is most faithful to thy will and most pleasing to thee, when the greatest number of men seek and receive her embraces.

APPENDIX D

Donne and Tilman: their Reluctance to take Holy Orders

EDWARD TILMAN, to whom Donne wrote his lines 'To Mr. Tilman after he had taken orders', is a shadowy figure. We know the poem he wrote on his motives in refusing to take orders and we know also the bare facts of his life. His poem is a feeble one, and Donne's lines to him are only a moderately good example of Donne's epistolary

[1] *Letters*, p. 164. See also *Sermons*, ii. 111.

manner. But both have interest beyond their poetic merits in the light they throw on a vexed question in Donne's biography: his own reluctance to enter the ministry.

Edward Tilman matriculated from Pembroke Hall, Cambridge, in 1609; became B.A. in 1612/13; M.A. in 1616 and B.D. in 1623. He was made a Fellow in 1613, before taking his M.A. His delay in taking orders may well have been on account of his having hopes of secular advancement, through academic distinction, such as George Herbert cherished. He was ordained deacon on 20 December 1618 and priest on 12 March 1619/20, and held various cures in East Anglia until his death in 1641/2.[1] R. C. Bald provided me with the additional information that he was granted his licence to preach in the dioceses of London, Norwich, and Lincoln on 14 March 1619/20.[2] There is also a reference to him in the *Autobiography of Sir Simonds D'Ewes*, in connexion with troubles in the parish of Stowlangtoft in the year 1625:

My father, being patron of the advowson there, had a little before presented one Richard Danford, a Fellow of Sidney College, in Cambridge, unto it, upon the resignation of Edward Tilman, a Fellow of Pembroke Hall, in the same University. They were both Bachelors of Divinity; but Mr. Tilman, whom my father had presented upon my motion, was not only a learned and able divine, but a religious and humble man; whereas on the contrary, Mr. Danford, having been many years president of his college, was of a most haughty and proud spirit, and utterly disused to preaching and unfurnished for it. Mr. Tilman having kept it a twelvemonth and having some unexpected disgusts given him, resigned.[3]

In spite of his learning and ability, Tilman did not obtain high advancement, and, as his will shows, did not acquire much wealth. It was proved on 5 February 1641/2,[4] and is a brief document, drawn up in his last illness. It gives his wife's name as Catherine, and presumably her maiden name had been either Tidswell or Brooke, since he leaves to his daughter Mary such legacies as had been bequeathed her by her grandmother Tidswell and her Uncle Brooke. The name Brooke suggests immediately a connexion with Donne, but this uncle was probably the William Brooke of the parish of All Saints the Less who was one of the sureties when Edward Tilman compounded for the first fruits

[1] See *Alumni Cantabrigienses*, ed. J. and J. A. Venn, pt. I, 1922–7.

[2] Lambeth, Archbishops' Register, Abbott, pt. 2, f. 187a.

[3] *Autobiography of Sir Simonds D'Ewes*, ed. Halliwell (1845), i. 274; this reference to Tilman was pointed out by John Butt, *T.L.S.*, 15 December 1932.

[4] Liber Vicarii Generalis Chaworth 1637–62, 15, Consistory Court of London, f. 102r.

of the Rectory of Rettenden, Essex, on 6 October 1626.[1] I have found
no evidence that Donne and Tilman were personally acquainted. Donne
may have come across his verses accidentally and been struck by the
parallel with himself. But the familiar apostrophe 'Deare' (l. 23) does
suggest some degree of acquaintance.

Tilman's own poem was discovered by Harvey Wood in a manu-
script now in the possession of the Duke of Portland, which I call
Welbeck, where it is followed by Donne's poem.[2] It is also extant in
Rawlinson Poetical MS. 117 (1), the commonplace book of Aubrey's
friend, Christopher Wase, where it appears without Donne's lines.
Since it is easily accessible in *Essays and Studies*, xvi (1931), I have not
reprinted it.

The interest of Tilman's poem lies in the fact that Donne's is a very
odd reply to it. The only reason that Tilman puts forward for not
taking orders is personal unworthiness. But Donne makes no reference
at all to the various accusations Tilman brings against himself: of in-
constancy, wantonness, wrathfulness, and ambition. He congratulates
Tilman for triumphing over 'Lay-scornings of the Ministry' and recurs
to the same topic later with a reference to 'Gentry' thinking it beneath
their dignity to take orders. If Tilman's own poem had not survived,
we should assume from Donne's that Tilman's hesitation had been
solely on the score of what Herbert, in *A Priest to the Temple*,[3] calls 'the
generall ignominy which is cast upon the profession' of clergyman.
Walton, whose account of Donne's conversation with Morton shows
a reminiscence of this poem,[4] says that Donne excused himself for
refusing Morton's suggestion that he should take orders on two counts.
He feared that the 'irregularities' of his early life might bring dishonour
on 'that sacred calling'; and he was afraid that if he accepted Morton's
suggestion, he would be doing so more for '*a maintenance*' than for
'*Gods Glory*'. I see no reason to dispute that both these motives may
have weighed with Donne. I would only suggest that the tenor of his
lines to Tilman points to another possible motive: the unattractive-
ness of the clerical profession from a worldly point of view. Men tend
to ascribe to others the same motives as have influenced them them-
selves.

[1] P.R.O., E. 334/17, f. 97ᵛ. I owe this information to I. A. Shapiro.
[2] See p. 100 for a description of the manuscript.
[3] Ch. xxviii, *Works*, p. 268.
[4] '*Remember*, Mr. *Donne*, no man's Education or Parts make him too good for this
employment, *which is to be an Ambassador for the God of glory, that God who by a
vile death opened the gates of life to mankind*' (*Lives*, p. 33). Cf. ll. 37–40.

There is plenty of evidence for Donne's complaint that it was thought

unfit

That Gentry should joyne families with it.

Richard Bernard in *The Faithfull Shepheard* (1607) speaks of the ministry as

an office more meet for the mightiest person of the best education and noblest birth, than for the basest of the people and lowest sort, upon whom for the most part it is cast; because the wisemen of the world, men of might, and the noble, hold it derogatorie to their dignities.[1]

The anecdote from Walton's *Life of Herbert*, cited by Grierson in his notes to this poem, shows the same attitude:

He did at his return to *London*, acquaint a Court-friend with his resolution to enter into *Sacred Orders*, who persuaded him to alter it, as too mean an employment, and too much below his birth, and the excellent abilities and endowments of his mind. To whom he replied, 'It hath been formerly judged that the Domestick Servants of the King of Heaven, should be of the noblest Families on Earth: and, though the Iniquity of the late Times have made Clergy-men meanly valued, and the sacred name of *Priest* contemptible; yet I will labour to make it honourable, by consecrating all my learning, and all my poor abilities, to advance the glory of that God that gave them.'[2]

Towards the end of the century John Eachard makes the same complaint in *The Grounds and Occasions of the Contempt of the Clergy* (1670); and although Barnabas Oley, replying to him in the preface to the second edition of Herbert's *A Priest to the Temple* (1671), declares that the Nobility and Gentry do not 'think their dear Relations degraded by Receiving H. Orders', and supports his statement by a list of persons of rank who had entered the ministry, the list is a short one, and the argument is rather damaged by a final appeal to the Nobility 'to think the Priesthood a Function not unworthy of them or their Relations'.

'Lay-scornings of the Ministry' were partly actuated by the economic position of the clergy. R. G. Usher, in his survey of the state of the clergy in 1603, which includes an examination of the incomes of dignitaries, as well as of the rank and file, says:

The wonder is not that so many incapable and poorly equipped men found their way into the Church, but that half the clergy had degrees; that any man, indeed, could be found to accept such posts, when their neighbours were becoming wealthy as merchants, lawyers, or doctors.[3]

[1] P. 5.
[2] *Lives*, p. 277.
[3] R. G. Usher, *The Reconstruction of the English Church* (1910), i. 220.

Although recent research has modified Usher's figures, and his picture is probably too dark, yet it remains true in its general outline. In comparison with other professions, the ministry was financially most unattractive.

Donne may well have felt, when Morton first suggested he should take orders, that it would be better to endure hard times for a while, in the hope of obtaining really remunerative secular employment, than to accept present relief by entering a profession which offered so little prospect of substantial reward. He had a wife and a growing family to support. He also belonged, by his associations, if not by his birth, to a class which did not normally think of taking orders.

Donne never speaks as if he ever felt any direct inward call to the ministry. He can hardly be reproached for this; nor need we question the religious beliefs or the piety of his middle years because, like George Herbert, he did not feel himself called to the priesthood. It has frequently been assumed that theological scruples were the real cause of his delay, and that the man who helped Morton and wrote *Pseudo-Martyr* was at heart unconvinced of the validity of the positions he was defending. Donne may be accused of many sins—of worldliness certainly—but this accusation of sustained intellectual dishonesty is one that I cannot reconcile with the character that is revealed in his works. The *Divine Poems* are relevant here. The majority of them were written during his middle period, for private pleasure and private circulation. Here, if anywhere, we should expect to find traces of his hankering towards the Church in which he had been brought up. We find just the contrary. His devotional temper is Catholic, but his devotion is a 'rectified devotion'; his theological position is Protestant.

In the end Donne accepted the advice of others, receiving from them, and particularly from the king, what he regarded as a calling.[1] It is true that by 1615 any hopes of secular preferment must have worn very thin. But Donne himself would not, I think, resent the implication that he took orders in the end because it was the only course open to him. He believed that each man's life is 'guided and governed' by God's 'good providence', and that the motion of the spirit may come through the voices of superiors or friends, or through the circumstances of daily life, as much—and perhaps with less danger of mistake—as through the voice of a man's own heart. Donne is to be honoured because,

[1] In the words of his epitaph: 'instinctu et impulsu spiritus sancti, monitu et hortatu regis Jacobi, ordines sacros amplexus'. Earlier, in the inscription he wrote in the Bible he gave to the Library at Lincoln's Inn, he wrote: 'Post multos annos, agente spiritu sancto, suadente Rege, ad Ordines Sacros evectus'.

having received his vocation thus indirectly, he tried to fulfil it worthily
and set himself an exacting standard of duty. In this poem to Tilman
he writes in a high other-worldly strain, to glorify the priest's calling,
which the foolish world 'disrespects'. There is an accent of warm
sincerity in the lines, as in all Donne's references to his late-adopted
profession.

APPENDIX E

The Date of 'Hymn to God my God, in my sickness'

THE date of this Hymn presents a problem. We have to decide which
of two good witnesses we are to accept. Walton, in the first edition
of the *Life of Donne* (1640), after quoting the 'Hymn to God the
Father' as written 'on his former sick bed', adds: 'And on this (which
was his Death-bed) [he] writ another Hymne which bears this Title,
A Hymne to God my God in my sicknesse.' In the 1658 edition he added to
the title the date 'March 23. 1630' (i.e. 23 March 1630/31); thus
placing the Hymn eight days before Donne's death on 31 March 1631.
In the 1670 edition he added the first verse of the Hymn, the begin-
ning of the second, and the last, with slight differences from the text
in *1635*, due probably to his usual carelessness in quotation. Our other
witness, Sir Julius Caesar, is equally definite. On the back of a sheet
which contains the Hymn he has written: 'D.Dun Dene of Pauls / his
verses in his greate / siknes. / in Decemb. 1623.'

John Sparrow (*M.L.R.* xix, 1924) argued in support of accepting
Caesar's statement, adducing Walton's notorious weakness in dates,
and bringing forward parallels to the Hymn from the *Devotions*, written
during Donne's illness of 1623. Twenty-two years later, Evelyn
Simpson took up the question and argued in favour of Walton's date
(*M.L.R.* xli, 1946).

Evelyn Simpson's strongest arguments were that the Hymn reflects
the mood of Donne's death-bed, when he was, by Walton's account,
ready, and even eager, to die, and not the mood of the *Devotions*, in
which, though resigned to God's will, he prays earnestly for recovery;
and that Walton, according to Bishop King's letter (published in the
Life of Hooker, 1665), was actually present at Donne's death-bed three
days before he died. She challenged John Sparrow's argument from
parallel passages in the *Devotions*, showing that it is also possible to

produce parallels from *Deaths Duell* and other sermons preached in Donne's later life.

Evelyn Simpson also argued that the fact that this Hymn appears in only one manuscript collection, while the 'Hymn to God the Father' (1623) appears in eight, is explained if we accept Walton's date, since most of the collections were made before Donne's death. This is a weak argument. *Lut* and *O'F*, both written after Donne's death, whose compilers collected all the poems they could, do not contain this Hymn. The Hymn may well be rare in manuscript because Donne did not wish it to circulate.

The most doubtful of Evelyn Simpson's arguments is that since the manuscripts abound in false statements and we have no evidence that Caesar was a friend of Donne's, we have no reason to take Sir Julius Caesar's statement seriously. Anonymous attributions and statements in manuscripts are not on a par with a statement by a man we know of, who was a public servant of many years' standing, accustomed by the routine of his profession to the accurate noting of information. Donne was by 1623 a public man: he had been chosen by the king to go on the important Bohemian embassy, and was often invited to preach at Court. Caesar, who was a considerable figure at Court, was a good Churchman; he was likely to be interested in Donne, even if he were not personally acquainted with him. We do not need to prove friendship.[1]

The case for accepting Caesar's statement, which cannot be dismissed as 'a random remark in some loose papers', must begin with an examination of his manuscript. *A 34* is a collection of letters, minutes, and poems, collected and indexed by Caesar himself. It has been rebound, and in the re-binding the contents have been rearranged; but the original foliation by Caesar corresponds with his index, so that we can reconstruct the order in which he put his papers together. The index has, under f. 237, 'Severall verses from severall men, concerning severall grave Themes, & Occasions. et fol.' The folios on which poems are to be found are then given, the last entry, f. 302, referring us to the sheet on which this Hymn appears. Almost all the poems are endorsed by Caesar with dates; but he did not arrange them chronologically by the datings. Apart from one poem, endorsed 'D. Latworths verses at the time of approching death in the Cales voyage. A chaplain to the

[1] Caesar had a property at Mitcham, where Donne lived in his obscure days; and Caesar had been closely connected with Lionel Cranfield, who was certainly a friend of Donne's. It is, therefore, not at all improbable that Caesar and Donne were personally acquainted.

then E. of Essex an. 1596', the dates of the endorsements fall between
13 July 1621 and 20 January 1633. In some cases it is quite certain that
the date Caesar has written is not the date of the poem's occasion; but
must be the date when he received it.[1] The endorsement on the Hymn
is set out as follows:

> D. Dun Dene of Pauls
> his verses in his greate
> siknes.
> in Deceb. 1623.

In view of Caesar's habits in dating it is arguable that 'in December
1623' is the date on which he received the poem; and, further, if he
meant the words to refer to 'greate siknes', it seems strange that he
set them on the line below, when he had room to run straight on.

If we accept Walton's story, we have to think of the poem coming
into Caesar's hands some time after 1631. How was it that he not only
remembered the year of Donne's severe illness, which is hardly, like
the Cadiz expedition, a memorable historical event, but was also able
to give a month?[2] Why should Caesar, or whoever gave him the poem,
if he did not receive it until after Donne's death in 1631, connect it with
Donne's illness of 1623 and not with his death-bed; and having done
so why should he, eight or more years after, remember the year of that
illness and approximately the right month? The weakness of Walton's
story is its extreme inherent probability. The Hymn looks like a death-
bed poem. We can see why Walton, if he is wrong, should have made
his mistake. But Caesar's error, if it is an error, is very difficult to
explain.

Caesar died in 1636; his statement is, therefore, at the latest, four
years earlier than Walton's. The title of the poem also agrees better
with his date than with Walton's. It is one of the few examples of a
title which must go back to Donne himself—writing above his poem
its occasion, 'in my sicknesse'. If he wrote the Hymn on his death-bed,

---

[1] A poem on the death of James I, buried on 26 April 1625, is endorsed '2 May
1625', a pointless date, unless it is the date of reception. Similarly, some verses on the
Nativity are endorsed '1 Jan. 1627'; and on another occasion Caesar has written
'Brought me by W.R. 9. April 1623 transcribed into books'.

[2] He does not do so when noting the year of Dr. Latworth's poem, like Donne's
written 'in an extreamity of Sicknes', but, unlike Donne's, in a sickness which oc-
curred in conjunction with an event of great public interest. It is actually rather
doubtful whether December is the right month. The *Devotions* were entered on the
Stationers' Register 9 January 1623/4. Donne must therefore have been convalescent
by December for him to have been able to prepare his book for the press. December
is rather too late for the crisis of his illness.

there was no need for a title—its occasion would be plain. Lastly, if the Hymn was written on Donne's death-bed, it is difficult to account for its non-appearance in *1633*; but if it was written in 1623, a good reason can be suggested for Donne's not wishing it to circulate. The Hymn is a solemn poem, written in expectation of death. He might well have been unwilling to publish a poem written in an expectation which had been falsified by the event.

On the evidence, my vote goes to Sir Julius Caesar; but the existence of Walton's statement makes me unwilling to say more of the date of this Hymn than 'most probably in 1623'.

APPENDIX F

'Paradise and Calvarie'

> *We thinke that* Paradise *and* Calvarie
> Christs *Crosse and* Adams *tree, stood in one place.*
> ('Hymn to God my God, in my sickness', ll. 21–22)

THE apparent meaning of these lines is that the tree of the Cross stood on the same spot as did the Forbidden Tree. Nobody has, so far, produced any authority for such an idea.[1] The difficulty can be solved if we take the word 'in one place' to mean not 'on the same spot', but 'in the same region',[2] and if we relate the lines to the train of thought in the poem.

In the previous stanza Donne asks

> Is the Pacifique Sea my home? Or are
> The Easterne riches? Is *Jerusalem?*

[1] The lines have been discussed by D. C. Allen in 'John Donne's "Paradise and Calvarie" ' (*M.L.N.*, lx. 1945). He states that there is no authority known to him for such a belief and my own searches in the Fathers and Renaissance commentators confirm his statement. His own explanation is that Donne has confused two legends: that the Rood was made from the wood of a tree which grew from one of the pips placed by Seth in Adam's mouth when he lay dying; and that Adam was buried on Calvary. He concludes: 'If the tree grew in Adam's grave and Adam was buried on Calvary; then Adam's tree and Christ's cross "stood in one place". But Adam must have been buried in the county of Paradise; hence Calvary must be in Paradise.' This is sufficiently refuted by the observation that the one place where Adam could not possibly have been buried is Paradise, since he was expelled from there after the Fall.

[2] This is a regular geographic usage; see N. Carpenter, *Geography Delineated* (162 5), II. i, where he gives 'a description of the *Terrestriall* Globe . . . divided into places'. On consideration it can be seen that this must be the sense. Paradise is a country of some extent: Calvary is a particular hill. They can only 'stand in the same place' in the sense that they are both contained in the same region.

Here he answers his own questions. His physicians have told him that he is to make a South-West discovery. This leads him to the thought that his goal is the Ocean of Peace, and then to the recollection that men had once thought that Paradise lay in the Southern Ocean. But they had also argued that it lay in the East, beyond a land of fabulous riches. Both these were exploded fancies; the view which was universally accepted in Donne's day was that Paradise lay in a totally different direction, in Mesopotamia, that is in the same region of the world as Jerusalem.[1] The Pacific Ocean and the 'Easterne Riches' may both be thought fine metaphors for the Heavenly Paradise, but Jerusalem is the true Scriptural name for the city of peace. From fancies Donne turns to the truth as his age conceived it. It is to Jerusalem he sails, to the region where both Paradise and Calvary can be found; for the Heavenly Paradise can only be reached by way of Calvary. The initial conceit of the map thus leads to the final comparison of the first and second Adam.

If we need a source for Donne's lines, there is an obvious one, *The Golden Legend*, and we find in it also the use of 'place' to mean region:

Adam was made and sinned in the month of March, and on the Friday, which is the sixth day of the week, and therefore God in the month of March, and on the Friday would suffer death, and at midday which is the sixth hour. Secondly, for the place of his passion, the which might be considered in three manners. For one place either it is common or especial or singular. The place common where he suffered was the land of promise. The place especial the mount of Calvary. The place singular the cross. In the place common the first man was there formed, that was in a field about or nigh Damascus. Where it is said in a place special, he was there buried. For right in the same place where Jesu Christ suffered death, it is said that Adam was buried. . . . In a place singular he was deceived, that is to wit in the Tree, not in this on which Jesus suffered death, but in another tree.[2]

If a field near Damascus and Calvary are 'the same place common', since both are in the land of promise; so may Paradise and Calvary be said to stand 'in one place', if Paradise is in Mesopotamia, as compared with being in the Pacific or beyond Cathay.

It may be objected, however, that there is a parallel passage in 'The Progress of the Soul' (stanza VIII), which cannot be so explained away. But there also we cannot take Donne to mean that the Forbidden Tree

---

[1] A lengthy and entertaining treatment of the question can be found in Raleigh's *History of the World* (ch. iii). Raleigh was rather flogging a dead horse; for, wherever we turn, to Catholic commentators such as Pererius or Suarez, or to the margin of the Geneva Bible, we find the same conviction: that the Terrestrial Paradise really existed, and that it was in Mesopotamia.

[2] *Golden Legend*, i. 76–77.

and the Cross stood on the same spot; for in a previous stanza (VI)
he declares that he 'launches at paradise' and weighs anchor 'at Tigrys
and Euphrates', thus placing Paradise again in Mesopotamia. After this
he goes on to say that the soul whose history he is about to relate 'had
first in paradise, a low but fatall "roome" '. This he then corrects:

> Yet no low roome, nor then the greatest, lesse,
> If (as devout and sharpe men fitly guesse)
> That Crosse, our joy, and griefe, where nailes did tye
> That All, which alwayes was all, every where;
>
> .   .   .   .
>
> Stood in the selfe same roome in Calvarie,
> Where first grew the forbidden learned tree.

The explanation I would offer here is that 'roome' means 'position'.[1]
The soul was not in a 'low roome', for though it inhabited an apple,
that apple hung on a tree that stood by the tree of life 'in the midst
of the garden', that is, in the position of highest honour. It was the
first of all trees to stand in this 'roome'. But when the Cross was raised
on Calvary, it 'stood in the selfe same roome'; for 'devout and sharpe
men' had held from Tertullian onwards that Calvary was the centre of
the habitable globe: 'hic medium terrae'.[2] Even in Donne's day this
tradition was so strong that Baronius in his *Annals* (anno 34) devotes
much time to citations from the Fathers declaring Golgotha to be the
centre of the world, rather weakly concluding that perhaps we may
take this to mean that it was the centre of Palestine. He is loth to
abandon the 'fit guess' that the central event in world history took
place at the centre of the habitable globe.

Christian sentiment has always linked the two trees: the 'lignum
perditionis' and the 'lignum salvationis'. Donne here makes a new and
ingenious connexion of his own: both 'stood in the selfe same roome',
for they were both 'in medio'.

[1] Cf. Luke xiv, the parable of the wedding guest who sits down in 'the highest
room', that is in the best seat or position.
[2] See Migne, *P.L.* ii. 1067 and 1113.

APPENDIX G

Donne's Latin Poem to Herbert and Herbert's Reply

DONNE's Latin poem to Herbert, with its translation, was printed among poems added on additional sheets in the edition of Donne's poems in 1650, the first over which the younger Donne had control. Some Latin verses by George Herbert 'In Sacram Anchoram Piscatoris', also with an English translation, were printed on the two preceding pages. It seems safe to assume that Donne himself kept no copy of his verses, since they have not survived in any manuscript. The fact that they first appeared with Herbert's points to their having been preserved by Herbert among his papers. There are three connected problems to discuss: the date of Donne's poem; its title and setting, both in *1650* and in Walton's *Life of Donne* (1658); and the nature of Herbert's verses which were printed with it. It is necessary, however, to begin with an account of Donne's seals.

Donne's Seals: The problem of Donne's ancestry, with which the question of his right to bear certain arms is connected, is for his biographers to solve. There is no record of any grant of arms to him or to his father at the College of Arms; and I have been informed there that the fact that he described himself as 'armiger', when taking his M.A. at Oxford in 1610, does not necessarily mean that he was armigerous. At this period 'armiger' was a recognized translation of 'esquire', and Donne may only have been claiming this description. Gosse stated that Donne as Dean of St. Paul's bore the arms of the Duns or Dwynns of Kidwelly, Carmarthenshire: *'a wolf salient and a chief argent.'*[1] He certainly used these arms on a seal when he was Dean, for a letter to Bishop Williams in 1626[2] has a seal with the device of a wolf salient, surmounted by a crest of five serpents entwined. A wolf rampant, or salient, was the arms of more than one family of Donne.[3] In Camden's description of the arms of Sir Daniel Dunn, Dean of Arches, Master of the Requests

---

[1] Gosse, i. 4.

[2] Lincoln Archives, L.T. 1626/11. I owe my knowledge of this letter and the description of the seal to its discoverer, Miss D. Williamson of the Lincoln Record Office.

[3] See Burke, *General Armory* (1884) and the Chatsworth Triptych by Memling, where Sir John Donne and his wife Elizabeth, the donors, both wear a wolf salient, depending as a jewel from a collar.

of London, we find it along with five serpents entwined.[1] It has been
suggested to me that Donne's words 'parva symbola' may indicate that
his family did not bear arms, but used this 'little emblem', taken from
the coat of arms of a family they presumed themselves to be related to.
On the other hand, the fact that the entwined serpents appear as the
crest on his armorial seal and on the arms of Sir Daniel Dunn suggests
that by 'parva symbola' he meant, as the English translator assumed,
'crest', as distinct from 'coat'.

Although the majority of Donne's holograph letters have lost their
seals, a number still survive in good condition. I. A. Shapiro informed
me that the only seals he had found on letters written before 1615 bear
the 'sheaf of snakes'. The earliest example of a letter sealed with the
emblematic seal of Christ upon the Anchor is the letter written by
Donne to Sir Edward Herbert, 23 January 1615, 'the very day wherein
I took orders' (Hayward, pp. 324 and 465–6). After he was made Dean,
Donne used the armorial seal of a wolf salient, but he continued to use
also his early seal of the 'sheaf of snakes' and his emblematic seal of
Christ upon an Anchor. Although I. A. Shapiro told me that he had
found no example of a very late letter with the seal of Christ upon an
Anchor, a bequest in Donne's will points to his having been in the
habit of using it until his death.[2]

Date: Walton, in his first revision of the *Life of Donne* in 1658, told the
story of how Donne 'not long before his death' had the figure of Christ
extended upon an Anchor engraved 'very small in *Helitropian* Stones,
and set in gold', and sent these to many of his friends 'to be used as
Seales or *Rings* and kept as memorialls of him'.[3] Walton then gives a list

---

[1] See Camden, *Grants*, iii. 7*b*, a manuscript volume preserved at the College of
Arms. The description runs: 'Dunn. Azure, a wolf rampant argent, one ermine
spot in his shoulder. 2. Branch. Argent, a lion rampant gules. . . . 3. Wilkinson.
Gules, a fess of varry argent and azure. . . . 4. vt. i. 5 Colubers internowed or.' Pre-
sumably the fourth quarter, for which no family name is given, is the same as the
first, and the '5 Colubers internowed or' is the crest.

[2] He left five pounds each to two officers of St. Paul's 'to make them seal rings
engraved with that figure which I usually seal withal of which sort they know I
have given many to my particular friends' (Gosse, ii. 360).

[3] Walton himself sealed his will with a seal with this device, and so did his son.
Bishop Ken, whose half-sister was Walton's second wife, also used a seal with this
device on his will; but his seal and Isaak Walton junior's seal were not identical.
Ken's seal descended to the Merewether family, and is now in the Library at Salis-
bury Cathedral. It is a ring seal. A pendent seal, cut in white chalcedony, with the
same device, but with a motto 'Sit fides sic fixa Deo' added, was in the possession
of the Crawley Boevey family of Flaxely Abbey, Glos., fifty years ago. This seal,
which was about twice the size of Ken's, also purported to come from Walton.

of those who had been sent these tokens, adding at the close 'in this enumeration of his friends, though many must be omitted, yet that man of primitive piety Mr. *George Herbert* may not'. After speaking of the friendship of Donne and Herbert, 'maintained by many sacred indearments', he added as 'some Testimony', the first two and a half lines of this poem in Latin, with the English version in full, and the first two and a half lines of Herbert's Latin verses, with a modified version of the English translation as it had appeared in *1650*. Walton headed Donne's poem 'To Mr. *George Herbert*, with one of my Seales of the *Anchor* and *Crest*'. In *1670* he corrected and expanded this to: '. . . sent him with one of my Seales of the *Anchor* and *Christ*'. It is plain that Walton means us to understand that when Donne sent his dying gift to Herbert, he sent with it this poem. He repeated the story of Donne's sending the seal to Herbert in his *Life of Herbert* (1670). He added there that, at Herbert's death, some verses, which he prints, were 'found wrapt with that Seal which was by the Doctor given to him'. On the authority of Walton, therefore, this poem has been dated 1630–1.

But we know that Donne used this seal of Christ upon an Anchor in January 1615, many years before he distributed copies of it as memorial gifts, and the opening lines plainly refer to a recent change of seal.[1] Although there is some difficulty in taking 'Adscitus domui Domini' as meaning 'having been ordained',[2] the presumption is that Donne had a new seal cut for his ordination, a new seal being a fitting symbol of a new life. We must accept Walton's twice repeated statement that Herbert was one of the recipients of Donne's memorial gifts in 1630–1; but, if we ignore the title of Donne's poem in 1650, there is nothing in the poem itself to suggest that it accompanied the gift of a seal. On the contrary, Donne says that all he sends is 'wishes and prayers' (*Vota, preces*). These pledges of friendship and rich gifts (*Pignora amicitiae, et munera*) he sends under his little seal (*sub*, not *cum*) to a friend who bears

---

Correspondents in *The Gentleman's Magazine* and *Notes and Queries* (see Grierson, ii. 261) mention various seals as 'the seal which Donne gave Walton'. I have to thank Henry Merewether of Lympne Hall, Kent, for answering queries.

I do not believe Donne gave Walton a seal. Walton does not tell the story until 1658—that is, after the publication of Donne's and Herbert's verses—and he does not include his own name in his list of recipients. The existence of more than one seal connected with Walton suggests that, in imitation of his hero, he had seals cut with this device for his own use and for gifts to friends.

[1] 'I, who used formerly to seal my letters with a sheaf of snakes . . . having been enrolled in the household of the Lord, take by right new arms.'

[2] See note, p. 111.

the name of the saint who rides on the Great Seal of the Realm. He hopes that under this more impressive seal, his friend may receive royal gifts. The poem is about a new seal which Donne is using to seal his letters. Its tone, particularly that of its closing lines, is entirely inconsistent with the supposition that it accompanied a memorial gift. It is incredible that Donne, if he were sending a dying token to Herbert, would end his poem with a mere wish for his friend's worldly prosperity. The poem must have been written at a time when Herbert looked to the Court for favour. I suggest, therefore, that we should date it about the time of Donne's ordination, in January 1615.[1]

That Donne should send a Latin poem of this kind to Herbert in 1615 is perfectly probable. Although Herbert was a much younger man, he was already launched on what promised to be a successful academic career. Donne's poem shows no signs of great intimacy; the friendship between him and Herbert developed later, when the gap in their ages would have seemed less large as both grew older. The poem is a natural one for Donne to send to a rising young scholar, who was the son and brother of close friends. He wrote on the day he was ordained to his friend Sir Edward Herbert, and sealed his letter with this seal of Christ upon an Anchor. I suggest that about the same time he wrote a Latin poem on his new seal and sent it to the younger brother, George Herbert, an accomplished Latinist, who was looking forward to a career of public service, with the wish that he should obtain royal favour. He probably felt that to write a Latin poem on a sacred subject did not conflict with his promise to 'inter his Muse': it was not in Latin that he had vented his licentious wit.

Walton's error is understandable. He apparently did not know that the seals which Donne sent his friends in 1630–1 were copies of a seal which Donne had had cut many years before for his own use. He writes as if Donne only thought of this emblem when he decided to distribute memorial tokens. Walton made a natural assumption: that the poem on the seal was sent with the dying gift. The editor of *1650*, the younger Donne, had made the same assumption before him; but fortunately he left a revealing slip in the title which he set above the poem.

Title and Setting: The title in *1650* ran 'To Mʳ *George Herbert*, with one of my Seal. . . .' All previous editors have followed Walton in correcting to 'one of my Seals'. I have emended by omitting 'one of'. I believe the

---

[1] This date was suggested by I. A. Shapiro, *N. and Q.*, 29 Oct. 1949. His arguments are rather different from mine, and I cannot accept his interpretation of Walton's words.

original title ran 'with my Seal', and that the younger Donne, assuming that the poem had been sent with one of Donne's memorial seals, altered this by inserting 'one of', but omitted to make the further necessary correction of 'Seal' to 'Seals'.

But when we have emended the title of *1650* some curious features of the title and setting remain. In *1650* Donne's Latin poem occupies the left-hand page of an opening (p. 378) and is headed

> To Mr *George Herbert*, with one of my
> Seal, of the Anchor and Christ.

The English translation occupies the right-hand page (p. 379) and is headed

> A sheafe of Snakes used heretofore to be
> *my Seal, The Crest of our poore Family.*

This is the translation of the first two lines of the Latin poem as printed on the page opposite, and consequently the English poem begins at what corresponds to the third line of the Latin: 'Adopted in Gods Family'.

In the *Life of Donne* (1658) Walton gave the poem the following heading:

> To Mr. *George Herbert*, with / one of my Seales of the *Anchor* / and *Crest.* A sheafe of Snakes / used heretofore to be my Seal, / the Crest of our poor Family.

He then printed the first two and a half lines of the Latin poem as it stands in *1650*, and the English poem as it is given in *1650*; that is, beginning at the words 'Adopted in Gods Family'.

What seems at first sight to be the obvious explanation of the setting in *1650* would be that the editor had a passion for symmetry, and moved up the first two lines of the English poem, setting them as prose, to balance the title of the Latin poem on the page opposite. We would then argue that this misled Walton into running the two headings together as one title. But this explanation is not wholly satisfactory, since it ignores the curious fact of the absence of a Latin heading to the Latin poem. Donne's Latin poem to Jonson is briefly but properly addressed in Latin; his poem to Andrewes has a longer heading, elaborately set out and explanatory of the poem which follows. It is odd that Donne, who enjoyed writing inscriptions, should have sent a Latin poem to Herbert without addressing it.

If we start from the assumption that a Latin poem must originally have had a Latin heading, we can give another explanation of the setting in 1650. This explanation reverses the previous one and suggests that the editor did not move up the first two lines of the English poem to make them a heading; on the contrary, he left them as he found them, standing as an explanatory heading to the poem that follows. But he removed the English address which preceded them and put it above his Latin poem, instead of the Latin address. Having done so, he then ran the Latin couplet, which should have stood as part of the Latin heading, into the poem it explained. He should have completed his adjustments by joining up the English couplet to the English poem, thus making the Latin and the English match, but, as in his emending of the title, he was careless, and left his work half done. The proper heading for the English translation should have been

> To Mr *George Herbert*, with my Seal
> of the Anchor and Christ.
>
> *A sheafe of Snakes used heretofore to be*
> *My Seal, the Crest of our poore Family.*

The Latin poem should have had a parallel title:

> Magistro Georgio Herberto, cum Anchora et Christo,
> sigillo meo,
>
> *Qui prius assuetus Serpentum fasce Tabellas*
> *Signare, (haec nostrae symbola parva Domus).*

When the editor decided to substitute the English for the Latin address, he left the English couplet where he found it, but he could not do the same with the Latin couplet which it translates. With the Latin heading we can construe 'Qui' with 'meo'; but the English heading leaves 'Qui' without an antecedent.

The weakness of this explanation is, firstly, that there seems no reason why the younger Donne should have tampered with the Latin title; and, secondly, that the first four lines of the Latin as they stand have such a natural and easy flow. They are reminiscent of the four spurious lines at the beginning of the *Aeneid*, which Spenser imitated at the beginning of *The Faerie Queene*: 'Ille ego qui quondam . . .'. This literary reminiscence is a strong argument for leaving the Latin text as it stands, and altering the setting of the English text to correspond with it.

Herbert's Verses: In Sacram Anchoram Piscatoris: In 1650 and subsequent editions of Donne's poems, Herbert's verses consist of seven iambic trimeters, three hendecasyllables, three hexameters, and an elegiac couplet. They are followed by translations into four decasyllabic couplets, two quatrains (the first of octosyllabic couplets, the second of decasyllabic), and a decasyllabic couplet. The Latin verses, without the translations, appeared in the same form in *Herbert's Remains* (1652). I give Herbert's verses as they appear in *1650*:

In Sacram Anchoram Piscatoris

G. HERBERT.

Quod Crux nequibat fixa, Clavíque additi,
(Tenere Christum scilicet, ne ascenderet)
Tuive Christum devocans facundia
Vltra loquendi tempus; addit Anchora:
Nec hoc abundè est tibi, nisi certae Anchorae
Addas sigillum: nempè Symbolum suae
Tibi debet Vnda & Terra certitudinis.

    Quondam fessus Amor loquens Amato,
    Tot & tanta loquens amica, scripsit:
    Tandem & fessa manus, dedit sigillum.

Suavis erat, qui scripta, dolens, lacerando recludi,
Sanctiùs in Regno Magni credebat Amoris
(In quo fas nihil est rumpi) donare sigillum.

Munde, fluas fugiásque licet, nos nostráque fixi:
    Deridet motus sancta catena tuos.

Although the Crosse could not Christ here detain,
Though nail'd unto't, but he ascends again,
Nor yet thy eloquence here keep him still,
But onely while thou speak'st; This Anchor will.
Nor canst thou be content, unlesse thou to
This certain Anchor adde a Seal, and so
The Water, and the Earth both unto thee
Doe owe the symbole of their certainty.

    When Love being weary made an end
    Of kinde Expressions to his friend,
    He writ; when's hand could write no more,
    He gave the Seale, and so left o're.

How sweet a friend was he, who being griev'd
His letters were broke rudely up, believ'd
'Twas more secure in great Loves Common-weal
(Where nothing should be broke) to adde a Seal.

> Let the world reel, we and all ours stand sure,
> This holy Cable's of all storms secure.

In the 1658 edition of the *Life of Donne* Walton only gave the opening of the Latin, and in giving the English version he attached the last couplet to the end of the first eight lines, omitted the second quatrain, and gave the first in a different form:

> Love neere his death desir'd to end,
> With kind expressions to his friend;
> He writ when's hand could write no more,
> He gave his soul (*for* seal), and so gave o're.

In *1670* he omitted this quatrain also. But in his *Life of Herbert* (1670) and in the same place in the *Lives* (1670) he gave two English couplets, which are plainly alternative translations of the first triplet and the final couplet of *1650*, stating that these verses were 'found wrapt up with that Seal which was by the Doctor given to him'. The verses run:

> When my dear Friend could write no more,
> He gave this *Seal*, and, so gave ore.

> When winds and waves rise highest, I am sure,
> This *Anchor* keeps my *Faith*, that, me secure.

Grierson believed the two Latin triplets, and their translation into quatrains, were of doubtful authenticity, and in printing the English version he followed Walton and moved the final couplet to stand at the close of the first eight lines.[1] F. E. Hutchinson followed Grierson in this, and, since he quoted it, he appeared to share his doubt of the authenticity of the triplets. But he added: 'The opening lines are addressed to Donne, but the additional stanzas seem to be written after his death.'[2] F. E. Hutchinson came very near here to what I believe to be the truth: that Herbert's verses do not form a single poem, and that separate poems written on two different occasions have been printed together.

The first seven lines, the iambic trimeters, are the answer to Donne's poem. They are extremely obscure, and even the title is puzzling. 'Piscator' would naturally be taken to refer to St. Peter, but Herbert cannot intend such a reference here. I would suggest that he is taking the promise: 'I will make you fishers of men', as applicable to all the Apostles and their successors in the priesthood, and that his title means 'On the holy Anchor of a Fisher of Souls', and is a reference to Donne's ordination. The gist of the lines is that Donne has substituted an

[1] Grierson, ii. 261.
[2] Herbert, *Works*, p. 599.

Anchor for the Cross, in order to 'hold Christ' better, and, not content with this 'sure Anchor', he has added to it a further token of certainty, a seal. (I take it that Herbert is using 'sigillum' strictly, for the actual wax seal which takes the imprint of the engraved matrix.) Thus water and earth, the elements which make up the seal, receive from Donne a symbol of their own certainty. There is no reference to a gift of a seal. The poem is an obscurely worded conceit on the fact that Donne has 'made assurance doubly sure' by sealing his letter with a seal, itself imprinted with an emblem of security, an Anchor. But the two following epigrams, the hendecasyllables and hexameters, both refer to a gift: 'dedit sigillum' and 'donare sigillum'. In both also Herbert speaks of Donne as dead. The final couplet, the elegiac couplet, makes no reference to a gift; it is simply a moralization of the emblem. But it cannot be attached to the first seven lines in the Latin, for it is in a different metre.

Walton's piety in wishing to preserve any relics of Herbert, which led him in his *Life of Herbert* to print two extra couplets and to tell us where they were found, gives us the clue to the whole story. I suggest that what happened was this. Donne sent Herbert in 1615 a poem on his new seal, which he used to seal his letter, and to this Herbert replied in seven lines of Latin verse as formal and impersonal as Donne's own. Herbert kept both Donne's poem and his own reply to it, and it is even possible that the English rendering was made by him. Sixteen years later, when they had become close friends, Donne sent Herbert, as a memorial token, a seal engraved with the same emblem of Christ upon an Anchor. On Donne's death Herbert wrote three Latin epigrams on this dying gift. Either he made two translations into English, or, possibly, he first wrote the two couplets which Walton printed in his *Life of Herbert* as drafts, which he turned into three Latin epigrams and then rendered back into English. Walton tells us that the two couplets were found with the seal, and I would suggest that all the poems were found there. It would be very natural for Herbert to put with Donne's dying gift not only the epigrams he had written on it but also the verses on this same emblem, which they had exchanged so many years before. This would account for the assumption in *1650* and in Walton that Donne's poem accompanied his gift, and that all Herbert's verses made up one poem. In *1650* the younger Donne printed what had been found, except that he did not give both English versions of the epigrams. Walton, in 1658, knowing that the three hexameter lines had no equivalent in the two couplets of English verse, dropped the second quatrain. He also shuffled the pieces of his jigsaw and moved up the final couplet to join the first eight lines. But reference to the Latin original shows that he was wrong in this, for the two scraps are metrically distinct in Latin, though not in English. Finally in 1670 Walton dropped the first quatrain also, recognizing that it had no real connexion with the first poem, but fortunately in his *Life of Herbert* he printed the two couplets, and told us that they were found with the seal which Donne had given to Herbert.

Herbert's first two epigrams, both in Latin and English, are very warm in tone; they reveal a deep affection. His elegiac couplet, though less obviously affectionate, is a moving expression of his faith, not, as the first poem is, a mere frigid conceit. Herbert thinks of himself still riding out the storm of life, and of his friend, who has ridden out the storm of death and now moors in the harbour, and of the sacred cable of faith which binds them both to their common Anchor. The couplet adds nothing relevant to the first seven-line poem, which is a complete and adequate answer to Donne's verses on his seal.

SUPPLEMENTARY NOTES

INTRODUCTION

AS it is now a quarter of a century since this edition of Donne's *Divine Poems* appeared, and the edition of Donne's poems in four volumes which it inaugurated is now completed, the time seemed ripe for a revision, taking into account work published since 1952 and new material and information that has come to light.

In addition to my edition of *The Elegies and the Songs and Sonnets* (1965) and W. Milgate's editions of *The Satires and Verse-Letters* (1967) and *The Anniversaries, Epicedes and Epithalamions* (1978), there have been two editions of Donne's complete poems: by John T. Shawcross (New York, 1968) and by A. J. Smith (Penguin English Poets, 1971). Evelyn Simpson's edition of *Essays in Divinity* (1952), Timothy Healy's edition of *Ignatius His Conclave* (1969), and the majestic Californian edition of the *Sermons* (1953–62), carried to completion by Evelyn Simpson after the death of her collaborator G. R. Potter, are of great assistance to any editor of Donne's poetry. The existence of a modern edition of the *Sermons*, available in libraries and to which reference can be made, would alone justify some revision of a book which necessarily had to refer constantly to Donne's sermons. (Unfortunately, there is still no modern edition of Donne's letters and reference has therefore still to be made to original sources.) Almost as significant as the edition of the *Sermons* was the publication of R. C. Bald's *John Donne: A Life* (1970), revised for publication after its author's death by W. Milgate, which dealt authoritatively with many disputed biographical problems and conjectures.

A great deal of work has been done on the manuscripts of Donne's poems, and many new manuscripts containing poems by him have been recorded. None of these are of much importance for an editor of the *Divine Poems*. Much more significant was the discovery that the Westmoreland manuscript was in the hand of Donne's friend Rowland Woodward, and, even more, the discovery of a copy of the Verse-Letter to Lady Carey in Donne's own hand. The first enhances the already high authority of the Westmoreland manuscript; the second is of fundamental importance to editors in considering the accidentals of the text.

Apart from minor corrections and additions, the General Introduction is unaltered; but the Textual Introduction has required considerable rewriting and additions.

TEXTUAL INTRODUCTION

I. *The Manuscripts.* The discussion of the nature of *X*, the common original of the five manuscripts of Group I, on p. lxii, has been replaced by a summary of the conclusions arrived at by Margaret Crum in her bibliographical examination of the manuscripts of this group in *The Library*, xvi (1961).

Two paragraphs on pp. lxvii–lxviii have been rewritten to summarize conclusions on *Y*, the common original of the four Group II manuscripts. MS. Lansdowne 740, a composite manuscript, contains as one of its items a collection of poems in a single hand, the great majority being by Donne. Both in the text and in the order of the poems common to *L 74* and Group II there are striking similarities. Details can be found in Gardner, *Elegies etc.*, pp. lxviii–lxix, and Milgate, *Satires etc.*, pp. xliii–xliv. *L 74* contains no poem that can be dated after 1609 and has none of the *Divine Poems*. It would seem that the compiler of *L 74* intercalated into an early collection of poems by Donne some poems by other wits, and that this same early collection was the basis of the large comprehensive collection in Group II.

Alan MacColl (*Essays in Criticism*, 17, 1967, and *John Donne: Essays in Celebration*, ed. A. J. Smith, 1972, p. 35) pointed out that Donne wrote to Sir Robert Ker before going to Germany in 1619 to send him a copy of *Biathanatos* 'besides the Poems, of which you took a promise' (*Letters*, 21–22). As he refers to *Biathanatos* as 'another Book', the poems must have been a fairly substantial collection. Two years later, Drummond wrote to Ker and referred to Daniel 'who, dying as I heare, bequeathed to you his scrolls' and 'Done, who in his travells lefte you his' (*Correspondence of Sir Robert Ker*, ed. D. Laing, Edinburgh, 1875, i. 24). This also suggests that the collection was a full one. MacColl puts forward the hypothesis that *Y*, the common original of the manuscripts of Group II, was made up by the addition of the papers Donne left with Ker to the early collection found in *L 74*.

My suggestion that *X*, the common original of the manuscripts of Group I, was derived from Donne's own collection of 1614, and this suggestion of MacColl's that *Y*, the common original of the manuscripts of Group II, was derived largely from the papers Donne left with Ker in 1619, are consistent with the absence of doubtful poems in the manuscripts of Groups I and II. They would explain also the general agreement of Groups I and II against Group III in the *Divine Poems*, and the fact that on the one occasion when Group II reads strikingly against Group I and all other manuscripts its reading can be shown to be the later one (see p. xlv).

The Dolau Cothi manuscript, now in the National Library of Wales, is, although not descended from *Y*, related to the manuscripts of Group II. It was discovered by Alan MacColl. It contains a very full collection of Donne's poems transcribed in one hand. The collection is canonical, but a handful of poems by other authors has been transcribed at the close. It opens with 'La Corona' and the first eight of the 'Holy Sonnets' of 1633. 'Good Friday', 'Annunciation and Passion', 'The Cross', and 'Resurrection' occur together towards the close, followed by a long series of Verse-Letters, after which the collection closes with 'The Lamentations of Jeremy' and 'A Litany'. In the order in which the poems occur there is no contact with Group II until the collection of Verse-Letters, which, with some small differences, is identical with the collection in *TCD* and *N*. There are other obvious connexions between *DC* and Group II. As well as containing poems otherwise only found in Group II, *Lut*, and *O'F*, *DC* has the titles of Group II. Its text is unequal. In the *Divine Poems*, it presents on the whole a good Group II text, avoiding at times errors in *TCC* and *TCD*, although it has some bad terminal readings. Its odd affinities throughout with the text of *1633* are discussed on p. lxxxv.

The section on the Westmoreland manuscript (pp. lxxviii–lxxx) has been rewritten in the light of the discovery that the manuscript is in Rowland Woodward's hand. This has made me pay more attention than I did in 1952 to the coincidence in the order of the 'Holy Sonnets' between the set of twelve in the Group III manuscripts and the first twelve of the Westmoreland manuscript. I now think this correspondence in order is more important than the, on the whole, trivial differences in reading between Group III and *W*, and that it is more likely that the archetype of the set in Group III was a corrupt copy of sonnets in Woodward's possession than that it was an independent version.

II. *The Editions.* The discussion of the relation of the Group I manuscript that was the main manuscript source for the edition of 1633 (pp. lxxxiii–lxxxvii) has been revised and rewritten to take into account conclusions reached in work on the text of poems other than the *Divine Poems*.

III. *Conclusions.* The first section (pp. xci–xciii) has been revised, and the first paragraph of the second section on the accidentals has been revised to take account of Donne's practice as revealed in the holograph Verse-Letter.

THE TEXT

The only alterations in substantive readings are: 'To Mr. Tilman', l. 29; 'The Lamentations of Jeremy', ll. 90, 250, 342; 'Hymn to God the Father', l. 8; see Commentary, and supplementary notes if reference to them is given.

I have abandoned the setting of the 'Hymn to Christ' in the edition of 1633 for the manuscript setting. This was adopted by Shawcross in his edition of 1968.

Contracted forms and elision marks have been supplemented extensively in this edition. In 1952 I did not attempt to improve on the practice of the early editions. The manuscripts, although helpful on contracted forms, give very little guidance as a whole on marks indicating synalœpha and elision, and I accepted what I took to be good seventeenth-century printing-house practice. In editing the *Songs and Sonnets* I came to the conclusion that inconsistencies by which a metrically necessary suppression of a syllable was marked in one line and left unmarked in another were confusing to a modern reader. A modernizing editor, while employing contracted forms, can discard elision marks between words; but the editor of an old-spelling text cannot remove so striking a feature of the early editions. The three subsequent volumes of this edition of Donne's poems supplied contracted forms and elision marks whenever they were metrically necessary, and this revision brings the text of the *Divine Poems* into line with them. Shawcross followed the same principle in his edition of 1968 and I have benefited by studying his treatment of this feature of the text, although not always agreeing with him. The holograph of the Verse-Letter to Lady Carey shows that Donne used more of these marks than are found in *1633* but fewer than appear in Milgate's text. As it is impossible to judge when Donne would or would not have placed a mark, there is no middle way between discarding all such marks and supplying them consistently. Owing to the boldness of the versification in the 'Holy Sonnets' and the editorial weakness of *1633* in 'The Lamentations of Jeremy', more supplementation has been required than in editing the *Elegies* and the *Songs and Sonnets*. All occasions when a mark has been supplied are noted in the apparatus, which also notes the readings of uncorrected formes.

COMMENTARY

The headnotes to each poem have been revised to include manuscripts containing a poem or poems that have come to light since 1952. Miscellanies containing only fragments of poems are not included.

P. 56. David Novarr (*P.Q.* xxxvi, 1957, pp. 259–65) rejects not merely 11 July but any date in July 1607 for the letter that precedes the sonnet to Mrs. Herbert in Walton's *Life of Herbert* (1670). He points out that the three letters from Donne to Mrs. Herbert that Walton printed in an appendix to the *Life of Herbert* in 1675, which are dated 'Michin, July 11. 1607', 'London, July 23. 1607', and 'August 2. 1607', make it clear that Mrs. Herbert was away from London throughout July. In the first Donne writes that he has no idea where she is and sends his letter 'as a Pinnace to discover'; in the second he writes that he has come to town and called at her house to find her still away and his letter there awaiting her return; in the third she is still away from home. But in the letter in question he writes that he has enjoyed her favours in London and on his return finds her Servant has come to whom he commits 'the inclosed Holy Hymns and Sonnets'. Novarr also notes that the tone of the three letters in the Appendix is formal, and points to their having been written when Donne was seeking Mrs. Herbert's closer acquaintance, while the letter sending the poems implies a settled friendship.

Novarr suggests that the date of the letter and of 'La Corona' is some time in 1609. He refers to the heading above 'La Corona' in H 49: 'Holy Sonnets written 20 yeares since', and the fact that the date 1629 occurs in the collection immediately preceding the Donne collection in H 49. As we do not know the authority for the statement in H 49, and it seems unsafe to take a round number as an exact one, it seems better to regard the date of 'La Corona' as uncertain. I would myself suggest ?1608 as more probable than 1609. This would link 'La Corona' with 'A Litany' as two poems inspired by liturgical prayer.

P. 57. Louis Martz has shown that the title 'La Corona' derives both from the form used, the Italian Corona di sonnetti, and from a special method of saying the Rosary, 'The Corona of our Lady'. Annibal Caro in 1588 published a famous 'Corona' linking nine sonnets in praise of his mistress. Donne was anticipated in using this Italian form by George Chapman whose 'Coronet for his Mistress Philosophy' (1595) linked ten sonnets. The Bridgettine Rosary, or 'Corona of our Lady', in place of the fifteen decades of the classic Dominican Rosary, had a set of sixty-three beads divided into six decades, with a final appendage of three Aves and a Paternoster. Directions for its use show that the material for meditation, events in the life of the Virgin, was divided into seven parts, either distributing the events considered into seven sections, or using the seventh part for some kind of conclusion. The method of saying the Corona was to run very rapidly in the mind through the events. Donne applies the Corona method to the events in the life of Christ, dividing the material into seven sonnets. Martz notes that in English treatises on the Rosary there is a reference to 'a Corona of our Lord'—a Rosary of thirty-three Aves, presumably divided into six sets of five beads and a concluding three. See Louis L. Martz, The Poetry of Meditation (New Haven, Yale U.P., 1954), pp. 105–8.

P. 66. The contraction 'wilt'not' (for 'winn't') in 1633, which has no manuscript support, has a parallel in the sonnet 'Batter my heart' (l. 9), where 1633 also has no support for its contracted form 'lov'd'; see note on p. 71. In revising I have rejected 1633 here for reasons given in the note on p. 66; but I have retained the contracted form in 'Batter my heart'. In the latter case an editor has to balance the lack of manuscript support against the fact that Donne does not use the uncontracted and archaic 'lovèd' in his poems, unless we are willing to ascribe to him the Elegy 'Variety' which I reject from the canon for reasons given in Gardner, Elegies etc., pp. xliii–xliv.

P. 71. Hugh Richmond has found a striking parallel to this sonnet in a sonnet by Ronsard:

> Foudroye moy le corps, ainsi que Capanée,
> O pere Jupiter, et de ton feu cruel
> Esteins moy l'autre feu qu'Amour continuel
> Tousjours m'allume au coeur d'une flame obstinée...
> Ou bien, si tu ne veux, Pere, me foudroyer,
> Donne le desespoir, qui me meine noyer,
> M'élançant du sommet d'un rocher solitaire,
> Puis qu'autrement par soin, par peine et par labour,
> Trahy de la raison, je ne me puis desfaire
> D'Amour, qui maugré moy se campe dans mon coeur.

He comments that we must note 'Ronsard's image of the death of Capaneus by thunderbolt at the siege of Thebes, a city usurped by Eteocles at the expense of the legal title of Polynices', an allusion that 'clarifies the military imagery of Donne's sonnet'; and also his emphasis on man's need for grace 'in view of the intransigent sinfulness of human nature, betrayed by its own best ally, Reason'. See H. M. Richmond, *N. and Q.*, cciii (1958), pp. 534–6, and *Comparative Literature Studies*, vii (1970), pp. 141–60; see also Clayton D. Lein, 'Donne and Ronsard', *N. and Q.*, N.S. xxi. 3 (1974), pp. 90–92, who adds to Richmond's examples of Donne's debts to Ronsard.

Rosemary Woolf (*The English Religious Lyric in the Middle Ages*, 1968, p. 161) cites four lines on the *ecce sto* theme from a translation of the twelfth-century Latin poem 'Philomena' by John of Howden, which anticipate the theme of Donne's and Ronsard's sonnets:

> Kyng of love, strengest of alle,
> I here thee at my dore calle.
> Thou fyndest it loke with barres stronge,
> But brek hem up, stond not to longe.

She comments that this call to love to break in by violence is characteristic of the mystical and ecstatic conception of love. For other medieval poems on the reluctance of the soul to respond to gentleness, see *The Oxford Book of Medieval Verse*, nos. 20 and 21.

P. 79.   *Since she whome I lovd, hath payd her last debt*
              To Nature, and to hers, and my good is dead,

There are two ways of reading the second line, which give three possible interpretations. (*a*) We may take 'and to hers' with 'To Nature', and paraphrase: 'Since she whom I loved has paid her last debt to Nature and to her family and friends, and my dear one is dead.' There is some difficulty in attaching the conception of the debts of affection and duty owed to persons to the commonplace of our 'debt to Nature', and even more in taking 'my good' as meaning 'she whome I lovd'. There is no example in *O.E.D.* for the use of 'my good' for 'my beloved'. But it is possible that Donne was echoing the common Italian use of *il mio bene* for 'my beloved'. It is not uncommon in post-Petrarchan Italian love-poetry. (*b*) If, on the other hand, we take 'and to hers' with 'and my good', there are two possible interpretations. Death ends the possibility of doing good to oneself or to others: she is thus 'dead' to her own good and to his. Or we may take it that the line points forward to the next two lines, and the sense is: 'Her death is for her good, since by it she enters heaven early, and it is for his good, since now all his affections are set on 'heavenly things'. This last interpretation may seem harsh, but it is consistent with the sonnet's whole theme and with the Christian view that all that happens to us is 'for our good'.

l. 10. *Dost wooe my soule, for hers offring all thine.* A. J. Smith retains the punctuation of Westmoreland and reads 'Dost woo my soul for hers; offring all thine:', strengthening its comma to a semi-colon. He interprets: 'God woos the poet's soul on behalf of the soul now in heaven, to reunite and marry them there, as a father might plead his daughter's case with a desirable young man; and the offered dowry of ransom is Christ himself, God's only son.' This is wholly inconsistent with the sonnet's theme of God's 'tender jealousy', and with Donne's thought on the subject of the death of those we love; see the letter to his mother, quoted on p. 78, and the 'Hymn to Christ', where he offers in sacrifice the 'Iland' that he is leaving,

> And all whom I lov'd there, and who lov'd mee.

Joan Bennett, also accepting the manuscript punctuation, has suggested that the antecedent of 'hers' is 'my soule'. God woos the poet's soul for *its* love. This is a possible defence of the manuscript pointing. It seems to me an unlikely interpretation in view of the strong stress throughout the sonnet on the personal pronouns. The sonnet turns on *She*, *I*, and *Thou*, and the swing from *her* to *thee* is its subject. It is difficult to supply any other antecedent for 'hers' in this line than the 'She whome I lovd' of the sonnet's opening.

P. 81. *Biathanatos*, to which Donne refers in the undated letter to Goodyer sending him 'A Litany', can be dated fairly precisely by its sources. Charles Mark informs me that it must be after 1607, since it makes use of Sedulius, *Liber Apologeticus* (Antwerp, 1607). But, according to S. E. Sprott (*The English Debate on Suicide*, La Salle, Illinois, 1961, p. 25), it makes no use of 'the third tome of Azorius (in which suicide was specifically treated), first published in 1612, or of Molina's fourth tome (in which suicide was discussed), first published in 1609 and soon widely influential'. This supports a date in 1608 for *Biathanatos* and 'A Litany', since in speaking of Sedulius Donne refers to him as having written 'of late', that is, recently.

Donne's knowledge of the litanies of Ratpertus and Notker, and the information he gives to Goodyer about them, have been traced to the *Antiquae Lectiones* (or *Promptuarium Ecclesiasticum*) by Henricus Casanius, a work published in five volumes at Ingolstadt between 1601 and 1608. In *pars secunda* of volume v, Canisius printed 'Litania Ratperti ad processionem diebus Dominicis' (p. 742) and 'Notkeri magistri cognomento Balbuli Litania rhythmica' (p. 746). See Dominic Baker-Smith, *R.E.S.* xxvi (1975), pp. 171–3. We do not know how early in 1608 Canisius's fifth volume was published. At this time, as *Biathanatos*, *Pseudo-Martyr*, and *Ignatius His Conclave* show, Donne was reading continental works very soon after their publication. Baker-Smith regards Donne's use of Canisius as consistent with a date in the autumn of 1608 for 'A Litany'.

P. 93. J. A. W. Bennett (*R.E.S.* v, 1954, pp. 168–9) pointed out that all the likenesses Donne notes to the Cross were noticed and collected by early Christian writers. The most concise list is in a Commentary ascribed to Jerome:

> Ipsa species Crucis, quid est nisi forma quadrata mundi? . . .
> Aves, quando volant ad aethera, formam Crucis assumunt.
> Homo natans per aquas, vel orans, forma crucis vehitur.
> Navis per maria, antenna cruci similate sufflatur.
>
> (Migne, *P.L.* xxx. 638)

They were collected together by Lipsius in *De Cruce*, chap. ix, Book I (Antwerp, 1595). Bennett notes that the separate editions of this work, as well as the collected works of Lipsius, include an illustration showing a swimmer, a bird, a praying man, a sail in the crosswise position, and similar figures.

Gibbon (*Decline and Fall*, ed. Bury, ii. 299) noted that 'The Christian writers Justin, Minucius Felix, Tertullian, Jerom, and Maximus of Turin, have investigated with tolerable success the figure or likeness of a cross in almost every object of nature and art; in the intersection of the meridian and equator, the human face, a bird flying, a man swimming, a mast and yard, a plough, a *standard*, &c. &c. &c.' and referred to Lipsius.

P. 98. Two manuscript copies of 'Good Friday' have come to light among the family papers of the Duke of Manchester. The first was sold at Sotheby's (23 June 1970, Lot 268), as the next lot to the holograph of the Verse-Letter to Lady Carey. It was bought by T. Hofmann, who kindly sent me a photograph. The second was found in the Huntingdon Records Office. It was the subject of a long article (*T.L.S.*, 16 August 1974), with photographs, in which it was claimed that it and some prose pieces found with it were in Donne's hand, and variants from the text in *1633* were listed and discussed. Nicholas Barker, in a second long article (*T.L.S.*, 20 September), which gave photographs of the Hofmann manuscript and of the holograph Verse-Letter, showed that both copies of 'Good Friday' were in the same hand and that the hand was not Donne's. He listed the variants between the two copies. In the following week (*T.L.S.*, 27 September) R. E. Alton and P. J. Croft, from their study of a number of other papers at Huntingdon, identified the writer as Sir Nathaniel Rich (?1585–1636), a kinsman of Lady Carey and her sister Essex Rich, who was also known to Donne since he delivered a letter to him at Paris in the spring of 1612 (*Letters*, p. 74).

Both copies present clumsily corrupt versions of the poem, the Hofmann manuscript being slightly the better of the two. Two questions arise: what was the source of the text, and why did Sir Nathaniel write the poem out twice? The errors the two copies share seem much more like the results of a faulty memory than of a failure to transcribe accurately from a written text. Differences from the text of *1633*, often damaging to the metre, in most cases substitute more conventional wording. The omission of two couplets (ll. 17–20) in the Huntingdon manuscript cannot be explained as an eye-slip as can the omissions in some of the Group I manuscripts set out on p. lxi. The summary Alton and Croft gave of the career of Sir Nathaniel Rich makes it seem highly unlikely that he would copy a document so incompetently, and even more unlikely that he would do so twice over. My own view is that he attempted to write out the poem from memory and, dissatisfied with his first attempt (the Huntingdon manuscript), he copied it with 'improvements' in the Hofmann manuscript. His omission in Hofmann of lines 5–6, which he inserted as one line between lines 4 and 7, can be explained as a eye-slip, the couplet omitted beginning, like the preceding one, with the word 'And'. He managed to remember one of the two couplets omitted at his first attempt, but got it wrong at first, writing 'It made the earth to crack and the Sun to winke!' which he corrected to 'It made his footstoole crack the Sun to winke!' The two similar corrections of his first attempt at a line in the Huntingdon manuscript (ll. 9 and 10) are incorporated into the text of the Hofmann manuscript.

Whether this suggestion is acceptable or not, the two copies present texts of no value to an editor; and the information given in the Huntingdon manuscript's heading, not in the heading in the Hofmann manuscript, that Donne was going from London to Exeter, which contradicts information given in other manuscripts, is inconsistent with what we know of Donne's movements in the spring of 1613.

Although Sir Nathaniel delivered a letter to Donne in Paris in 1612, this need not mean that they were closely acquainted, and although the copies in his hand may well be early ones, it is a common fallacy in textual criticism that an early date is any guarantee of the value of a text.

P. 99. Rosalie Beck has pointed out an anticipation of Donne's reversal of Sacrobosco's moralization of the heavenly system in Lydgate's translation of Guillaume de Deguileville's *Pilgrimage of the Life of Man* (ed. F. J. Furnivall, 1899–1904, ll. 12, 257–70). She comments that Sacrobosco, uneasy in making the motion of the *primum mobile* from east to west *motus rationalis* and the motion of the inner spheres from west to east *motus irrationalis*, attempted to make this consonant with the usual significance of the east for Christians by describing the motion of the *primum mobile* as being 'from east through west back to east again', thus resembling rational motion in man 'whose thought goes from the Creator through creatures to the Creator'. Lydgate, on the contrary, takes movement westward as movement away from God and equates the *primum mobile* with 'Lust of the body' and 'Sensualyte'. The movement of the inner spheres towards the east he equates with the movement of the spirit in man. 'The significance of the East in Christian thinking', writes Rosalie Beck, 'has prevailed over the Aristotelian significance of the outer wheel as "First Mover".' She makes clear that she is not intending to show that Donne was directly influenced by Lydgate or his French original, but that 'a moralization of the heavenly system more compatible with accepted Christian symbolism than that of Sacrobosco was current well before the seventeenth century'. See *R.E.S.* xix, 1968, pp. 166–9.

P. 106. The setting in *1633*, which divides what the manuscripts all write as a fourteener into lines of eight and six syllables, is not unsuitable in the first, third, and fourth stanzas where the long line pauses after the eighth syllable, but it is unsatisfactory in the second stanza where the line runs without a break. Donne used a fourteener to conclude a stanza in 'The Will', 'A Valediction: of Weeping', 'The Funeral', and the Somerset Epithalamium, and, to conclude a poem, in 'The Dissolution'.

P. 107.

ll. 12–14.   *As the trees sap doth seeke the root below*
         In winter, in my winter now I goe,
   Where none but thee, th'Eternall root of true Love I may know.

Kitty Datta cites two striking passages from Augustine on the 'root of true love'. The first is from the *Enarrationes in Psalmos*, a work, she notes, that Donne commended in his sermons. 'Now is the season of winter, your glory is not yet apparent. But if your charity is deeply rooted, like many trees in winter, the cold passes away, and the summer, the Day of Judgement, will be at hand: then shall the greenness of the grass wither away, then shall appear the glory of the trees. *For you are dead*, says the Apostle, just as trees during the winter; they appear as if withered and dead. Well, then, what have we if we are dead? The root is deep within: where our root is, there is our life also, for there is our charity' (Dame Scholastica Hebgin and Dame Felicitas Corrigan, *St. Augustine on the Psalms*, 1960, vol. 2, on Psalm 36. 1–2). The second is from the eleventh homily on the first epistle of St. John, where

Augustine is speaking of the truly loving soul: 'Shall we get at that soul, think you, that we may address it? think you, is it here in this congregation? is it here, think you in this chancel? think you it is here on earth? It cannot but be, only it is hidden. Now is the winter: within is the greenness in the root' (*Homilies on St. John's Gospel etc.*, Library of the Fathers, 1849). See 'Love and Asceticism in Donne's Poetry: the Divine Analogy', reprinted from *Jadavpur Journal of Comparative Literature* in *The Critical Quarterly*, Summer, 1977.